The
Liberty
Club

The Liberty Club

Marianne Aleck

ISBN: 978-0-9970485-0-6

dedicated to

my wonderful

parents Johnny and Monique

and all my ancestors who have walked this earth

who lived your lives on your own terms

who endured hardships, loss, and tragedy,

continuing the only way you knew how.

who drank, laughed, enjoyed, and smiled

who cried, shared, led, and strengthened

drudging your way through life

dancing your way through life

and loving your way through life

until there was no more life to live

I am so very honored to have been the one to tell your stories

Preface

I would never have written **The Liberty Club** had I not been inspired through the years by my mother's words, *"Someday I should write a book about my life."* I'm sure Monique, the sassy stubborn French lady I called Mom would have had a best seller! When I was twelve years old I made a promise to myself that I'd be a published author by the ripe old age of thirty. But when my thirtieth birthday rolled around, all I had was a handful of unpublished poems. In hindsight, authorship and the book I was born to write wasn't ready to be birthed. Many of the events that would fill these pages had yet to take place, and the technology to gather important documents and information was in its infancy.

Still, the desire to write her story never left my mind, and finally in retirement I knew the timing was right. As I mused about where to start it was apparent I couldn't write about her life without including her husband's rich Greek heritage. And I couldn't write their story without going back even further, including their parents, and bits of their grandparents. As I slowly uncovered generations of my ancestors it became clear the addition of their siblings would give the storyline more breadth. And with that, my Greek and French roots morphed into a book I call **The Liberty Club**.

I describe their fascinating journeys as a *"Slice of Americana with a European Twist."* That's the shortest description I can think of to encapsulate twenty-five chapters of immigrants through survival, love, tragedy, war, and the tenacious human spirit. It's about the great sacrifice of those who left loved ones behind to start anew in route to the land of milk and honey. As you follow their stories you will lose yourselves in the everyday lives of immigrants who, with a "wish and a prayer" came to America in hopes of making a better life for themselves and their children. **The Liberty Club** is a non-fiction narrative family memoir that drifts back in time from the late 1800's, through the 10's, 20's, 30's, 40's, 50's, and beyond.

The majority of this book covers the lives of my parents and grandparents, born to become part of the Greatest Generation. My ancestors' determination is a reflection of the lives of thousands, even millions who came to America during the early 1900's. But the men and women who lived during those difficult yet exciting times weren't aware of their greatness. They didn't know they were the Greatest Generation. Their humility didn't allow a thought as to the legacy they'd leave behind. They were just doing what needed to be done to survive.

Clearly, post generations admire their gumption, resourcefulness, patriotism, and fortitude while faced with perplexing decisions that earned them this extraordinary title. Yes, they would laugh at such a notion of being the Greatest Generation, but you and I recognize their bravery. It was as though they lived by the motto "Never Say Die" and bravely died by that motto. The individuals within these pages are a reflection of a yesteryear never to be forgotten.

I was extremely fortunate to have the personal stories, as told by my parents, in recordings done by my brother John in the 1980's. The wealth of information about their lives and those of their parents and grandparents filled both sides of four cassettes. Those recordings, coupled with my own research built the foundation for this labor of love. My father shared stories about the strength and character of his father, and tales of his own youth living through the Great

Depression and so much more. My brothers eagerly supplied several of our dad's WWII stories, and I found more in newspaper clippings when my dad was interviewed about the famous battles in which he had fought. Years back my mother mailed them to me, and naturally I kept them as keepsakes, not realizing then how valuable they'd be in the writing of this book.

Likewise, my ancestors' family dynamics coupled with growing up in France before and during WWII are told by my mother within these same recordings. Her tales left snippets in my mind of how she was raised and lived as a pampered, yet lonely child. The stark difference between my parents' lives is obvious. In addition to the cassette tapes I was blessed with finding two very precious mementoes my mother had kept which became irreplaceable gifts in writing **The Liberty Club**. One was a bag filled with love letters my dad had written to his French beauty during the war. The other was my mother's journal, also from the 40's. It spoke volumes about family life and events while living under German occupation. As I listened to the contents of her journal it was as though I sat quietly in their living room witnessing the dysfunction to follow.

Prior to typing a single word, I did three years of research collecting personal stories, pictures, and documents. My mother's younger sister Colette was a godsend, translating my mother's journal, sharing her own stories about the war and other amazing anecdotes enriching **The Liberty Club**. I combed websites including Ancestry.com, which helped narrow down dates. In addition, I searched for books to assist in keeping my dad's war stories in context. *"Stand in the Door"* by Charles Doyle and *"Bloody Clash at Sadzot"* by William B. Breuer provided further information to showcase the bigger picture of the battles in which Johnny had fought.

Being a stickler for detail, I was thrilled and very fortunate to have my father's war chapters fact-checked by WWII historian Matt Anderson, who is also the webmaster for the website about the battalion of brothers my dad fought with, the 509 PIB. www.509thgeronimo.org

I searched for major events during my ancestors' time to help put their lives in perspective. Timeless tales from at least a dozen family and friends "who were there" added a unique personal perspective. I visited the library and found articles on microfiche regarding tragic events I'd heard about as a child. I was even able to get my uncle's military records from the Veteran's Administration, and I visited the county records for grant deeds, and birth and death certificates.

After I wrote **The Liberty Club** I realized it wasn't just about *my* ancestors. It's the story of so many who walked boldly on this earth not even aware of just how strong, courageous, and self-sufficient a people they really were. I believe many of you will relate in some way to the characters and lives within these pages; especially those of you who had parents and grandparents yourselves who passed through Ellis Island on their journey to the land of plenty. The tales within this text will bring tears, make you laugh, cringe, and experience a host of other feelings as you become a part of **The Liberty Club**. And as you watch their lives unfold I urge you to invite them into your imagination, into your heart, and find yourself living, eating, and breathing amongst the Greatest Generation within the pages of a book I call **THE LIBERTY CLUB**

Chapter 1

THE GREEKS HAVE LANDED

When I was a teenager, my Aunt Joy came over with an old picture. My dad, Johnny, held it with pride and said it was his grandfather, my great-grandfather Nicolaus Alexiou. The worn wooden frame and faded oval mat appeared to be original. I'd say the man in the picture looked to be about thirty or so, and felt familiar even though his hair was more blond than was typical for our family. All of us, except for my brother Gregg have the same dark brown hair. As unoriginal as it was, we teased him, saying that his father was the milkman. As soon as we saw the picture of Nicolaus, we knew where Gregg had gotten his fair hair. In fact, my brother has such a strong resemblance to our great-grandfather it was decided that someday the picture would be his.

The image looked like a painting. Instead of the usual black and whites from long ago, this one had a green hue in the background. It was a head and shoulders shot with part of his brown suit showing. Nicolaus was wearing a white shirt, knotted two-toned dark tie, and a small red flower in his lapel. But what really stood out, what you just couldn't tear your eyes away from was Nicolaus's handlebar mustache! It was very thick above his lip and extended outward five inches in both directions, with ever so slightly upturned ends. He wore it proudly, and I suspect it certainly would have required just as much upkeep as a small pet. As with other family photographs I had found from this time period, there was no smile as his gaze drifted away from the camera. His complexion was the smoothest I have ever seen on a man. Nicolaus's light-brown hair was parted on one side and flowed just over his forehead with a natural lift on the ends. He was quite handsome, and I can see where my grandfather had gotten his good looks.

Nicolaus Alexiou

Through the years that picture remained in our family's living room, and not once did I or anyone else ask anything about him. In hindsight I can only blame the unfortunate self-indulgence of our youth. I had correctly assumed that he was born in Greece, but other than that, I walked past his picture hundreds, even thousands of times, and it was as though my dear great-grandfather had disappeared into the wall.

As they say, with age comes wisdom, and now I was wise enough to appreciate the stories I was about to hear. Immaturity finally vacated my mind and I was giddy with excitement to decode our families' colorful lives. My dad didn't have a wealth of information about his grandfather, but a little was all I needed to get started.

Nicolaus Alexiou was born in Gerakiou, Greece on the island of Evia, the second largest island in Greece. Nicolaus married Vasiliki, which is the Greek version of the name we would know as Bess. My Aunt Bess was named after her, and Uncle Nick was named after Nicolaus. The couple had two sons: Gus, the oldest, and Tom, plus a daughter whose existence and name our family was not aware of until I started writing this book. I learned about her when I found my grandfather's draft notice online, but unfortunately there was no name listed to satisfy my curiosity.

My great-grandfather Nicolaus came to America around the turn of the 20th century. There was no work in his homeland so hundreds of thousands of Greek immigrants poured into the United States in search of a better life. In order to understand what caused this mass exodus, it's important to know a little about the history of Greece. Way back in 1453 the Turks captured Constantinople, which is now Istanbul, Turkey, which resulted in Greece becoming a part of the Ottoman Empire. Four hundred years later, revolutionary uprisings sprung up for various reasons in Western Europe, as well as North America which inspired Greeks to rebel against their own Ottoman state. The Greeks united against the Turks, and along with their strong sense of

Greek nationalism, the Greek War of Independence (also known as the Greek Revolution) ensued between 1821 and 1832. The result allowed Greece to regain its freedom from Ottoman rule.

The years to follow found the newly independent nation faced with many economic challenges. The country was slow to industrialize since 80% of its population lived in rural communities. Currants were its chief export, and when the prices declined, farmers went bankrupt and were unable to pay their taxes. With this dismal economic forecast the Greek government encouraged young men to sail to America in search of work. The exodus began around 1880, with the bulk leaving between 1900 and 1920. More than 350,000 Greeks emigrated; 95% of which were men leaving their homeland. Upon finding work, they often sent money back home to the women left behind, which was also used as dowries for their sisters. In 1905 alone, Greek immigrants sent more than four million dollars back home to their loved ones who remained in the old country. Most had no intentions of staying in America, yet only 30% returned to the motherland.

Many were single young men, but some, like Nicolaus, left their families, and upon finding work, sent money back to loved ones. It must have been a punishing decision. Especially for those like my great-grandpa Nicolaus, who had to leave a wife and children behind and sail halfway around the world. These were brave men who felt they had no other alternative. For to remain in their country was to go hungry, or worse yet, to watch their children go hungry. It showed enormous strength and a sense of unselfish commitment to uproot oneself from all one had ever known, and step into the vast unknown. The possibility of never seeing family again was part of the sacrifice needed for Greeks to survive.

My Greek relatives boarded small boats that took them to their awaiting steamship bound for America. Patras, Greece 1910 - (Library of Congress)

After Nicolaus came to America he settled in Butte County, which is at the northern end of the Sacramento Valley in the great state of California. With such a vast country to choose from, I don't know why he chose Oroville to be his home, but I do know the Greeks networked with their compatriots, as did many other immigrants. My dad said that the climate and countryside of our hometown of Oroville was similar to many parts of Greece. Perhaps that played a role in the choice of America's west coast. Nevertheless, with such a mass exodus I'm sure a buzz was created that propelled this forward momentum. The Greek immigrants were united by their roots which brought about a sense of belonging. A camaraderie was formed with total strangers; a kinship that united their drive. Once in the states, the men lived in rooming houses in order to keep their own costs down. The more they saved, the more they were able to send back home. Nicolaus didn't read, write, or speak English, so finding fellow Greeks made the adjustment for him a little easier.

When his boots first made their imprint upon American soil my great-grandfather was already forty-five years old. Not an old man by today's standards, but in 1900 the life-expectancy for men was just forty-six. And yet he was able to secure a job and work for the railroad as a laborer. Greeks are a tough breed, and I'm sure he pulled his weight in spite of his age. Fortunately, his son Gus was the next to make the long trek across the Atlantic through Ellis Island. He continued west all the way to California to start a new life and be with his father again. I imagine the pair lived at the same rooming house, enabling Nicolaus to see his young son grow from adolescence into manhood. He was proud to see Gus had inherited his strong work ethics and knew he would continue to thrive in this new land.

Unfortunately their time together would be short-lived. As it turned out, this man who had brought our family to America became gravely ill. In 1910, just four years after his son arrived, Nicolaus Alexiou, took his last breath. Even though his wife and two other children weren't able to be at his side, at least his oldest was there in the end.

I learned from my dad's recording that Nicolaus was buried right here in Oroville. This was a pleasant surprise since I now had a chance to find both his death certificate and his grave marker. I wasn't living in Oroville when I first began my family's research so I enlisted the help of my cousin Lydia, my Aunt Joy's oldest daughter, and asked her to search the old cemetery to find our great-grandfather's marker. We knew approximately where he was buried, again, thanks to my dad. Lydia had also developed an interest in learning more about our Greek side, and soon we began collaborating on the bits and pieces we had discovered.

One day, not long after requesting Lydia's assistance, I opened a most wonderful email. There it was – a picture of his grave marker. The inscription read, "Father" on top, then "Nickolous Alexiou, 1852-1910," and on the bottom, "Born in Greece." On one of my own trips north I had gone to see for myself this somber piece of our history. It took a little while but I finally found him lying right where he had been for over a hundred years.

His marker lies beside a large scraggly tree with exposed roots that come right up to his gravestone. The tree is probably as old as my great-grandpa would be now. It was befitting as I was discovering my roots and learning about my own family tree.

Seeing my brother Gregg, who is now in his mid-fifties, gives me an idea of what great-grandpa would have looked like in *his* fifties. It might have been how his son Gus saw him back in 1906. My dad had said Nicolaus died in 1914, but now we had a marker that showed 1910. So with that information I went to the Butte County records department to find his death certificate. They don't store them that far back on the computers, so the gal behind the counter showed me the huge books that carried all the older death certificates for the county. There was volume upon volume of hardback books at least two inches thick and two feet tall. The packed shelves reached to the top of the ceiling, and about ten feet in length for an impressive collection of history. All those death records preserved well over a century of lives. I gave the clerk his name and year of death, and told her he was my great grandfather. She entered it into her computer then scribbled down some numbers. After musing over the volumes she grabbed one with both hands as I helped her set the mammoth book on a table. I wondered when it had been opened last. She flipped pages this way then that while glancing at her notes. Finally, as with the grave marker, she pointed and said, *"That's him!"*

I poured over the perfectly handwritten script and saw his name as Nicolaus A. Alexiou, not the same spelling from his grave stone which was Nickolous. And instead of his birth being listed as 1852 as on the marker, the death certificate said he was born in 1855, and died at the age of 55. I was able to read that he was still married at the time of his passing and his father's name was written as only A. Alexiou.

My young grandpa Gus, at just 22 years of age would have been burdened with the unpleasant task of writing his mother, brother, and sister a letter no one ever knows how to start, and worse, no one ever wants to read. He had to grieve his father's passing amongst newly formed friendships and without the comfort of family.

The cause of death was Acute Spinal Meningitis, and he also suffered from Inflammatory Rheumatism. My poor dear great-grandpa must have been miserable and ready to leave this earth. He was hospitalized for forty days before his death on August 25, 1910. Two days later he was buried, and according to my father, didn't have a grave marker for years.

Gus finally had one made prior to his own death, and without it, we may never have found his final resting place.

When Nicolaus's son, my grandfather Gus, found his way to America, it was on board the S.S. Georgia, dropping anchor in New York Harbor on May 24, 1906. The ship set sail from Patras, Greece, which was about 250 miles from the small village Gerakiou, where I believe he was born in the northern region of Evia, also known as Euboea. His name on the ship's manifest is his Greek given name, Constantinos Alexiou although it should have been spelled with a K instead of a C. Grandpa was only eighteen when he journeyed west with just $16 in his pocket, which went a lot farther back then. The vessel was completely filled with fellow Greeks like he and his father who were in route toward the land of plenty. As with many immigrants who passed through Ellis Island, my grandpa changed his name to simply Gus Aleck. My mother told me that everyone was upset with him for changing our last name. For many years, I, too, was upset with his choice as I would have loved to have had my last name Alexiou. But as I matured I realized Grandpa was simply doing his best to blend into the overwhelming American melting pot.

When Gus came to Oroville much progress had been made from its frontier beginnings in the early 1850's. As a result of gold being discovered in "them thar hills," the town grew to become one of the largest cities in all of California. Its name literally means "Gold City" or "City of Gold," with *oro*, from the Spanish word for gold, and *ville* from the French for city. With the great gold rush the town became a whiskey drinking, saloon-riddled, rowdy community reminiscent of old western movies. Hordes of men took a chance with the sweat of their brow to strike it rich, but more often than not they scratched out just enough to cover gambling, booze, and barroom harlots.

Gus Aleck

Oroville became the county seat of Butte County in 1856 and remains so to this day. A year later in March of 1857 it was incorporated as a city. Then the goldmines started to dry-out and with the dwindling boom it was dis-incorporated in 1859. Almost fifty years later dredge mining was introduced and once again Oroville became an incorporated city on January 3, 1906. When Gus arrived in that same year, gold was still being uncovered from the all-important Feather River, allowing Oroville to continue to grow and prosper. By 1906, besides dozens of saloons, the town supported billiard halls, stables, hotels, eateries, mercantiles, rooming houses, banks, meat markets, and more, filling the brick and wooden buildings. Old dusty miners with long straggly beards could still be seen walking their pack mules down dirt roads. These streets were named after the city's founding fathers and important businessmen such as Montgomery, Myers, Huntoon, Downer, and Bird. And of course, Johnny Law was still a force, hoping to tame what remained of the wild, wild, west. This was the ripe new world my grandfather entered. The turn of the century was full of promise for any ambitious newcomer with a can-do attitude. And Grandpa Aleck had that in spades!

Straight away, as soon as Gus was settled, he was in search of work. In my father's own words he speaks of how his father landed his first job in America. *"I remember my dad telling me they were building the sewer system in Oroville, see. He tried to hire out and the guy looked at him and said, 'You're too young,' and all this and that. So he just grabbed a pick and he started knocking out bigger chunks and tossing them out of there than the whole damn crew was doing. And so they hired him. He had to prove himself on his own without even being hired."*

And with that, Grandpa Gus did indeed prove himself to be worthy of his salt and helped install miles of sewer line.

Notable projects that would appear later on his resume were powerhouses such as Bucks Lake and Rock Creek Reservoir in the Feather River Canyon.

After the installation of the sewer pipes, the first two streets in town were paved. Prior to their paving, the downtown dirt roads were spread with gravel in the winter months to soak up the wet rains, and in the summer the gravel was hauled away because it proved too bumpy, dusty, and dirty. Paving the streets made sense – especially with the increase of automobiles. In 1913 the first dirt streets in Oroville to be black-topped added up to less than a mile. Montgomery Street was paved from Bridge to Oak, and Myers Street from Montgomery to High formed a T through the busiest routes in town. Change is never easy and many objected, but soon they saw the benefits of a cleaner, smoother surface. This was especially true for the women who grew tired of the bottoms of their dresses constantly being soiled.

A photo taken in 1914 shows men and equipment busy paving Oroville's streets. Workers spread the asphalt by hand while the tractor waits to press it down. Note the beautiful trees the townspeople preserved at their residences, many of which survive to this day.

Downtown residential streets being paved in Oroville. Picture courtesy James Lenoff from his book, "Images of America- Oroville California." circa 1914

Gus capitalized on the opportunity and proved he was more than just brawn. Living in a rooming house, young Grandpa recognized the potential for making a decent living by renting out furnished rooms to the growing number of newcomers. In 1914 well over a dozen such establishments flourished in the downtown area. It was in this same year, Grandpa, at just twenty six years of age, together with a fellow Greek partner opened the Oro Vista rooming house on newly paved Montgomery Street near Myers. The brick building they chose, known as the Friesleben-Howard Building had been built in 1878, thirty-five years earlier. With Grandpa still working in construction, his partner Bill Anagostou stayed behind to manage their new sixteen-room venture.

PHONE 552

Oro Vista Rooming House

GUS ALECK, PROP.

609 ½ MONTGOMERY ST.   OROVILLE, CAL.

One of Grandpa's business cards.

Two years earlier, Gus's younger brother Anastasios Alexiou sailed on the S.S. Themistocles in April of 1912 to the land of milk and honey. Upon his arrival at Ellis Island my sixteen year old Great Uncle changed his wonderful Greek name to a more homogenized, Tom Aleck. His WWI draft card dated May of 1917 stated he was born in 1896. Also typed on the card was, *"Does not know month or day born but brother says from letter read from mother in Greece that he is 21 years old."* Tom took up stakes at his brother's rooming house and soon got a job as a laborer with Great Western Power Co. on the Feather River. From there, Tom worked for a while at the Lumber Mills in Feather Falls, but decided to turn his attention toward his true passion of boxing.

Being of small stature, the younger Aleck was a welterweight at just under 5' 3" and took on the professional boxing name of George Gilmore. Held in Woodland, CA on April 9, 1919, his debut bout would prove promising, ending in his first professional win. From there he squared off at the Municipal Auditorium in Oroville where Tom had one draw and one win with his proud brother rallying in his corner. This was a major social event in Oroville with ringside crowded by men in three-piece suits topped with derby hats and dolled-up broads at their sides. There was an intoxicating yet familiar smell of cheap perfume mingled with cigar fumes, of testosterone, and hooch that adrenalized the spectators. They heard the thud, thud-thud sounds of human punching bags taking their hits while ambling about the ring. The shouts of the rowdy crowd cheering and jeering echoed throughout until, ding-ding-ding, and the arm of the victor was raised high.

George Gilmore continued traversing the boxing circuit, reaching as far south as Hollywood, CA. Then in 1925, by now a seasoned scrapper, this Greek found himself bound for Havana, Cuba for a couple three matches, followed by a quick stop in Florida, and finally landing in New York City. Most of his fights in the Big Apple, as with his other contests, were fought in military armories, and boasted more wins than losses. As a bonus, my great uncle's manager booked a toe-to-toe in Perth, Australia where he had the chance to take in the local culture down under while adding another win to his resume. Once back in the states, his final bout took place May 11, 1934 at the Convention Hall in Utica, New York. George Gilmore, at the ripe old boxing age of 38, won with a TKO. Throughout his adventurous career Tom duked it out in 49 matches going a total of 251 rounds over his 15 year career. His statistics stand with 19 wins, 15 losses, and 14 draws. The little Greek from Evia had the time of his life!

Tom Aleck aka George Gilmore with his niece on his lap.

While his brother fought his way across the countryside, Gus continued to capitalize on his own good fortune. In 1916, just two years after opening the Oro Vista, Grandpa bought out his partner and became the sole proprietor. To manage his enterprise he hired an older Greek gentleman, one John D. Stefanis who already lived at the rooming house situated on the second floor of the building, and had come to America about the same year as young Gus. Mr. Stefanis was tall for a Greek, with a square jaw, robust build, and thick graying mustache. With full cheeks when he smiled, welcoming eyes, and a congenial disposition, Gus had picked the right man for the job.

Now that Grandpa was diversified it helped ease his financial burden of sending money back home to his mother and sister. Upon his father's death, providing for loved ones had become Grandpa's sole responsibility, which he dutifully fulfilled. I can only imagine how proud his mother Bess must have been of her first-born. Being a single young stud, as my dad described him, he could have been very careless with his earnings. Instead, Gus made life happen, and reaped the financial rewards. After all, coming from nothing and having the opportunities to make something of himself was what the American dream was all about.

Along with that dream comes the desire to have a wife and raise a family. He had his priorities in order: first establish a solid means of support, then get married. It is important for many cultures to marry within their nationality. There was just one problem in that the inventory for a suitable Greek bride was slim at best. Over the next few years he and Mr. Stefanis became good friends, and as it happens, John had two daughters as potential wives to fill that role. What could be better for Mr. Stefanis? Not only

16

was young Gus his employer, but now he had the opportunity to have him as a son-in-law.

View of the south side of Montgomery Street between Myers and Huntoon Streets was taken around 1918. Historic Washington Block is shown at left. The pointed roof at the end of the block is on the Hecker Building.

The second building from the left with the three large upstairs windows was Grandpa Gus's Oro Vista Rooming House. Picture courtesy James Lenhoff, from his book, "Images of America- Oroville California." Montgomery Street - 1918.

John also had a son who was a Greek Orthodox priest and lived out his life in Greece. At one time in his young life Gus also had aspirations of becoming a priest and was well-schooled in the Greek Orthodox teachings. I can see how John, who was just five years younger than Gus's own father Nicolaus, and Gus would have filled the void left in each other's lives. My father expressed that they had become very close, and having a wife to bring them together as family was only natural.

So, with that it was settled. In 1920 my great-granddad Mr. Stefanis made the arduous journey back across the United States and boarded a ship bound for Greece. Having been away for fourteen long years, it must have been an awkward yet joyful reunion.

While John was in California, he and his wife Joy, whom my aunt Joy was named after, wrote letters to each other so he could watch his young children sprout through her words. Besides providing the necessities of life, the money John sent home also paid for an occasional picture that allowed some sense of family cohesion. Upon arrival at his home in Greece, he found his eldest daughter Anastasia ill with the measles. She most certainly would have been quarantined, and the risk of traveling such a distance was out of the question. John was determined to have at least one of his daughters marry his good friend Gus, and decided his younger daughter Angelica would take her place.

Grandpa had requested a recent photo of his new bride-to-be, so the pictures were switched and my grandmother Angelica's picture was sent instead. With Gus's curiosity satisfied, a Greek wedding was in the forecast. Once again, John Stefanis, said goodbye to his beloved wife and adult children. It was another bittersweet moment – siblings saying goodbye to each other; one anticipating a fresh new life, the other still waiting. A wife who would once again miss the warmth of her husband, as well as the presence of her youngest daughter. Yet it was expected that at a certain age the women would marry and the men would go off to make their own way. And so this was true for the Stefanis family as their son had already decided on priesthood and now their daughter would begin her own family. Grandchildren were in the future. Pictures and letters would have to do. That's the way it was in those times as sacrifice was synonymous with life.

Angelica

On December 16, 1920 John and Angelica docked in New York harbor having sailed on the Calabria from Patras, Greece. It was the same town Gus had sailed from fourteen years earlier. John took ill on the voyage, but recovered quickly and they were allowed to "step ashore" four days later on the 18th. According to the ships manifest, John had a nephew living in Keene, New Hampshire whom they were able to stay with until he felt strong enough to continue the exhausting journey west. At the age of sixty, Mr. Stefanis was not a young man, but as I have said, Greeks are a tough breed. Finally they arrived in Oroville and soon-to-be husband and wife met for the first time.

Angelica was relieved to find her soon to be husband well put together from his years in construction. Grandpa was a very handsome eligible bachelor with perfectly arched dark eyebrows over coffee brown eyes. His short black hair receded slightly on each side, and a manicured mustache extended to the corners of his mouth. In most of the pictures I've seen of Gus in his twenties and thirties he's impeccably dressed in business suits complete with hats, ties, and a pocket watch tucked neatly within his vest. It was apparent Gus was a solid businessman to whom prosperity soon would follow.

Gus had already seen a picture of the woman who would bear his children, but still there are nuances in a person's personality a photo is unable to reveal. He knew his bride would have an olive complexion, round face, and very short wavy brown hair parted to one side. Grandma had a nonchalant gaze in most of her younger pictures, with soft brown eyes and simple features. Her dresses were very stylish yet modest for the era of the roaring twenties. Living in a small Greek village during the early 1900's there was much farm work including tending to animals, gardens, and picking fruit and olives. Her chores also included making food from scratch, like breads and pasta. The list was never ending. As a result, Angelica was amazingly strong with a short, sturdy body that plumped through the years. The pair complimented each other, bringing their own set of skills to a soon to be union.

As for love, it either would or wouldn't find its way to their hearts, but both possessed the character and openness for the seed to grow. An arranged marriage comes with no guarantee, but then what marriage does? I do believe having come from poverty, both embraced the allure of making money, and Angelica saw with her own eyes her new husband-to-be had wasted no time in that department.

With the wedding date set, all that was needed now was an appropriate altar. The closest Greek Orthodox Church was in Sacramento, California which is a good seventy miles south of Oroville. The Northern Electric Railway ran from Oroville to Sacramento during those early years providing convenient transportation for the wedding party. Our family is fortunate to have three wedding photos taken that day with expressions that would lead one to believe the next stop was divorce court. Grandma and Grandpa, bride and groom, were without smiles, and yet from Gus's posture I detected a very proud moment. Angelica, on the other hand, looked woefully unamused.

In my research about their wedding day, I found an email address for a priest at the only Greek Orthodox Church in Sacramento. I emailed the priest and attached the three photos of my grandparents' wedding day, along with their names and Greek last names, Alexiou, and Stefanis. I estimated the year they may have gotten married, and requested any tangible information he might uncover. A few days later I was ecstatic to receive this email.

Good afternoon Marianne,

We do have marriage records going back to February 12, 1921. Your grandparents actually were the 5th recorded marriage at Annunciation.

Konstantine Alexiou and Aggeliki Stefani were married by Father George Sardounis on May 13, 1921. The groom was 33 years old and it was his first marriage. The bride was 23 years old and it was her first marriage. Both were living in Oroville, California. The sponsor (koumbaros) of the marriage is not listed. Attached is a scanned copy of the original entry from the parish archival records.

Father James

I could not have been more pleased!

Gus and Angelica Aleck

Gus and Angelica Aleck wedding party with John D. Stefanis far right.

Chapter 2

OUR FRENCH BEGINNINGS

It wasn't until after my maternal grandmother Simone died that we began learning more about the French side of our family. That's when my mother displayed some old black and white photos we had never seen before. Mame, which is what we called our grandmother, must have kept them tucked safely away somewhere since I don't remember seeing them in her house. There was much to discover about my French bloodline. Growing up, we had heard the scandalous story about my mom's father Jean, followed by constant declarations of his innocence, and a little about our great-grandmother, whom we called Grand Mame` MeMille. For the longest time I never even knew her real name. Our ancestors on my mother's side were all natives of France, but names and personal stories remained as distant as the relatives who bore them.

Amongst the photos my mom brought out was a small picture of my great-great-grandfather Sebastien Stoll. It was a military picture of him from his waist up as he sits with arms crossed, staring straight ahead. Sebastien's dark uniform has a double row of brass buttons, and shoulder dressing called epaulette, worn during that period. On his upturned collar is the number 140. I assume the number was that of his regiment. Maybe I'm biased, but as with my great-grandfather on my dad's side, I think he is a very handsome man with fair hair, again, genes Gregg must have inherited, a handlebar mustache, and a well-manicured beard. I had never given much thought as to what uniform he was wearing or from what war he may have fought. As before, I was busy with my own life, and just knew he was Grand Mame` MeMille's father. It wasn't until I began my research that I discovered that the uniform was worn by French soldiers during the Franco-Prussian War. My mother confirmed that he had indeed fought in that bloodbath.

Sebastien Stoll

As with most conflicts, the Franco-Prussian war had its roots in the struggle for power. In 1870, France declared war on Prussia, and the Second French Empire battled against the much stronger, more organized Kingdom of Prussia. One thing that France hadn't counted on was the North German Confederation joining forces with Prussia. Napoleon III was the ruler of France at the time, and during that same year in September was captured at the Battle of Sedan. Not long afterward the war came to an abrupt halt on May 10, 1871. The French territories of Alsace and part of Lorraine (both bordering Germany in the North Eastern part of France) were taken by Prussia and annexed to Germany. Over the years these French regions had many Frenchmen with German surnames who identified with their French nationality and had lived for generations as French nationals. Even so, there was for some, a nagging emotional attachment to their German homeland. Where one's loyalty lay became an internal battle in the minds of those afflicted.

So, this was the era my great-great-grandparents had lived in. The mere mention of Napoleon makes it seem like so very long ago. As I continued searching for tidbits of his life, I had a wonderful surprise when I found a document online that read; Alsace-Lorraine, France Citizenship Declarations 1872. It was a simple one-page document which showed my great-great-grandfather Sebastien Stoll had retained his French citizenship after the war. The document also stated he was born in Kaysersberg, France about 1853. By 1872 he was only 19; still a very young man who had lived through the gruesome reality of war. Having fought in the battles, it must have been extremely punishing to continue to live in a region that was now a part of Germany. After the conflict, German families began making the region their new home. Even though much of Alsace and parts of Lorraine had German influences from centuries before, there was a noticeable shift in attitude as resentment set in among the French. The emotional landscape had changed due to the thousands of men who had lost their lives in some of the most horrific battles ever fought. Even women and children fell victim to the senseless slaughter called war. And those who survived, those who lived through the horror, would never forget. They became prisoners in their own country. Their new government took on a foreign appearance, for now they had the mark of Germany upon them as the French flag was lowered and replaced with the German Imperial Coat of Arms.

I for one don't think I could have stomached the aftermath. But stomach and survive they did. A few years later, Sebastien met and married his bride Philomene Zimmerman who was five years younger than he. She was a sturdy, plump woman with a round face and jolly smile.

Philomene had a daughter out of wedlock by the name of Augustine. Even though during those times it was very rare for a woman in that compromised position to find a suitable husband, the pair fell in love and soon married. When we were young my mother told us we had relatives living in the Alsace Lorraine region, and that it had become part of Germany at one time. Her mother would write letters to the Zimmermans in Molsheim, France, and referred to them as the "cousins Alsace." Now, I had a name of at least one of the relatives that was somehow related to the "cousins Alsace," who had lived in that region.

Wanting to live as true French citizens Mr. Stoll decided it was time to leave the scars of battle and German rule behind. Part of survival includes knowing when it's time to leave, so Sebastien packed his dignity, along with his new loving family and traveled west across the French countryside.

France's railways and locomotives were being improved upon and traversed all regions of France with Paris as their final destination. It was the first time either had left the Alsace region. What an adventure it must have been, what a breath of fresh air, and yet a bittersweet moment leaving their beloved friends and family behind. The military had shaped my great-great-grandfather into a disciplined man. His confidence was his strength, and he would continue to walk boldly on this earth, never looking back. They settled in a small village by the name of Saint Lubin des Joncherets in Upper Normandy where he soon found work in the local spinning mills.

Sebastien and Philomene weren't my only ancestors who were born in the Alsace region. With a letter my aunt Colette (my mother's sister) received from an inquiry to Colmar, France, I was able to determine that Emile Wacker, my great-grandfather was born in Colmar, France on April 6, 1876 to my great-great-grandparents Mathias and Marie Anne Wacker. Marie's maiden name was Hirtz, a confirmation of the German lineage in that region. Colmar is also in Alsace which was still annexed to Germany while Emile was growing up. His father Mathias worked as a *tisserand*, which is French for weaver. When Emile was old enough, and after his schooling, he followed in his father's footsteps and labored in the spinning mill. Employment alone wasn't enough to fulfill the youthful spirit of his early twenties. And so just before the turn of the century, Emile was ready to make his own way in the world. Surely there had to be more to life for a Frenchman than living under the German's thumb. Many Alsatians had made the exodus to the region of north-western France where small spinning and weaving mills had sprouted. He settled in the quaint village of Nonancourt which lies in the southern portion of Upper

Normandy and borders the region of Centre to the south. With his experience as a weaver he soon took a position at one of the local mills; the same mill where Sebastien worked.

Emile Wacker

And that is how both my great and great-great-grandfather left the region of Alsace and settled in neighboring villages a stone's throw from each other. Sebastien, who was twenty-three years older than Emile had settled in Saint Lubin des Joncherets years prior to Emile's trek to Nonancourt. During that time, Sebastien and Philomene raised four daughters: Augustine, whom Sebastien adopted, Victorine, Melanie, and Louise. It was Louise Stoll, born October of 1884 who later became my great-grandmother, my Grand Mame` MeMille.

The Stoll children were raised in a very disciplined, yet loving environment. The family enjoyed a small piece of land with a humble home where sisters shared bedrooms, and the well-placed out-house was just the right distance and downwind from their home. They had the usual horse and buggy for transportation which was kept securely in their small barn.

As a means of self-sufficiency the family tended to their seasonal gardens and fruit trees. The Stoll's had a cow for milking, chickens for fresh eggs, pigs for meat, and other farm animals. Framed with wild flowers and green hillsides their little farm captured the true essence of the French country side.

Everyone pitched in as it was the way all families lived back in the day. Sebastien continued his position at the local mill as Philomene tended to their children and farm. As they grew older, some of the sisters, including Louise, joined their father in his trade. It was tedious work with long hours, but in such a small village one did not complain. Instead, they talked amongst one another, allowing the time to pass effortlessly, while the small community wove together, becoming one large extended family.

It wasn't long before Louise and Emile had an interest in one another. Her father, of course, knew the handsome young man since they toiled at the same job. Like Sebastien, Emile was intelligent and well-read; a fine suitor who qualified to be a husband for his youngest daughter. My Aunt Colette recalled her grandmother Louise's tale that many women in the village made their interest in Emile known, but his gaze fell upon her, and her alone. They truly did love one another, and with her family's blessing, Emile and Louise were married on March 19, 1904. Our family is fortunate that my grandmother saved her parents' wedding photo and tattered wedding certificate, and unlike the marriage of my Greek grandparents, they genuinely appeared as cheerful newlyweds.

Emile and Louise Wacker

Emile had higher aspirations than working as a *tisserand* the rest of his life. This seemed like the perfect time to break free of the family profession of spinners and weavers. So he and his wife made the transition into owning and operating their own *Laiterie et Buvette*, which translates to Dairy and Barroom. The Wacker team became *fromage* or cheese makers, getting their raw milk from the locals. My mother referred to it as a creamery, or one could say, a very small cheese factory. As the name suggests, their storefront also kept plenty of aperitifs and wine available to quench the thirst of the Frenchmen. When the creamery was well under way and business steady, the timing was right to have a child. Two years after their marriage, my grandmother Simone Sebastienne Clementine Wacker was born on July 6, 1906, the year of the Great San Francisco earthquake. Louise's oldest sister Augustine, who had her own child by now, acted as midwife and had the honors of delivering her newborn baby niece.

Once again, my grandmother, who was an only child, had come through by saving a picture that may well be one of my favorites. It appears to have been taken around 1911, since Simone is in the picture and looks to be about five years of age. My great-grandmother Louise and her daughter are standing outside the door of their business with two other young girls alongside them. I don't know who they are, but with Louise having three sisters they could easily have been my grandmother's cousins. Two large metal milk cans sit in the foreground, while the four are holding different sized ladles. All appear cozy in layered, long sleeve, hand-sewn dresses and aprons, with only Louise summoning a half smile. The charming brick building has a plaster finish covering all except a one-foot border leaving the brick exposed on either side of the oversized front door and tall narrow windows. They even have wooden shutters to protect the glass, and a sign affixed above the doorway which reads, *LAITERIE et BUVETTE* in caps.

On the dirt road next to them stands my great-grandfather Emile, proud business owner, holding the reigns of his white horse hitched to a small covered wagon with two large wooden spoke wheels. His flat cap shades deep brown eyes while sporting a thick untamed mustache. Great-Grandpapa was a true working man with dark baggy pants, frumpy buttoned-down jacket, and worn work boots. How I love the simplicity of this image; one they would look back on with much fondness when all were healthy. A magical time that the family would wish they could go back to and remain in.

Wacker family with horse and wagon.

I remember visiting my grandmother one day while she was in the hospital. I'm not sure how we got on the subject but she told me in her thick French accent how when she was a little girl her father had a horse and buggy. She said she loved going for rides with him as they traveled the beautiful French terrain. Her old eyes lit up as she remembered how beautiful the flowers were, and how hillsides always seemed to be lush and green, unlike the dry brown fields where we live now. She expressed a deep love for her father and said that he was a caring hard working man. I couldn't help but think as she lay in the hospital that she knew her time was drawing near. There was comfort in reliving the days of her youth. Mame's body may have been withering, but her mind remained clear and focused.

She told me a story of how on one of their trips her father had a basket full of plums in the back where she liked to sit. With eyes gleaming, she recounted how they were so sweet, tasting like candy, that she kept eating one after another. She didn't know how many but said she ate plenty! Then Mame laughed a little to herself, and said softly to make sure no one else in the hospital could hear. *"I had to use the cabinet for three days after that, but it was worth it."* We laughed as I knew the word 'cabinet' can be used in French for bathroom. What a wonderful memory to have lived such a simple life as a child, when eating a sweet juicy plum was the best thing in the world!

As Simone grew older she attended the local school and continued to help with the family business. Mame had cousins to play with, including Roger, Augustine's only child. Being close in age, the two cousins grew up much like brother and sister. Simone relished her time with her grandparents on the family farm. Years later she would share with her own daughters that this was one of the happiest times of her life.

A very young Simone with her grandmother Philomene on the family farm.
About 1911.

Augustine left and her sister Louise right on bikes with Augustine's son Roger looking on. About 1911

Cousin Roger

All was going as planned for Emile and his little family. He had no regrets for having left the Alsace region, since after all, he would never have met his cherished wife, or had such a perfect child. But there are situations that can arise in our lives where we have no control. In 1914 when Simone was but eight years of age, France and Germany were at war again. It escalated into The Great War which would later be known as World War I. Emile was thirty-eight at the beginning, and without hesitation, joined the ranks of fellow Frenchmen to once again fight for their freedom. He still held the childhood memories of the effects of the Franco-Prussian war, and the horror stories his father-in-law Sebastien shared over bottles of wine. In fact, my mother confided in me she had learned in her own history classes that France had never fully put the humiliation of losing that conflict to rest, and shared a united consciousness for revenge.

Simone, age 7

The assassination of Archduke Franz Ferdinand of Austria by a Bosnian Serb on June 28, 1914, was the match that ignited this blaze. Austria retaliated by invading Serbia a month later on July 28, 1914. Soon afterward Germany invaded Belgium, Luxembourg, and France, while Russia attacked Germany. The carnage had begun. One of the first battles the French engaged in was the Battle of the Ardennes, in the Lorraine region, August 21-23, 1914, which was part of the Battles of the Frontiers. Through my mother I learned that Emile fought in this dreadful slaughter of the French third and fourth armies.

Fighting continued in northeastern France, including the Alsace region. Technology had advanced since 1870, along with new ways to kill one another. Literally millions of shells exploded from both the Allies and their enemy, the Central Powers. This war brought about the birth of trench warfare, with miles and miles of trenches dug within the landscape housing millions of soldiers. The Western Front became a city unto itself with supply lines from both sides continuous in their efforts to keep the weary troops armed, fed, and alive. These were the grunts of war that lived in the trenches for months, even years on end. The conditions were deplorable, with mud, hunger, sickness, and the constant fear of death, with death being the norm. The unfit who could no longer continue the fight were routinely replaced with fresh faces.

From February 21, 1916 until December 16, 1916 the famous Battle of Verdun took place. After ten exhausting months it is said to have been one of the lengthiest and deadliest of battles ever fought. In the end, an estimated 700,000 died, were wounded, or were considered missing on a tiny patch of land less than a square ten kilometers. Much is written about this senseless display of inhumanity that Emile also fought in and somehow survived.

All of this and the introduction of chemical warfare had taken root throughout Emile's and Sebastien's homeland. Rows of canisters of the deadly poisons, such as tear gas, mustard gas, phosgene, and chlorine were placed in strategic locations. When weather conditions allowed, the gasses were released, resulting in torturous deaths for thousands.

Emile Wacker in his French uniform

At such a young age Simone would have had a hard time understanding why her father had left their happy trio. Louise was barely able to keep the doors to the *Laiterie et Buvette* open. I imagine others stepped in to fill Emile's boots, and being surrounded by family eased the burden. Still, each day would begin with a prayer to bring their loving husband and father home safe to their arms. The wait seemed like an eternity, but finally with Germany's surrender, The Great War came to an end on November 11, 1918, dubbed Armistice Day. Almost fifty years had passed since the War of 1870, and at long last, with the Treaty of Versailles, Alsace-Lorraine once again flew the French blue, white, and red.

Upon Emile's return, it soon became apparent that the effects of noxious fumes that filled the battlefields had its effect on this brave soldier. At first glance his infliction wasn't as visible as some war injuries can be, for he had been subjected to mustard gas. The effect would leave him with permanent respiratory damage that was progressive as he aged. I have a picture of my great-grandfather prior to his illness, standing proud in his French uniform. He looks very healthy with two war medals pinned to his chest. And I have another of Emile, Louise, and Simone taken a few years later. The hardships of the Great War are clearly visible as Emile's face is drawn and his clothes hang two sizes too big. Louise aged more quickly than she would have liked, while my grandmother in her early teens appears immune to the situation. Internally though, she knew their lives had changed.

With the family reunited, they did their best to continue with some sense of normalcy. Although not in the best of health, Emile insisted on continuing the dairy runs. The townspeople and farmers knew of his condition and would assist him in placing the heaving cans of raw milk in his wagon. As it was a family business, I imagine a nephew could have assisted in much of the heavy lifting. This was the new normal for the Wacker family, but in spite of his difficulties, all felt blessed to have Papa and husband home again.

Emile, Simone, Louise

Simone continued her schooling and her duties at the *Laiterie*, but within a few years, at age sixteen another event would disrupt Simone's world, changing it forever. Unbeknownst to her, a woman by the name of Celina Poulain approached Louise, searching for a suitable wife for her nephew Jean Andre. The two women knew one another since they lived in such a small village. Louise was made aware of Celina's nephew and of his ambitious nature, exceptional schooling, and how he was seen as an eligible bachelor to many available young women. This may well have been the answer to Louise's prayers as she always feared what would become of her and Simone when Emile's health was beyond consolation. The year was 1923 – five years post WWI. Her husband was no longer able to make milk-runs, so that duty had been handed to another who was more than sympathetic to assist an ailing comrade.

Celina had noticed young Simone about town, and was aware of the family, who was Catholic, but did not attend church consistently enough by her standards. Regardless of the lack of regimented hours spent kneeling in the pew, my grandmother had been raised in a very strict religious household. She was not allowed to date, and most of her friends were her cousins. As a teenager she still had hormones as there was a young man Simone fancied. He would frequent the store to buy cheese and other foods. This naive adolescent was unaware of the sizable crush the pretty girl behind the counter had developed on him. She kept her feelings close to her chest, fearing that if her mother found out, she would banish him from the store forever. It had been made clear at work she was not to speak to the male gender except as necessary since it would have consequences.

Apparently her mother felt she knew best in choosing a suitable husband for her sheltered Simone. First though, because of what Celina perceived as an inappropriate Catholic upbringing, she wanted to test the character of young Simone and devised a most unconventional means. One day, with Louise's approval, she walked into the store, and without making a purchase asked for change. It was not customary to provide the service of giving change if a transaction hadn't accrued. After all, the small shop owners needed their cash for paying customers, not window shoppers. Simone accepted the bill from the woman and cheerfully gave the change she had asked for. And with that small gesture of a willingness to go above and beyond, she passed the character test. In Celina's world this was proof-positive my grandmother would make a fine wife for her nephew since she did not get grumpy or refuse to give her change, regardless of the fact that Celina hadn't spent one single Franc in their shop. I must admit, when my aunt told me this story I was quite amused. If only life was this simple today.

A meeting between the potential bride and groom was set. But there was one small unknown in this equation that the meddlers hadn't considered – Simone herself. What if Simone had no feelings toward this man who was six years her senior? It never even occurred to Louise or Celina that this naive young woman might shun the advances of such a suitable young bachelor. That she might, in fact have a mind of her own with emotions and desires that didn't agree with theirs. Celina viewed her tall, dashing nephew as a real catch. To her there was no alternative. They would be married, live happily ever after, and that would be that! In such a strict home, one did not sass or disrespect one's parents. Although I can't imagine that she, as a young hormonal teenager remained silent. Even though she knew her protest would fall silent upon her parents' ears, rebel she did. Her tears were met without sympathy and it was Louise who was angry at her daughter for being unappreciative.

As far as Louise was concerned this young suitor was their savior, and her daughter the snare to catch him. What could Simone do, run away, refuse their demand? And it most certainly was a demand that would squeeze tightly around her ring finger. It would be a constant reminder of the helplessness she wore, mixed with the betrayal of her mother. I say 'mother' because she was keenly aware of the influences her mother had on her ailing father. Later in life Simone related this story to my mother and told her, *"Right up to when I stood at the altar, I told myself, I'm going to say no, I'm not going to say yes."* What torment for such a young woman. In the final seconds as she stood with a strange man by her side, Simone's ingrained obedience to her parents would declare itself the winner as she whispered, *"I do" en Francais.* They married on July 16, 1923, just ten days after her seventeenth birthday. I can't even begin to imagine how their wedding night must have played out. Not just for her, but for her new unwitting husband Jean, for he too was a victim of family intervention.

I have the family tree on my grandfather Jean's side dating back to the 1700's. On it I found Celina Poulain's name listed as Jean's father, Emile Louis Poulain's sister. It stated she was *"celibataire,"* or single, when she passed in 1946 at age seventy-three. I wondered what would possess a single woman who never married to play matchmaker. My mother recalled that Celine had worked at the local post office and later had become my aunt Colette's Godmother. Unfortunately, other than Jean's mother, two brothers, and a sister listed on the family tree, the names and information of all the others are just names on paper. Long lost relatives I'll never come to know.

Simone and Jean's wedding. July 16, 1923

Even though I have no stories to go with my grandfather's side of the family, I do have Simone and Jean's wedding photo. I counted twenty-five people seated and standing in the black and white photo taken in front of a wonderful brick building which I assume is the church where they wed. Jean and Simone are seated in the middle front row with family behind and to each side. Jean's mother Noel Marie Poulain is seated by her son's side. She was born Christmas day, 1871, hence her name Noel, which is French for Christmas. Jean's two brothers and a sister attended the wedding. And of course, Simone's parents, and even her grandparents, Sebastien and Philomene were present. Sebastien, who if you recall, had fought in the Franco-Prussian War, was now in his seventies. He had balded some and was sporting a thick, greyer goatee and mustache, but looked healthy; the years being very kind to this old solider. Of his wife Philomene, my mother said, *"She looks like someone you'd want to sit next to and have a conversation."* With her rounded face and cheerful smile I think she was the only one having a good time that day. Emile is seated next to his daughter, and at the age of forty-seven appears a bit thin and older, but still holding up better than one would think, given his condition. Louise is seated next to Emile and appears to have put on weight, looking very robust indeed. My mother pointed out the matchmaker Celina Poulain standing in the back row, far left, with a sternness that would make a Drill Sergeant quiver!

Lastly, my grandmother has her arm entwined with her new husband's as they stare straight away. A simple white gown is accented with a thin wired headband laced with petite flowers. Above the shoulder, her wavy brown hair is reminiscent of 1920's hairstyles as Mame seems to do her best to force a smile. Seated by her side, Jean appears debonair in a three-piece suit with upturned white collar and matching bow tie. The ensemble is complete, sporting trendy spats over well-polished shoes. I had to grin at my grandfather's disheveled hair that held a Krameresque flair, and his tightly pierced lips. Looking at the photo, one would never know this was an arranged marriage. Young Simone put on a good show to please her parents while fooling the others, as this was supposed to be the happiest day of her life.

Jean and Simone Poulain

Chapter 3

JOHNNY'S EARLY YEARS & THE GREAT

DEPRESSION

The cultural landscape of America is constantly evolving, with the surge of immigrants at the turn of the century a huge contributing factor. Millions from both European and Chinese descent along with a splattering from other countries swelled the large metropolitan cities, overflowing into rural America. I don't believe there was a single town across this vast nation in the 1920's that didn't house at least one new family from abroad.

Gus and Angelica were one of these families getting better acquainted as husband and wife. Gus continued his work in construction while Angelica was able to spend time bonding with her father after all those years apart. She followed him around the rooming house as he did his daily routines, slowly learning her version of broken English. Husband and wife became one under the roof of the Oro Vista as Gus had yet to purchase a proper home. With a double bed, bathroom down the hall, and small kitchen near the back office, all necessities were in place. It was a huge adjustment for my grandma. American customs, language, dress, and even diet, is so different from that of her homeland. Then to be married to this man she barely knew would have required a strong woman indeed. What a different time, a different way of life my grandparents lived.

Soon Angelica tired of their lack of privacy and yearned for a home of their own with a larger kitchen and room for future children to roam. Gus found a suitable house in the downtown residential area within walking distance to his business. The timing couldn't have been better as a few months after their first wedding anniversary Angelica started showing. In March of 1923 they had their firstborn, my aunt Bess. It wasn't long before my dad Johnny was born in May of '24 followed by the twins, Joy and Nick in April of '25.

Gus stands proud in back, John Stefanis sitting with toddler, Johnny, Angelica carrying twins Joy and Nick, and lovely Aunt Bess as a little girl.

My mother told me on several occasions that my grandma Angelica was a very superstitious woman. Still I was amazed when Aunt Joy shared that her mother made sure her and Nick's birth certificate stated they were born on the eighth of April when in fact they were both born on the ninth. The ninth apparently had bad ju-ju and could result in a curse upon her babies. I wondered how she was able to legally do this, and if it in fact it actually happened. I'll never know for sure. Joy went on to say that Nick, the younger of the pair, was born a "blue baby" from lack of oxygen, and required a nurse to care for him for a short while before Angelica could love on him full time. Maybe there was some truth to Angelica's mythical ways after all.

Regardless, Gus was a very proud man with his successful business, machismo construction career, and now a beautiful Greek family. It was hard to conceive that had he stayed behind in the tiny village of his birth all this could have been possible.

Grandpa lived to work, and my father would say, *"My dad believed in dumbbells, and wrestling and being strong."* That would explain his motivation to get up each morning before daybreak full of energy and vigor. Gus was a snappy dresser with his multitudes of suits. Likewise, he was very conscious of his image amongst his work peers. He was most comfortable in what I would call a Mountie style uniform. Khaki in color, his shirts were collared, button-down, with long sleeves, pants that billowed on the sides known as breeches, rugged lace-up work boots, and to top it off, a matching wide brim hat for protection against the blistering summer sun or rainy wet weather. His days were long, and the crew even worked half days on Saturday, but not once did he complain. He was small in stature yet unstoppable in pure grit. Being just 5'4" and weighing less than a buck fifty, young grandpa was able to pack not one, but two bags of cement, one on each shoulder for a combined weight of just shy of two hundred pounds. As if that wasn't impressive enough, he would run the bags up a ramp, lap after lap. Work turned into an exhibition of strength as the men made a game of it to see who could out work the other. The word "lazy" didn't exist in this world of virile competition. The strong truly did survive, as this brotherhood, by the sweat of their brow, helped build the greater Oroville area.

While Gus did his part, Angelica stayed home raising their young family. My father recalled his earliest recollections of living in their first house as a child of about three. *"There were three homes that were built way up high for when the water would rise. The river would rise and eddy back in. It wouldn't be a force, it would just eddy back in. You lived above so nothing would get wet then the water would go back down. I think we lived in the next to the last one, there were three of them there. As a kid, just a little brat, I used to run up and down those stairs then go up to the corner where it widened out to the cribbage. Of course I didn't know what it was at the time. The cribbage was where all the hustling girls worked, and was up against the levee. There was a couple of bootleg joints and all that too. But on this side it was all Chinatown businesses clear up to the Ford garage where they used to sell Packards."*

It was pure joy listening to my dad talk about his youth. You could hear the enthusiasm in his voice, as he could see in his mind the images he portrayed through words and hand gestures. The area he spoke of, though still residential, has changed since his childhood memories. The river is the Feather River I mentioned earlier, and at this time the full height of the levee had yet to be built. Flooding was always a concern for the downtown businesses and residences as is recorded in the town history. Today, little remains of the

Chinese who populated the downtown area except for the historic Chinese Temple now owned and maintained by the city of Oroville. I had to laugh, knowing my father's first impressions were of call girls and bootleggers since both prostitutes and alcohol would be part of our families' future ventures. It must have been a colorful neighborhood for this wide-eyed, snotty-nosed kid.

When Johnny was still a youngster two to three thousand Greeks lived in what he called a colony at the end of Linden Avenue, east of the downtown area. They used to have huge parties near the river, and he remembered the cops being called on more than one occasion. Gus and Angelica would pack up the kids and travel the short distance up the hill on Montgomery, as the entire family thoroughly enjoyed the diversion from Gus's long work week and joined in the fun. It was a way for all to get out and catch up on local gossip while enjoying delicious food with friends. On the property was a sizable outdoor clay oven the men had built for the women of the community to bake bread. On those days a wonderful aroma filled the air, but when not in use the younger children, including my dad and his sibling, were allowed to crawl in and out of it. The cooled oven served as a lone babysitter, as the Aleck children thrived in the carefree wholesomeness of yesteryear.

As a community of immigrants, the children and adults spoke their native tongue, and only their native tongue. As my dad put it, "We spoke Greek, we ate Greek, we danced Greek. We would go from house to house on the weekends, and all get together. It was a good life!"

My father's earliest recollections of living in the downtown area would be his last, as Gus sold that house and bought another one, including the lot next-door, located on C Street in Oroville's South Side. At the old house downtown the constant intrusion of the river wasn't conducive to having a garden. Now with the additional lot they had plenty of room for both winter and summer vegetables. Drainage was an issue in their new neighborhood as the South Side was not annexed to greater Oroville. In fact, that wouldn't happen until 2015. Eight by ten inch trenches could be seen looping around the neighborhoods to divert water when it rained since there were no sidewalks or gutters. Likewise the city sewer lines were still years away, and each home had it's own out-house. My dad got a good laugh as he described theirs as being *"a two hole-er, and we even strung a line out to it. We were rich!"*

When Johnny was still a little tyke, too young for school, he used to take off from the house on C Street and head toward town to see his Grandpa Stefanis at the rooming house. Even though he was only four or five at the time, he knew his way to town and would walk, skip, and run the mile and half from their house.

"I used to run off from home and see my grandpa, because I knew he would give me donuts and ice cream if I went there, but I knew my way down, as little as I was, see. And Grandpa would always treat me good, and that's when pops hired old Jim Hunter, the old black garbage man. He had a Model T truck with a bunch of cans on it, and you could hear him coming up the road 'cause the Model T made lots of noise. If you looked down the street when he came to get your garbage, you'd see it had flies swarming all around it. Yeah, no kidding," he laughed. *"He'd pick up the garbage, and charged fifty cents a month. But he never wanted fifty cents – he'd come with his empty jug and my dad would give him a gallon of wine. And then Pop and him would have a nice glass at the same time. I can remember that."*

"Dad hired him to put me in a gunny sack to break me from running away from home. And he come after me and I fought him,

and my brother and sisters – everybody fought him, and finally I got away from him and went through the crawl hole under the house where he couldn't get me. He was laughing – I remember that, and having a ball. He thought it was funny, you know, and all that. And the kids were climbing over him and he finally left, then I come out of there. But it cured me from running away, see."

Bessie, twins Nick and Joy, Johnny

My father had made it clear as a kid he didn't know a lick of English. He does, however, vividly recall the first word he ever learned. The South Side had immigrants and blacks alike in the neighborhood, and C Street sits right in the heart of the small neighborhood. Still too young for school, my dad had this story: *"When the school would let out, or in the morning, I used to go out to the fence. It was a chicken wire fence and I used to put my nose to it. And these colored kids would all walk by and they'd all call each other [the n-word], and that was the first American word I ever learned, and I learned it from them. I couldn't speak a word of nothin' but Greek".*

The children were growing, as was Gus's wallet, and it wasn't long before he purchased three more lots – this time across the street from the Oroville High School. Two were side by side with one of the two on a corner. The third was another corner lot that sat across the street on the opposite corner. All were in the Orange Heights subdivision, so named due to the flourishing Orange orchard that once combed the rolling hills.

While the family continued living in the house on C Street, construction began on the lone corner lot that would soon become their brand new home. The kids enjoyed watching the progress, as they'd climb into the family car – a Falcon Knight made by Willys-Knight. Pops drove them and Mama the short drive around town to the new site and watched the crew as they dug out the basement. With Gus in construction I'm sure he hired fellow Greeks for the task. Even grandpa and his sons occasionally grabbed picks and shovels to help in the cause. It was demanding yet satisfying work for the two athletic boys, baptizing them into healthy work ethics.

During the next several months family trips continued, and with each, a growing anticipation of what seemed like a castle rising into the skies. Then finally, at long last their beautiful new home was complete. Their house on C Street was rented out, belongings packed, and the young family moved into their new abode around 1932 or 33.

Several wide steps led to the front covered porch that ran the full width of the front of the house. It was unique in that instead of having both ends open with short pony walls or railing, the builders created two very large circular openings on either side to look out through. They must have been at least six feet in diameter. When I was a kid we used to play on these foot-wide circles, laying in them since they provided a natural curve for our little bodies. Even though it felt like a mansion compared to the C Street home, their new house was a modest two-bedroom, one-bath with high ceilings and an open combined dining/living-room area. Later, my grandparents filled this space with heavy dark wood furnishing, including a long polished table and chairs for entertaining. A brick fireplace provided extra warmth and ambiance for chilly winter months. Entering through a door from the dining area, a small yet comfortable kitchen was situated, and off that was a screened-in back porch. The full basement below was thoroughly used throughout the years.

It was as if Gus could do no wrong. He had made one lucrative decision after another, but no sooner had the youngsters begun exploring their new stomping grounds than the financial storm was upon them. The hand of the Great Depression had taken hold, and in order to save his properties while keeping his family sheltered and fed, Gus had to come up with a plan, and quick. With his residence on C Street already rented (and fortunately to a couple who were of financial means to continue,) Grandpa made a bold yet difficult decision. Survival tactics kicked into gear as he put the word out that their new home was for rent. It was a great disappointment for all; one the children didn't fully understand. Even though grumbles could be heard, the family trusted the judgment of the head of their household. As luck would have it, a gentleman who at the time was in charge of one of the local lumber mills answered that call.

Grandpa secured a job in the canyon, so now, with the second house leased once again, he packed the family car for an adventure that was sure to stick in any youngster's mind. Following the banks of the north fork, the Falcon Knight served the family well as Gus maneuvered around one treacherous turn after another. The road through the Feather River Canyon was just a narrow strip of dirt winding through towering mountainsides and steep embankments. With the combination of Grandpa's cigar smoke and the coupe rattling around death-defying turns, Joy and her siblings got car-sick and threw up all over the back seat and floor boards. Fortunately, an occasional turn-out provided for off road pit stops. With a quick clean-up, and pink returning to the youngsters cheeks, the Greeks were on the road again until finally reaching their destination in the Pulga.

Once fully recovered from the nauseous ride the clan pitched two tents; one for sleeping, the other for cooking. Others, also hit by the Depression, had already arrived and made a community of tents, housing not just blue collar workers, but now their families too. No one knew how long this economic disaster would last. Without minute to minute updates as in the 21st century, all focus was in the moment, setting up cots and bedding, paying no mind to the "what ifs," just the "what is." There was an adjustment period to be sure, but having come from rural Greece, husband and wife embraced the peasant simplicity from their homeland. As for the children, my dad, who spoke fondly of these days, would reflect, *"It was one of the happiest times of my life."*

Gus worked as a blaster on one of three tunnels being carved out of the mountainside. A dangerous job to be sure, using dynamite and powder to bust up large portions of the solid granite. With his invincible demeanor I can see it was well within the realm of his personality to shout, *"Fire in the hole!"* He was an alpha male through and through and was meticulous in every aspect of his hazardous job. Other, less difficult projects put convict labor to work. With women and children in the area, my aunt said they were housed up the road and kept separate at all times.

Unable to build around the massive granite mountains that jutted down to the canyon floor, highway engineers blasted tunnels through the Grizzly Dome area east of Oroville. These tunnels are still used today.

Grizzly Dome, one of three tunnels blasted out of the thick granite mountain side in the Feather River Canyon. Photo courtesy James Lenhoff from his book, Images of America - Oroville, California. Date of picture unknown.

During the daytime hours the children did their book learning at a one-room school house called Injun Jim's. My dad said it was brand spanking new and he had built the first fire in the wood burning stove. It was packed with forty children, many of whom were Native American, for one lone schoolmarm to wrangle. Their teacher, Mrs. Hedge, whom Aunt Joy described as *"skinny and mean, with a long nose,"* one day accused Joy of stealing her lunch. For her punishment, Joy had to stay after class for an hour for the next five days to ponder what the teacher alleged was her crime. Johnny, who knew full well his sister hadn't taken the teacher's lunch, told Joy he wouldn't have accepted any punishment. Later, when the tough old coot learned my aunt was innocent, not a word of apology was heard. But my aunt never forgot, and years later, to her surprise, one day Mrs. Hedge showed up at her sister Bess's business. All Joy could think of was approaching her old teacher with the hope of hearing a heartfelt, "I'm sorry. I was wrong." For Joy, it was a matter of being vindicated. Since Mrs. Hedge was one of her sister's clients, Bess talked her younger sister out of the confrontation. Even now at age 90 my aunt still hasn't forgotten or forgiven her teacher for the penance she didn't deserve. That's a mighty long time to hold a grudge. As for my dad, he would eventually be held back that year. He said it was because there were too many other kids in school, but I think he just liked to daydream and couldn't wait for the bell to ring.

It was pretty hard to sit patiently and pay attention knowing the freedom that lay just beyond those walls. With a step into the great outdoors my dad and Nick lived their own Tom Sawyer adventures. One of the favorite pastimes for the brothers was to go fishing at one of many fishing spots along the river. It wasn't uncommon for them to walk two to three miles each way, hiking along switchback trails that opened to lush green hillsides. The pair gingerly crossed a swinging bridge that led them to an old wooden cabin. Once there they'd spend a few minutes swapping stories with the old Greek who called the mountains his home. Rested and watered, the two would continue on to their favorite fishing spot.

Nick was a natural fisherman, and even as a young squirt he fished often when they were still living in Oroville. He could sniff out the best place to drop a line with never an objection from Johnny. Once at the river lined with huge boulders and beautiful deep blue pools, the young brothers would kick off their shoes. The feel of the wet sand on their bare feet was cooling as they dragged railroad ties to the water's edge, making a small pier to fish from. It never took long for that familiar tug of the line to bring excitement to these two young anglers, pulling in their catch and comparing trophies. On Sundays when Gus was rested, he joined in many of these fishing expeditions. The rule was, he who caught the least had to haul the days catch back to camp. That was usually my dad. But when it came time to eat, he wasn't complaining.

When they weren't fishing, the boys were off hunting for small game, including quail and squirrel. This time it was Johnny who took the lead. Armed with just a .22 caliber rifle, his steady aim helped put food on the table. My dad always shot at the head to ensure there would be more meat to eat. Pops had taught his sons how to field dress their kill even though they weren't even in double digits yet. Living in the mountains, food was plentiful as long as one had the skill and gumption to take advantage. Mama did her part cooking up whatever the boys brought home. With a community garden and plenty of garlic and onions Angelica could flavor up any meal.

Deer was also a favorite and was abundant in this wilderness region. But big game was reserved for Gus and the men. My dad told a story about one of those hunting trips in which a good sized buck had been shot at the bottom of a steep ravine. After it was gutted, the hunters were having a difficult time packing the deer up the precarious incline. Gus finally handed his rifle to one of his buddies, crouched down and grabbed the carcass by the front and hind legs. Slinging it over his shoulders, Grandpa stood up, and with shot put calves, switch-backed his way clear to the top. The story was a keeper as brother John would hear this same tale repeated by old man Theveos, one of the venerable Greeks that witnessed his tremendous strength that day. Like I said, the Greek are a tough bunch!

With hundreds of people living in the area, stores had been set up to buy much needed supplies and dry goods. Gus still had a business in town, so instead of buying locally, he took his family to Oroville once a month by rail. While there, he and his wife gathered a stockpile of necessities and checked in on John at the Oro Vista. The family always stayed overnight, sleeping at the rooming house, or sometimes the kids lodged with friends. The following day, with provisions purchased at a much better price and business duties tended to, another scenic train ride back to their home away from home was a great way to break up the long months living in the canyon.

My Aunt Joy shared one more story that decades later, still raises the hair on the nape of her neck. Near their tents was a large shed where firewood was stored to keep it dry throughout the rainy winter months. One day my young aunt was walking past it and let out a death scream! Under the shed, rolled up in the dirt, flicking its forked tongue, was a poisonous rattlesnake. The rattles shook to the core of this little girl's fears as she had been taught full well the ill effects of their venomous bite. Fortunately for all, Pops was home and flew out of the flaps, rifle in hand and shot it dead. Pure fatherly instinct prompted him to grab that rifle which always sat loaded near the opening just in case. Excitement filled the air as neighbors took a good look around their own sites. There was never a dull moment during those lean years living in the Pulga. While the rest of the nation struggled through the Great Depression, this little Greek family created memories to last a lifetime.

Chapter 4

FROM RICHES....

Jean Andre Poulain

Born in 1900, my grandfather Jean Andre Poulain was too young to enlist in the French Army when The Great War first began in 1914. When he was of age a few years later, they accepted his enlistment, and, as luck would have it, the battles came to a halt just months afterward. His mother must have felt a huge relief since she had been a widow since 1905 and feared she may lose a son as well. Jean came from a well-to-do family; an important attribute that sold my great-grandmother on arranging for him to become her son-in-law. As my mother would suggest later, *"He was her meal ticket."* He originally wanted to be an architect, and as a talented artist, designing would follow suit. But Jean soon realized the salary of an architect wouldn't equal his ambitious appetite so he abandoned the idea.

Instead, he was hired as an insurance salesman where he deduced no cap would be placed on his earning potential. My mother had said, *"He could sell anything."* Tall, handsome, and charming was a cocktail for true success. After they married, Mr. Poulain moved his wife away from her family in Nonancourt to Rouen which is further north in Upper Normandy. My poor grandmother must have been miserable. They took a modest apartment above a *"Tabacs"* or tobacco shop, which is still there today. From the Tabacs one could see the place nearby where Joan of Arc was burned at the stake.

Mame wasn't one to sit still, and with Jean's business taking him on the road for days on end, to have something to do she took a position at the downstairs shop. The owner was more than happy to have a fresh young face with experience behind the counter. One day, to her complete disbelief an unexpected customer made an appearance. It was the young man she'd had a crush on when she worked in the creamery. My grandmother had once told me in a fleeting conversation that she had feelings for a young man prior to her arranged marriage. It must have been a very strong tug for her to have shared such personal information with me. He of course knew she was married, as they had come from the same small town. Her face blushed as her old feelings for him were rekindled. He was cordial, bought his goods, and then was off as quickly as he had appeared never to return again. With her heart pounding, Mame placed her cool hands on the warm flush in her checks. In her mind it was an awkward moment, but once again the blond-haired, blued-eyed young man was oblivious to her infatuation. It was a stabbing blow to her emotions as the excitement she felt in the presence of this young man was absent in the union with her husband. She felt a deep emotional desire that she knew would never come to fruition. How my young grandmother longed for just one tangible, passionate embrace. But in reality, as the years would drift by, the fire she felt in this puppy love moment would wash away and be shelved forever.

On the road, Jean's role with the insurance company was growing as he acquired large vineyards to insure as his clientele. His name floated amongst the well-to-do and prosperity was soon to follow. During this time my mother Monique was born in February 1927. When she was just six months old the Poulain's relocated from Rouen to an apartment in Dijon where they had a second child, my aunt Colette, in November of '28. During this same time it became apparent that Louise was no longer able to fully care for her husband's needs. The day had come to close the little creamery doors forever. In those days it was expected of a son-in-law, and Jean would have been seen as selfish if he did not care for his wife's ailing father. So, with that chapter behind them, the Wacker couple prepared for the big move. Now with a wife, toddler, newborn, and in-laws to support, Jean moved his family once more finding much larger accommodations that would suit their new living arrangements.

MONSIEUR ET MADAME JEAN POULAIN

SONT HEUREUX DE VOUS FAIRE PART DE LA

NAISSANCE DE LEUR FILLE

COLETTE.

25 NOVEMBRE 1928.

7, RUE EUGÈNE GUILLAUME, DIJON

Baby announcement for my Aunt Colette. Translated, it reads, Mr. and Mrs. Poulain are happy to share with you the birth of their daughter. Colette - November 25, 1928. 7, Rue Eugene Guillaume, Dijon.

When my mother spoke of her childhood, she spoke often of this new house. I had always envisioned it in my mind, but never knew the address to do an online search. One afternoon while eating our fromage and crackers over storytelling out of the blue, she recalled the address. I promptly wrote it down and found it on Google maps that evening. To be sure, this was the place. I printed the image and showed it to her. As soon as my mother saw it she exclaimed, *"That's it, that's the house!"*

From the picture I was able to view the detached two car garage which at one time housed the family car, a Renault, and Simone's symbol of wealth, a convertible Bugatti. Learning that my grandmother once had her own car was a real shock as she had never ever driven the entire time she lived in the US. In fact, we were not even aware she knew how to drive. And then to learn she had a vintage convertible Bugatti.... well, flabbergasted is a word that comes to mind.

A block and rock wall surrounded the house that sat on a corner with streets on three sides. The front entrance has large pillars made of block with two gates to access the property. One, an iron walking-gate for pedestrians, the other, a double-entry iron gate for their automobiles. The yard has plenty of room for trees and shrubbery which were abundant on the property in the 1930's. Along with a maid the family had a full time gardener who kept the flower beds perfectly manicured. In the backyard my aunt fondly remembered her grandfather Emile, who even as sickly as he'd become, devised a swing for her and her sister and hung it from one of the over-hanging branches. From the street view I could count two chimneys in front and two in the back for a total of four separate fireplaces.

My mother described in detail the interior of her childhood home. She recalled a flowing staircase with elaborate banisters and marble tiled steps that led to the upstairs bedrooms. The lodging included the master suite with a bathroom, a bedroom for the children to share, Jean's office with thick masculine furniture, and a separate upstairs apartment for Emile and Louise. Walking up and down the stairs was, to say the least, challenging for my great-grandfather, so he spent most of his days in his room. As time went on and his condition worsened he would stay weeks on end in a sanatorium for breathing treatments and care.

The downstairs had a kitchen, pantry, living area, and two of the fireplaces. The living space was accented with a built-in cabinet to display my grandmothers beautiful Fine China and shelving nooks showing off decorative figurines, vases, and the like. The cabinetry was constructed by the finest craftsmanship available, and the room, accented in

71

marble inlays and crystal chandeliers. They were surrounded by elegance.

Just off the living room was a "salon," or sitting room for after dinner conversation while the body rested from the gastronomical delights of a well-prepared French meal. Due to the nature of his business, the Poulains routinely entertained friends, clients, and potential clients. Much of the schmoozing would take place over an aromatic pipe or cigar, and settling glass of *"digestif"* which was usually brandy or a preferred liqueur.

When I asked my mother about her relationship with her mother as a child, one enduring memory came to mind. *"My mother was an exceptional seamstress, and she used to sew clothes for my doll. She would hand stitch beautiful dresses and even made silk panties for her."* But other than this one precious memory my mother would most often say, *"She was always gone with my father."* I sensed a sadness in her voice as her mother wasn't demonstrative with her feelings of affection during my mother's childhood. Young Monique diverted this loss of tenderness toward her doll as a way of coping. Even though she had a sister, they were very different in that Colette was more of a tomboy, playing outside while my mom preferred the solace of children's books and the comfort of her baby dolls.

With Simone's mother now a live-in babysitter, it was true she often accompanied her husband on his long business excursions. Jean's territory extended throughout the region of Champagne Ardenne and Burgundy, of which Dijon is the capital. It is evident purely by name recognition alone that Jean was in the midst of multitudes of vineyards all awaiting his arrival. It was customary in those times to invite businessmen who traveled such long distances to be invited as dinner guests. It wasn't uncommon for these meals to last three to four hours with the best the winery had to offer being un-corked and sipped with enthusiasm.

Wives traded stories of their children, favorite restaurants, and the latest Paris fashions. While the men embellished on anecdotes too grand to be real. Everyone knew and expected larger than life tales as a means of entertainment not to be taken seriously. As the evening wore on, voices boomed, polite laughter turned to roars of thunderous applause, and deals were made. Client and salesperson became friends, and as every good salesperson knows, people prefer to buy from people they know. It was the early 1930's and the world was the Poulain's oyster.

In their private lives however, life would not be so forthcoming. As to whether or not Simone ever changed her emotions for Jean, my mother's response was a quick, *"No, not really."* But I do believe she fell in love with a certain *"savoir-faire"* her husband possessed in the art of money making. He wasn't her first choice, nor would he have been her last, but her basket of lemons had turned to cases of champagne, and Simone was along for the ride. And ride they did, frequenting Paris as often as some shop Walmart. They attended the theater and plays, dined at the most exquisite restaurants, tossing money like peanuts in a zoo. They didn't just act like high society – they *were* high society, rubbing elbows with other well-to-do's. In Paris they shopped the finest clothing stores. Outfits were tailored to their exact measurements. Even at home my grandmother had a favorite seamstress who would come to their house with bolts of fabric to choose from. Mame would make her choices, measurements were taken, and beautiful one-of-a-kind outfits would set the family apart. Furs, diamonds, silk scarfs, all were the norm for this young woman who had once squeezed cheese through a cheese cloth.

Simone Poulain

Jean too was most fashionable in his tailored three-piece suits, with double-breasted overcoats, sporting velvet collars, and a kerchief accenting the pocket. He continued to wear spats over his polished shoes which were reserved for the upper echelon, and his pocket watch was worth thousands. Jean wouldn't be a very good son-in-law or father if he didn't make sure the same standards weren't enjoyed by his entire family. His mother-in-law had her share of furs, and I can only wonder what conversation between mother and daughter would have been like. Was it customary for the "I-told-you-so's" to emerge from Louise's lips? Or was it unspoken with subtle glances of "See, I was right." One can only guess.

Our family has three photos taken of my grandparents as they vacationed along the *"cote d'azur"* or French Riviera in Nice, France. They were strolling along the *Promenade des Anglais* when a professional photographer captured the essence of affluence Jean had showered upon his family. In the black and white photo my aunt who was just a baby is being pushed in a fancy carriage by her grandmother. My mother looks to be just shy of two in this picture, so it would have been taken in the winter of 1928 or early '29. The clothes I had described are what my grandparents were wearing. Keeping my young mother warm was a one of a kind designer jacket. It is two-tone with the darker color on top, and what I can only describe as a resemblance of thick blades of grass wrapped around the bottom in a lighter color. She's swinging a child's bucket, and of all things, little Monique also has her own small fur draped gently about the neck. As with mother and grandmother, a stylish *chapeau* is snuggled atop her head to stay warm.

The Poulains on Holiday in the South of France. Winter of 1928 - 29.

At home, all was going as well as one could expect under the stress of a masked marriage. Then in 1932 news came from Nonancourt that Sebastien, who by now was just shy of eighty, had died from kidney failure. A few years prior in '27, the year my mother was born, his wife Philomene had also left this realm at age sixty-nine. Mame had been especially fond of her grandfather and it was heartbreaking that she had not been able to spend time with him in his later years, although they did correspond through letters. She would carry the most precious of memories of Grandpapa.

Philomene Stoll

Likewise, this was Louise's father, who she idolized. From what my aunt had said, both women felt as though Sebastien could do no wrong and had always let their affection for him be known. With these thoughts, the Renault was packed and the family traveled in silent remembrance, mourning the passing of one so loved, grieving for weeks. My mother, although a very young girl at the time, still remembers the cemetery.

Sebastien Stoll

Within the same year, Emile's condition deteriorated, and by 1933 Simone found herself staying at home more while Jean continued his rounds. The inevitable was upon them as my great-grandfather was spending more time in the sanatorium and less at the grand home in Dijon. I learned enough to know my great-grandfather had lived an honest life, took chances on the family business with success, and above all, dearly loved his family. The war had caused irreversible damage to his lungs, but his will to live had extended his life by another fifteen years. This precious time allowed him to watch the unfolding of his only daughter's life, and so he knew she would be just fine. There was joy in his heart with the gift of two beautiful granddaughters. And of course, even in sickness his gaze upon his wife was undeterred, for as the years passed he still saw her as fresh and youthful as the day they met.

Even at six years of age my mother recalls the morning her grandfather passed. Her mother was distraught as they had brought him home from the sanatorium knowing his days were few. Simone sat alongside his bed while doing her best to console his weeping wife. Through the night they kept vigil, as no one should die alone. In the morning, after Emile took his last breath, Simone emerged from the room as both women sobbed over the loss of such a glorious yet humble man. Jean returned home upon hearing the news, and once again arrangements were made. The family packed suitcases and children, and this time, a grieving widow. Emile Wacker age 57 was laid to rest in Nonancourt where he had lived the best years of his life.

Shortly after Emile's passing Jean made the decision to move his family again, relocating from Dijon to Vichy in the region of Auvergne which is located near the center of France. The moving company packed the belongings from their magnificent home as the family said good bye to a host of memories, from exhilarating to somber. Jean was anxious to get settled and take on the new responsibilities he had earned with his earnest dedication. Their new home was now a luxury flat in the heart of Vichy. Once again, the spacious apartment was well out of reach of the vast number of Frenchmen in those times and would be by today's standards as well. The wide brush strokes of plenitude encapsulated their very existence.

Emile Wacker

With all that prosperity could buy, still, the affections of Jean's wife would never come to fruition. The arranged marriage did not come without its own price or consequences. Jean had fallen in love with Simone but his desires were more often than not met with indifference. This did not bode well for a healthy relationship. The constant trips, dinner parties, and shopping sprees were distractions to the obvious. With the setting sun, lovemaking was void of interest or desire. It was a one-sided affair with my grandmother only doing her wifely duties and never pretending to enjoy his advances. Both my mother and aunt had said when they were teenagers, their father referred to his wife as *"frigid and a cold fish."* Hurtful, unnecessary commentary for his daughters to hear, coming from a thoroughly frustrated man.

Jean's threads of love slowly began to unravel and were replaced with knots of resentment. It had in fact become more than he could bear. The Poulain's had a few married couples in their inner circle. One in particular, a Mr. and Mrs. Pedrotie, were of the same mindset and when in town shared many an evening over bottles of wine. Mrs. Pedrotie had become one of Simone's closest friends while Mr. Pedrotie was away on business far too often. My mother remembers Mrs. Pedrotie well. She recalled how kind she was and that she and her sister used to cut out pictures from Mrs. Pedrotie's magazines and place them together to make little nonsense stories. But this may well have been a ploy to nudge closer to her true prize. Why is it always the best friend who pretends to admire your witty conversation while covertly luring your husband? With Jean's own wife not aroused by his good looks, charm, and wit, Mrs. Pedrotie's advances were fetching. Grandpapa just wanted the same as anyone, to love and to be loved. Deep down, I think my grandfather may have believed he could buy the admiration of his wife with extravagant gifts of jewels and furs. But Simone could not feel what was not there. Her underlying resentment of being forced to marry him was always alive and well. She had never forgiven Jean or her mother for sentencing her to a life void of passion.

And so, Jean responded favorably to the alluring glances of Mrs. Pedrotie. At first their liaisons were held in secrecy.

The other woman would become his mistress, accepting, and even inciting his desires time and time again. Jean felt like a new man reborn in this adulterous affair. He did his best to keep this new love secret but a wife knows when her husband is cheating. Ultimately, after weeks of denial her husband finally cracked under the constant interrogations. His admission lacked any feelings of guilt. *"You do not want me, so why should you be mad?"* And with that, not a word she hurled would be heard. He had won, and they both had lost.

As irony would have it, he was right. My grandmother didn't want his advances but loved the prestige, the affluence that was a benefit of their marriage contract. She wasn't jealous so much as she was fuming mad at the lies and betrayal from husband and best friend. Being a proud woman there was an even deeper wound that would fester. The mockery of their marriage was displayed for public view. How the salt did burn. For Jean on the other hand, it was a day of liberation.

While at home in their new apartment, the frosty air between husband and wife was felt by the Poulain children. It was a tense household to say the least, but the children were not allowed to ask questions. My mother and aunt were eight and six years old and I'm certain they felt the weight of this tumultuous relationship. They were enrolled in the nearby private Catholic school that was reserved for families of means. Both told stories of the strictness of the nuns who taught and ran the school. My aunt described to me how the classroom would be so quiet you could hear your own breathing. The students were never allowed to use the bathroom unless it was during recess or lunch. Mind you these were mere children who were forced to wait until at times it was too late. It was not uncommon for both little girls and little boys to wet themselves and then be forced to spend the rest of the day in soiled clothing. When this would happen the other children did not laugh as one might think in today's world, but felt pity, as they too had fallen victim to this demoralizing excuse for discipline. Colette hesitantly confessed the indescribable humiliation of having been one of those very unfortunate children. She still had an uneasy squirm while admitting this extremely personal disgrace. Other bodily functions such as sneezing and coughing in class also were not tolerated. My mother recalled having to stand at the blackboard and write over and over, *"I will not cough in class," en Francais,* of course.

My mother Monique to the right of the boy in her Catholic school play

I can't even begin to understand what the purpose of this inhuman practice was. I do know however, if it was fear they wished to invoke, they succeeded. Nevertheless, my mother would get A's as it was expected from her parents and grandmother. To escape Louise's strict hand and constant day to day control of her, my mother escaped by delving even deeper into the world of books and make-believe with her dolls. My aunt Colette was her grandmother's "pet," and as a reward she was allowed far more freedom.

Our grandfather, while still working in the insurance business met some very influential Frenchmen holding high positions in France. Both my aunt and mother referred to them as Ministers of the French government, with names they recalled as Lalla and Dassy. According to Colette, Lalla was a very large man with a bellowing voice who commanded respect from all within ear shot. Dassy, much smaller in stature, is only remembered by the thick goatee that hung from his chin. Both had befriended Jean and both where highly influential and of great financial means. They visited the Poulains house often. The pair sought the partnership of Jean and he was both intrigued and flattered. The proposal was for the three of them to pool their resources and open a bank. Jean would maintain his position with the insurance company while their new business was in operation. It was a win-win situation and as time went on the venture was so lucrative Jean was able to quit his position with the insurance company and become the bank president.

Jean Andre had grabbed the brass ring and wasn't about to let go. It didn't seem possible he could achieve a more lofty goal than the life he was living. Strolling into work one day he took his position behind the baroque crafted desk. As usual he smiled at the employees as they filtered past with *bonjour* salutations. But it didn't take long before everyone noticed this wasn't an ordinary day as someone shouted from the back that they'd been robbed! Running to the vault doors my grandfather saw for himself that the shelves were empty. The police were called and all were questioned. Lalla and Dassy were nowhere to be found, but someone had to pay the price.

The police must have surmised it was an inside job and my grandfather was accused of the theft. They decided he had showed up for work that day to make himself appear innocent. My aunt and mother didn't know the full details as to why their father had been arrested. They were both very young and the accounts of that day were retold to them years later by their mother. But both swore he'd been framed. My mother and aunt believed Lalla and Dassy had absconded with the entire lot, split the loot, and went their separate ways; one to Spain, and the other to South America. Again, they were paraphrasing the events as told to them by Simone. And so, when the authorities were summoned, only Jean Andre was left holding the proverbial bag.

I had always believed one hundred percent that the pair had duped my grandfather from the start. It was obvious Jean was an obliging target. The ministers were seasoned con-men, possibly left over from the Stavinsky debacle of the same era. (Stavinsky was a famous swindler who had made front page news.) They attacked Jean at his weakest point, his complete trust and ego. The fortune Jean had built which allowed his family to live as royalty was swept away with one poor business decision, leaving the Poulain's flat broke. As this tale was told and retold to us dozens of times throughout our lives we all felt sorry for the grandpapa we never knew. I wondered how my French family would have fared had Jean not been wrongly accused of such a scandalous crime. I tried to imagine what life would have been like had he never met Lalla or his sidekick Dassy. What I do know is that my grandfather's life changed forever afterward, and like dominoes, his family felt the heaviness of his fall.

It was 1935 the last time my mother saw her father before he was taken away. As she was peeling potatoes in the kitchen he joked with her and asked if she wanted him to help, and she told him no that she could do it herself. But she loved his attention, and knew he was just kidding anyway. As he continued on toward the master bedroom she heard arguing between him and her mother. Her parents had turned arguing into a ritual with the children never privy to the subject *du jour*. As any child would, my mother hated the shouting between her parents and did her best to tune them out. Her father left that evening without having dinner. Unbeknownst to her and her sister, it would be the last they would see of their Papa for a very long time. Outside their flat the police were waiting as Jean was taken away to be booked on charges of embezzlement. At the end of his trial he was found guilty and sent straight to prison.

I had always believed the stories of my grandfather starting a career in insurance and having an adulterous affair were both true. But now, years later, the story of the bank theft made no sense to me. Why would the only man who did not flee be considered part of the scheme, and why didn't he run? Where was the money and what of his trustworthy character? I still questioned, was he really framed as my grandmother had told her daughters years later? Was he really innocent, or was Simone doing what any good mother would do, fabricating a wild tale to protect her children from the harsh truth? The story does not end there – not by a long shot, as I would soon uncover the truth through court documents straight from Paris itself!

Colette and Monique just seven months before their father went to prison. Their mother sewed the sisters matching outfits which were pale blue with yellow and white accents. Picture taken during Easter Holiday April 22, 1935 at Albert 1st Gardens in Nice, France

Chapter 5

YOUNG JOHNNY - GRANDPA STEFANIS

By 1936 work in Pulga barely had a pulse as the devastating effects of the Great Depression made its full impact on the region. The workforce thinned as one by one, the men received their final wages, and families returned to civilization. Even though the last tunnel wouldn't be completed until 1937, Gus and Angelica were anxious to get back to city life. The Falcon Knight greeted the family once again for the stomach churning trek back to Oroville. It had been two long years since the Aleck's pitched their tents – much longer than any on the mountain had ever imagined.

Feather River Canyon Highway officially opened in August 1937. Locals and dignitaries near Grizzly Dome Tunnel to celebrate the occasion. From Plumas County: History of the Feather River Region. Info by Jim Cook. Photo from the Plumas county GenWeb Project

The future was still unstable so Gus made the decision to continue renting out the houses and took his family to his empty lot on C Street where the garden once flourished. The family re-pitched tents, set up cots, rolled out bedding, all without skipping a beat, just as they'd done in the mountains. This would be their new residence while America continued its recovery. Work was very scarce, but Gus was able to eke out a living working for the Civilian Conservation Corps which he called the C.C. It was during the period between 1933 and 1936 that President Roosevelt implemented his New Deal which was a series of economic programs to bring about the 3R's: relief, recovery, and reform. The New Deal helped keep Gus's family and many others afloat during this devastating chapter in American history. The C.C. provided work for those who couldn't find jobs. They had limited funds and thus limited equipment. The men worked for little pay, but it was enough to put some food on the table and that's all that really mattered. When he first started they had one shovel for every four or five guys. While one was digging, the others stood around waiting their turn. My grandfather, who was there to work, started bringing his own shovel since he was just happy to have a job. Besides, getting paid to watch didn't sit well with his strong work ethic. It wasn't long before the others mimicked his actions and soon the entire crew had ample picks, shovels, and sickles to get the work done properly.

Living in tents began to wear on the family so they built a very small house on the second lot. It had a kitchen and just one bedroom, with the living room doubling as a second sleeping quarters for the children. In the warmer weather the kids could always sleep in one of the tents or under the stars in the summer evenings. In the backyard the two hole-er out house by the mammoth fig tree was shared with the rental house tenants. Having never had indoor plumbing except for a very short stay at the new house, it was business as usual.

A few months after returning to the real world, word got out of a gold mine being resurrected from the great gold rush days. Gus hired on and was in charge of riding one of the rail buggies away from the mine, dumping the ore further down the site. My dad recalls:

"He was dumping the load and it was overloaded, and the handle got caught in his sleeve. It threw him over with it down this big ravine where they was dumping everything and the load dumped on him. He just barely had his head out of the water – he was in water, see. And they missed him. About forty five minutes later they realized that he hadn't come back with the little train, you know, for the ore. And so they went and got him. They got him out of there and he ended up in the hospital. He was there for quite a while, about six or seven months. Broke his shoulder, broke his ribs, he was really hurt bad."

Gus had worked in a variety of dangerous jobs throughout his career. And then in just one swift moment his twenty-nine-year work span came to an abrupt halt. At the age of forty-seven he had plenty of time while recuperating to plan his next business venture.

The four siblings returned to Burbank school just a couple of blocks from their C Street home. With their dad in the hospital and money scarce, they had to be smarter than they were poor. *"We were so poor out there on C Street sometimes the school would repair your shoes for you and all this and that. One time I went there and the lady had just run out of material and she started crying."* The soles of my dad's one and only pair of shoes must have been down to nothing. *"I said, 'Hey, forget about it,' you know, and I went home and cut up an old tire. I stuck it under there, taped it up, just the same as all the other Okie kids did. I wore them to school and everywhere; the tops were still good. But we couldn't afford to go to a cobbler, see. But everybody was poor out there. We were all in the same boat nobody was any better than anyone else. There was no such thing as welfare in those days. It was measly pickin's and once in a while you might get a dollar bill or something. Everybody was strictly on their own.*

Those were the days when all the families were coming here from Oklahoma and all from back East. Families on freight trains with their cows, and goats, and chickens. And you know, during the dust bowls they had what we called the railroad bowls. They wouldn't dare do anything with them people, because they tried it at first and they found some of those "bowls" dead. The Railroad decided to let them all get out here, and when it's through it's through. And that's what really built the west."

He certainly was right in that an estimated 200,000 men, women, and children migrated from the Great Plains to California alone in what was the largest exodus in a short period of time in American history. The term "Okie" was coined from this period of the "dirty thirties" referring to the homeless displaced from Oklahoma. In fact, it was estimated that in just one year over 86,000 migrants relocated to northern California – more than that of the great 1849 Gold Rush.

My dad certainly knew his history. To me he was a walking, talking history book. In school, Johnny was an average student, and above average in his athletic skills. He was also quite capable of defending himself. My dad chuckled as he shared a story from his grammar school days, *"I got into two fights, one, I don't know why this Mexican kid Albert Vasquez – we became friends later – he threw a bottle of ink at me once. And for no reason. I don't know what it was that made him do it. I just give him an upper cut, I hit him once, and he ended up with his feet sticking out of a garbage can".* My dad's voice lit up. *"Just once I hit him! I felt bad about it – I pulled him out and everything, you know. We were the best of friends after that. And another time, Gilbert White who was wounded real bad in the second war, he got me in the corner of the steps going up, and he just wouldn't leave me alone. I just came out swinging and I bloodied him up. I felt so bad I took him in and washed him up and everything. And we became the best of friends. Only two fights I ever had in school. Both times, you know, there was nothing I could do about it."*

Johnny's 5th grade class picture at Burbank School taken May 5, 1935. Provided by the Butte County Historical Society.

I imagine the boys were just testing my dad since the family had been gone for a while. I don't think they knew him yet and certainly weren't aware of his strength. The new kid in school had to prove himself so the schoolyard pecking order could be determined.

During rough times when money was scarce, having farm animals helped families make it through the lean years. Coming from the old country everyone knew you weren't a true Greek if you didn't own at least one farm animal, preferably a goat. Goats provided milk, cheese, and sometimes meat. Plus, if you had a yard they kept grasses and weeds mowed. Any discarded table scraps one didn't want in their compost pile would be eaten by the goat and became fertilizer. My dad's family was no exception.

"We had this goat that gave us a gallon of milk a day when we lived on C Street. When the other kids would go to school and play until the bell rang, I'd have to take the goat up to where Piggs Club

is. That used to be a big empty lot up there at one time – all of it. In fact, they used to put the circus there. I'd take the goat up there with the chain and a big spike and sledge hammer, drive her in, and then the goat would eat around as far as she could eat, see. Then when I'd go to school I'd have to give the sledge hammer to the teacher." My dad and brother had a good laugh at that one. *"Then there'd be recess, and I'd go get the sledge hammer, and I'd go change the goat again then bring back the sledge hammer. For lunch, I did the same thing, see. Then at 3' o'clock, I'd knock the stake loose and walk the goat home and have to milk her."* Then my dad gave another little laugh and said, *"Everyone used to tease me and called me "Johnny the Goat."* I think he wore the name proudly.

Another great story my dad told is the one about Gypo the horse.

"Skeet Smith had a horse and his name was Gypo, and he was proud cut. When they tried to castrate him he fought them off and they only got one of them, see. He was a quarter-horse and I used to ride him as much as I could. One day I'm riding him way out on Upper Wyandotte road out there and a lady had two big fences and she had two thoroughbreds in there and one of them was in heat. I couldn't stop that goddamn horse – he went at full gallop when he caught wind of her, you know. Just before he went to jump the fence, and I didn't have a saddle, I was bareback, see, I pushed myself off of the horse, but when he hit the top of that fence, the fence sprung him back and his neck caught me right across the chest and knocked me out colder than hell. All I remember was this lady who owned the place had a hose on me, hosing me down, bringing me to. I walked the horse home after that, cause I wasn't going to put up with that anymore. So I walked Gypo home, see."

I love how freely my dad roamed the hills of Oroville, and how nice the neighbors were to let him ride their horse. It warmed my heart to know that in spite of the Depression he was having a great childhood, and years later these stories would remain vivid as some of the best years of his life.

"The horse got to know me real good 'cause I used to go over there and feed him apples and whatever I could find. Coming home one night, just as you come up where Raley's is as you start up the hill on your left where there is a tire shop now, there used to be a little store and gas station. On up Myers there was just a small road that went to the rock piles. There was no Oro Dam Blvd back then, see. And what happened was, Gypo got loose somehow or another from El Noble, and some car hit him. I mean he was down! They had a whole bunch of cars parked around him with their lights on, you know, trying to decide what to do and all this and that. I was walking from town and I got there and I said, 'Hey, I know this horse.' I started talking to him and everything, as he just laid there. He had his eyes open, he could see me, but he couldn't move or anything. He was still stunned! They wanted to shoot and kill Gypo, and drag him off with a rope. I fought the hell out of them men! I threw rocks at them and everything. I really put up a battle! I heard them say, 'We can't do this with the kid here.' They re-routed the traffic and a few cars stayed there with their lights on. I was screaming at those guys! I kept throwing rocks at them, and threatened to bust out the windows in their cars and everything. I warned them, 'Don't you dare do anything to this horse.' I even laid across his head so they couldn't shoot him. I just wouldn't let them do it.

"Then all of a sudden he got up. I had stayed there with him fighting those guys off for two and half, three hours, and then all of a sudden the horse got up. I got a rope from one of the guys and looped it around his neck, and walked him home. He limped something awful. I walked him all the way back, opened the gate to the corral, and locked him in there. I didn't even wake up the people to tell them anything about it. First thing the next morning I went up and told Skeet before I went to school. As time went by,

he got back all of his composure and all, and he was still a real fine horse. He lived for a long time after that. I just loved that horse – you know, that was my pet. When you're poor you have to have something like that. People talked for a long time afterward – they couldn't believe how I had fought for that horse."

Johnny, age 11. Picture provided by Butte County Historical Society.

Knowing my dad, I believed it. Someone had to advocate for that poor horse, and he was the likely candidate. Besides, Johnny loved that horse. I do not believe for one second that it was purely by chance he was walking by that evening. Call it what you will, but I do believe it was divine intervention. A kindred spirit between boy and horse that transcended the physical realm as we know it.

Young Johnny got his first paying job as a newspaper boy delivering print to the downtown shops. This made it easy for him to drop in for a quick visit with his grandpa while he managed the boarding rooms. They had formed a wonderful relationship which was evident from his days as a toddler running downtown to sneak a doughnut. Sadly, in all likelihood, the very doughnuts and ice cream Grandpa Stefanis loved sharing with his favorite grandchild was his own undoing.

It was the winter of 1937. By now, Gus was healed enough that he had left the hospital and it was apparent his father-in-law was very ill. Unable to go back to construction, he took over the rooming house responsibilities. Angelica stayed by her father's side while the children continued going to school. In the final moments of my great grandfather's life, all would be by his side. *"I remember I went up to the hotel and he was very sick up there. He died of sugar diabetes, I think it was. And all the Greeks were just there, you know. I cried like the devil 'cause I really loved my grandpa. But um, after we buried him, it took me quite a while to get over it."*

I'm sure the same held true for the entire family. My dad was thirteen at the time and this was the first family member during his lifetime to pass. Prior to my grandfather's accident, Gus's construction job took him out of town all week working on power houses in the surrounding area. When the children were young, (except for their time in the

Pulga,) they spent more time with their Grandpa than they did with their own father. And out of the four, my dad had the closest relationship with his grandfather, possibly because he had John's namesake, but more likely because they had formed a special bond. They shared the same easy going disposition; one that may have been influenced from older Grandpa John to young grandson Johnny.

By all accounts it can be said John D. Stefanis had made some very good choices in his life. Difficult at times, but necessary. He had played matchmaker with his daughter, and was not only blessed with having her in his life again, but gained an exceptional son-in-law. And the result of this marriage brought the love of four Greek grandchildren into this old man's heart. Boarders would become friends, and a smaller community within the larger circle was formed. I can't help but think that he was loved and greatly missed by the entire Greek community. Even listening to my dad's voice in the recordings you can feel the heartbreak as he relived his grandpa's last days.

I was able to find my great-grandfather's grave marker in the same cemetery where Nicolaous Alexiou had been buried. It is a bronze flat marker that reads simply, John D. Stefanis, 1860-1937. No reflection of the magnitude of the loving gentle spirit he possessed. I also found his death certificate when I had searched for Nicolaus's. My father was correct in that he had died from diabetes mellitus, on December 2, 1937.

John Demetrius Stefanis

Dr. Kusel, whose office was in the upstairs building next door above Johnson's pharmacy, documented that he attended to him throughout his last twelve days on this earth from November 20th. My thoughts are that it was John's preference to die amongst family and friends at the Oro Vista rather than in some sterile unfamiliar hospital room. At the age of 77 and having lived in California for thirty-one wonderful years, John Demetrius Stefanis was laid to rest.

After the funeral both parents spent the majority of their time running the boarding house while working through the loss of Angelica's father. The fact is, with their children now young teens their parents decided they were old enough to fend for themselves. Kids grew up quicker in those days. Both my mother and father said with the jobs my father had as a young teen and through high school, he bought all his own clothes and basically raised himself. With the strong personality Johnny had, I don't think it bothered him. It was just the way it was growing up during the Great Depression.

Thankfully after Gus's accident he received a small settlement for his troubles. The Oro Vista sat atop a bar that also served food. The owner of the business and entire brick building, Jesse M. McClung, had recently passed in April of 1937. According to Jim Lenhoff, Oroville's well-respected historian, the back alley entrance to the building from Miner's Alley led to McClung's speakeasy during prohibition. Since Mr. McClung had died, Gus saw an opportunity to purchase the entire brick structure. Gus had a buddy who was a carpenter by the name of Andy, and as before when he bought the Oro Vista, the two pooled their resources to become partners purchasing the business. With both men having spent decades in the construction trade they knew just about everyone in town. After the purchase, and deciding to keep the business as a bar it didn't take long before the place was packed day and night. It became a favorite amongst blue-collar workers as a place to unwind, network for who's hiring, and just hang out with the gang. Gus's new calling would be as bartender and he learned to pour left-handed since the injury had caused his right shoulder to freeze.

My grandpa named their new venture, "The Liberty Club" which provided an escape from the woes of the Depression that drudged throughout one communal mind. It was a time to hoist your pints and cheer to the smallest of good fortunes. People made due with less: a cot, a meal, a bath once a week, for what was truly important was family and a place to gather with friends.

The air in the club was thick with exaggerated tales, foul jokes, and billowing smoke over back room card games. It was the perfect name with many of the patrons immigrants entering through Ellis Island, admiring Lady Liberty just as my great-grandfathers and grandparents had done. More than just a bar in an old brick building, the Liberty Club was a collective state of mind, knowing that no matter how bad it was outside those swinging doors, life inside looked pretty rosy.

The Liberty Club matchbook. It was royal blue with yellow letters.

Chapter 6

....TO RAGS

My curious nature demanded that the unsettling incarceration of my grandfather was a mystery to be solved. I wanted hard evidence of the truth, and in my search I came across a French government website that I hoped would provide answers. I wrote to them (using an online translator) explaining what I was searching for, and they in turn led me to a website for the Vichy Archives. Again I sent an email in French and English, and within two weeks was amazed to be holding copies of Jean's actual booking documents from his imprisonment in Cusset, France. One of the pages even had his thumbprint.

My grandfather Jean Poulain's booking document with his thumb print.

When I took them to my aunt it was a very emotional experience. She was uncomfortable reading the sentence of her father. It was tangible proof of his jail time for a crime she fervently declared he was not guilty of committing. *"He was innocent Marianne. I mean it – he was innocent."* With some urging she translated the documents as she read aloud, *"By arrest of the prosecutor, appellant of Paris 29 November 1935, the Mr. Poulain, Jean Andre, age 35 is condemned for publication of false facts, embezzlement, and abuse of power."* My grandfather was given a four-year prison sentence and had to pay 3,000 francs.

Booking document for Jean Poulain - November 29, 1935

Along with the booking documents was a letter with information on how to contact the Paris Archives to retrieve copies of the actual court documents. Was I really going to learn all the dirty little details surrounding Grandpapa? Deep down, I wanted to believe that Jean was the victim, the fall guy who was cut down during the prime of his life. But my rational mind wasn't so sure. I sent a letter to the Paris address and within three weeks received a letter asking for six euros in order for them to send the documents. Where was I going to find euros in California? I did the rate conversion and decided to mail a U.S. ten dollar bill. Before my letter even reached the shores of the Atlantic I received a large brown envelope. The truth had arrived.

Letter from Vichy Archives in France, sent with Jean's booking documents.

I earnestly ran into the house and carefully opened the envelope, finding eleven old-school typewritten pages, all in French. On the two-inch margins were handwritten notes with underlined words. I could only make out the prison sentence my grandfather and the others had been given. Finding someone to translate the documents would prove to be more difficult than it had been to acquire them. I wasn't about to ask my aunt as it would have broken her heart to have learned that her father was in fact guilty. And I truly believed his guilt would be revealed in these papers dated April 23, 1936.

I was able to locate some teachers at the local university willing to do the translation, but in my opinion, they wanted way too much money. Three years passed before I was finally put in touch with a French woman by the name of Anne-Marie, who, as it happened, had studied law in France and loved family history. She was the perfect candidate for the job.

I brought my brother's cassette player, the documents, and a bottle of wine to her house and we went to work. I was to learn that my grandfather had actually gone to prison November 29, 1935. Four defendants were listed, and all of them had appealed the conviction. The documents were actually from the appeals court as the heading read, *"Extract from the minutes of the Court of Cassation."* It listed all the defendants' employment, with Jean's entered as insurance investigator instead of salesperson. This would be the least of the indiscriminate information. My aunt and mother were correct in that there was a Lala and a Dassy listed along with Poulain, but there was also a fourth accomplice by the name of Vidal. Unlike the story I'd been told of them absconding with the money and leaving the country, each of them actually had their own day in court.

It all begins in late 1927 while Jean and his family were living in Dijon. I can only assume the men met during my grandfather's business travels. Although the circumstances of how they met is unknown it is evident they were of like deviant minds. The court documents referred to Lala as *Remarkable* stating he was the mastermind of the con game they devised. It was true my grandfather had become a very rich man, but insurance hadn't been his goose that laid his golden eggs. The brilliant deception was to start a company which they called Franco Equatorial Mining and Industrial, or FEMI. It was an impressive name, to be sure, as it was presented as a French gold mining venture. Its diggings were said to be in the French Guiana territory of South America near the equator, thus the addition of 'equatorial' in the business name. In order to build capital the company put a release for 38,500 action bonds at 100 francs per bond. This was equal to $3,850,000 in late 1927. The verbiage of the bonds led investors to believe they would see a return on their investment in three to five years. Through subsequent years the dummy company released up to five million francs more in action bonds. That was equal to five million dollars by today's rates; an enormous amount of money in the late 1920's making them filthy rich.

Apparently, there were limits as to how much a company could issue in bonds so the foursome opened a second company they named CICO. My grandfather became the manager of this second dummy venture and was dubbed the sole salesperson for the bonds. His commission was between fourteen and twenty percent, of which he would share a smaller percentage with Lala. My mother was correct; he could sell anything, including fraudulent bonds. In 1930, the CICO company started distributing commercial brochures advertising the sale of bonds and had the gall to send them to government officials at the French ministries level. This would be equal to presidential cabinet members in the United States. They also solicited bankers, promising a very serious return on their investment to engage them to buy the bonds. The advertising stated that even though there is *"loss of value in domicile construction, there are values that can be protected from speculation. FEMI and CICO promise a good return on investment."* They went on to promise a profit within a fixed date with their capital intact. The four crooks had covered all the bases, making this venture sound too good to be true. Even so, their smooth, convincing ways and the lure of making a quick buck on a sure thing was too appealing for the unsuspecting investors.

As they, say go big or go home. I can only assume that Jean and his three cohorts thought they'd never get caught, or didn't care if they did, for to solicit top officials was surely a one-way ticket to prison. They must have become drunk on power to continue this game of chicanery. Brochures continued to circulate listing an influential local Frenchman as a board member while omitting my grandfather's name who actually was on the board. This individual who was present at the hearing stated he was not happy that the company had used his good name. The man was viewed as an honest and upstanding citizen in the world of finance and had many influential connections. Using his name had helped lend credibility to FEMI and CICO. In reality, unknowingly being associated with such a scheme was to have one's well-earned reputation slandered.

FEMI had contacted government officials of French Guiana to get concessions for their mining exploration. Concession is the right to use land or other property for a specified purpose granted by a government. It was denied, so they tried to bribe the ministers to gain land for mining, but that too failed. And yet the brochures continued with bold, false statements with a map of French Guiana. Circled on the French territory was 200,000 prime acres of land said to be granted by Guiana for the purpose of research and development for the mining operations. Another bold-faced lie. The pamphlets boasted that their R&D proved there was in fact gold, and more capital was needed to purchase equipment with which to unearth the millions of dollars' worth of gold that lie beneath the surface. These precious selling tools also boasted that FEMI and CICO had also expanded mining operations to the Congo in Africa. The court saw differently when it came to the R&D report. They stated the findings from the research and development department was precarious. In other words they didn't believe any of it.

Yearly profit and loss statements were naturally falsified since they were "cooking the books." Board meetings were manipulated to sway the votes. Whenever a meeting did take place, those present would receive a separate documented payment for showing up. Since only administrators were on the board, records of who attended these meetings would come back to bite the four accused as it proved they were in a position to make and change business policy. I don't know if the other members besides the four men really knew they were working for a fake company, but I do know two of them quit because the pawns didn't appreciate how they were treated by Lala according to court papers.

For those potential investors who were on the fence, so to speak, extreme tactics were in the ready. They would be invited to Lala's house for dinner where his sweet little old mother would vouch as to the trustworthiness of her son. She believed in him even as he pulled the wool over her eyes. Whatever it took, even a home-cooked meal from Mama if it meant selling more bonds. For Jean, his last resort sales pitch was using his friend Mr. Pedroite, whom it was fabricated was the son of a prominent Commodore, well respected in all of France. I had to wonder if Mr. Pedroite was aware of the affair his partner was having with his wife, or if he even cared. Name-dropping certainly was not off limits as my grandfather told an outlandish lie, saying that even the Commodore had purchased bonds from FEMI and CICO. Neither men personally knew the Commodore, yet his fabrication was so believable Jean was able to sell the bonds at a premium by falsely using his name. The court referred to Mr. Poulain as a *"gifted and a talented director in his behind the scenes manipulation."*

Page 1 of 11 of Jean Poulain's appeals court documents. April 23, 1936

It was clear that Lala and Poulain were the main instigators of the embezzlement and fraud they had been accused of. The court papers declared, *"They were taking the cash register of the companies and splitting it."* Remember, we are talking about millions of francs! I had to wonder how long they thought they were going to get away with the falsehoods. What was their exit plan when the five years was up and investors were demanding their fortune? The house of cards finally folded as a lone investor suspected fraud. He had invested $138,000 francs and sued for "Breach of Trust." Surprisingly, there were no other plaintiffs in the civil suit.

In his appeal, Jean Poulain hired the best attorney in the Dijon region – the president of the French lawyers' bar. Now penniless, I'm not sure how Grandpapa planned on paying for his counsel. They had three witnesses for their defense, but after hearing just two, the court dismissed the third, seeing right through the untruths and not wanting their precious time wasted. As their only defense, counsel tried to prove their clients were not administrators of FEMI or CICO and therefore had no influence on the outcome of the companies. Court documents from the original trial in November of 1935 were thoroughly reviewed. They disclosed, among other incriminating evidence, the payments each accused had received for attending the administrative meetings. It didn't take long for the judgement to be rendered. The appeal was denied to all and the men were sent back to prison. Both my grandfather and Lala continued their four-year prison sentence and had to pay the 3,000 franc fine, while Dassy and Vidal, having played lessor roles received three-year terms, and paid 2,000 francs each.

My translator found the story intriguing, frequently blurting out, *"Oh my God."* Having unlocked the shameful secrets that had been dormant all those years, I admit I was a bit taken aback. I sat throughout with jaw dropped, as she read the events that had actually taken place. I thought to myself, who does these unconscionable acts? My Grandpa? True, I had suspected he was a guilty man, but not knowing the whole story, guilty of what? Never had I imagined the truth would reveal his involvement in such a deceitful elaborate plot, stealing millions of dollars with bold faced lies! My interpreter was also amazed at the brashness of their deeds, as she looked me squarely in the eyes and said, *"I'm sorry, but your grandfather was a crook."* Images of today's Bernie Madoff played in my mind as I wondered, *"Was he really that bad?"*

Now when I look at the pictures of my family strolling along the French Riviera I see Jean Andre in a different light. It isn't one of judgment, but simply of knowing the events as they really happened. It might have been better to have left well enough alone, sharing the same belief as his daughters that Grandpapa had been framed, and in reality was innocent.

I had to wonder if my grandmother was privy to her husband's fraud. They traveled together in the early years when he had a legitimate job. Was she aware when the change took place? Mame was a very devout Catholic. I can't fathom for a moment she would have condoned this behavior. I do know that during that era men kept a lot of secrets from their wives. I suppose this is the case in today's world as well, but it was more the norm back then. As convincing as my grandfather was, he could very well have led her to believe there really was a gold mining operation in South America. She could have thought everything was on the up and up. Why would he lie about such a thing? And why would she even question him? Yes, he had broken her trust with his affair, but would he deliberately put the future of his children at risk?

My deepest belief is that Mame had no idea Jean was engaging in fraud – not that she could have stopped him anyway. I imagine she sat in the courtroom and learned the truth as it was revealed in legal jargon. Hopefully, Jean came clean when the sham company was first being sued, to ease the shock factor. The arguing my mother endured from her parents could have been the result. Either way, my grandmother went through hell.

The family's Renault and Simone's prized Bugatti were seized, along with her diamonds. Their bank account was emptied as the embezzled money was taken by the court. The scandal became the talk of the town with newspapers reporting the sordid details for all to read. Simone and her family were shunned yet pitied by many of the wives. They were able to keep the furnishings from the flat along with their clothes. It became obvious the family had to move.

Through it all the children were unaware of the truth about their father's sudden disappearance. As a mother, Simone couldn't bring herself to disclose the truth to her children; the truth that their father was a criminal and had been sent to prison. Instead, she fabricated a story telling her children their father had gone to Africa to manage a gold mine. At six years of age Colette believed the account, and shared it with the children at school as it was a tall tale indeed. My mother, a couple of years older, wasn't as certain about the gold mine theory and thought maybe her father was sick and hospitalized somewhere.

The two sisters were sent away to stay a week at the Catholic school which also provided boarding. Their attendance would be kept hush-hush, while Simone found another apartment for her mother and two daughters to live in. My mother said the school had a bulletin that came out weekly. The bulletin kept other families informed of new arrivals, listed people who were ill, who had passed, and other information for the parishioners. To this day she recalls that her and her sister's names were not on the list of new boarders, as would've been the norm. Nor was her father mentioned in the prayer list which was reserved for those with an illness. She knew then there was a more serious reason that their father wasn't coming home. What she didn't know was that the school would never print the names of children in their bulletin whose father was an accused embezzler. The other parents would be less than understanding. All she could do was wonder since she and her sister were not allowed to ask questions regarding their father's absence.

My grandmother's heart was layered with another coat of armor that day, as she too became the victim of vicious, shallow falsehoods. Her world and that of her family's, would forever bear the inward scars of the devastation left in the wake of Jean's arrogance and greed. As if she didn't already have enough reason to despise her husband, his blatant disregard for their future had drained the last inkling of respect she may have still had for this man. But in her eyes, he was the lucky one. Placed behind bars, he was able to hide from public scrutiny. Simone was the one who faced the firing squad daily, absorbing the humiliation, the sneers, the pity. But my grandmother was always a very strong woman, or at least that day, she became a fortress.

Simone found an apartment on the other side of town. It had two bedrooms, a bathroom with no door, and no bathtub. There was a poor excuse for a kitchen, and they would have to wash from the bathroom basin. Swallowing her pride, and without another option, it would have to do.

What didn't fit in the apartment was sold, but she did keep a few items held dear. Crystal cut glasses, two beautiful blue vases, a marble Madonna statue, her good china and silver ware, and two delicate figurines were among her most prized possessions. I was surprised that the government didn't take these as well, but they too could have seen her as a victim and knew she had an aging mother and two small children to care for. She may need these later as bargaining chips. Mame also had a small bag of Napoleon gold coins she had tucked safely away that the officials were unaware of. Colette had seen these coins and said her mother would cash in one or two over time when funds were minimal.

My grandparents had gone from riches to rags, affluence to pauper at the speed of light. Now it was survival mode as the children returned from their dreaded week at the convent school. They found their world transformed; reduced to a meager existence. Questions about their father went unanswered, or at best, the answers given were vague. All that they knew was that their father was far away managing a gold mine, and no additional details, such as when he would be coming back were forthcoming. Neither adult in the house ever spoke his name, but for the young sisters to do the same would've caused further dysfunction in an already broken family. Simone turned her back on him, as she had decided he had turned his back on her and their family. The arranged marriage, humiliating affair, and now an excommunication from normalcy had practically turned Simone into a pillar of salt. My mother recalls that Simone was so emotionally damaged from the marriage that she, *"wasn't very affectionate with her or Colette."* I don't think there was even any love left for herself.

In the aftermath of the storm, Mame went back to what she knew and found a position as a clerk at a nearby deli that specialized in a variety of cheeses. It didn't pay well, but one did not complain. With four mouths to feed she was happy to have found work at all. The shopkeepers knew of her plight and allowed my grandmother to take home a loaf of bread or a hunk of fromage from time to time. She had two choices, to feel sorry for herself, or to delve into her job as a distraction from the poison that brewed within. Simone became a workaholic, withdrawing more and more into her own little safe place. The children continued going to school while Louise, left home alone during the day, stared in disbelief at the walls of their new apartment. Her savior had failed them. Her life was ruined and she was overcome with grief and self-pity. My mother said that her grandmother, *"changed forever after that."*

It wasn't long before Simone was approached by the Jewish owner of the dress shop she used to frequent. Naturally, he understood full well her circumstances and offered her a position at his store. My grandmother was a very smart dresser, and he was keenly aware she possessed a talent for fashion and fabrics unparalleled from other high-end customers. Plus, she was available. With an increase in salary, Simone discarded her apron to start a new career. In just a short time she became manager of the small yet extremely busy dress shop. Many of the ladies who frequented the store either knew, or knew of Simone and the shocking events that led to her standing on the other side of the counter. As at home, she would not engage them in small talk of her private life. She was there to offer her expertise, and help to design dresses others would envy. Try as she may, the gossipers were much more obsessed with my grandmother's fall from grace than she was. Simone approached the owner and let her feelings be known that she wanted to move her family away from the whispering busybodies. He was well aware of the scandal-mongers who made it their business to drag the misfortunes of his manager out ad nauseam. He sympathized, and as luck or fate would have it, he had a fellow Jewish friend in Nice who had a position open in his dress shop. His friend was looking for a reliable manager he could fully trust, and the only name that came to mind was Simone Poulain.

Once again, the Poulain family, with Simone as acting matriarch, gathered their belongings in search of a fresh start. At the age of twenty-nine she was still a young woman, but the years of a loveless marriage, infidelity, and now an imprisoned husband made her feel twice her age. The dress shop owner provided a moving company for their belongings, and Simone found a much more suitable three-bedroom apartment in the seaside city of Nice. Mame was beginning to feel relief from the crushing pressure that had been pinned to her chest. She was determined to provide the best she could for her family, even if that meant being absent both emotionally and physically. She buried the shame of her husband by completely immersing herself into her new profession. Louise once again resumed her role as full-time grandmother while her daughter toiled. Monique and Colette were enrolled in the nearby Catholic school, blending in with the other uniformed children. The geographic change was a blessing.

While at home when the mail was delivered, one of the children would gather the letters and promptly bring them inside, handing the bundle directly to their grandmother. There was a strict rule that they were not to read the outside of the envelopes since some of the letters were from their father in prison. Of course, the children didn't know this at the time, but were steadfast in their compliance to the rule. I asked my mother if she or Colette ever took a peak at them, and she answered in no uncertain terms, *"No, never, we never looked. We did what we were told."* I wondered if they had ever spoken between them about their father, and again my mother's words were clear. *"I'm sure we were very obedient."*

Since they both were so young when their financial lives were turned upside down, amazingly it didn't make as much of an impact on their young lives as I had thought it would. My mother said it was just the way it was. She knew something had changed; they both knew. The family lived in a new city and their apartment was different, but to them, they were still going to a Catholic school, their mother was still gone more than she was home, and they still were being raised by their grandmother more so than their mother. Except for their father not being home on weekends, it wasn't much different at all. But I know that they really missed those cherished weekends, and now each member of the household kept Jean's memory deep within their own solitary confinement. Each with a different perspective, never mentioning his name nor sharing their emotions with one another. Life without Jean marched on, as months turned to years, and all along another march had been brewing, to the east.

Shortly after Germany had surrendered in the Great War, Adolf Hitler made his bid for power to unite his defeated country. In July of 1921 he became the leader of the National Socialist (Nazi) Party. From this platform he emerged as the Chancellor of Germany in January of 1933. His assault on the Jews had begun. One unjust law after another was introduced, methodically stripping the rights and livelihood away from the Jewish people. Upon the death of Germany's President von Hindenburg, in August of 1934 Hitler became the Fuhrer. SS troops, the Gestapo, and concentration death camps were well-established by the time Germany invaded

Poland on September 1, 1939. Two days later both France and the United Kingdom declared war on Germany, but no military action was taken during what became known as the "phony war." It only took a few months for Germany to respond to France's declaration of war, and so on May 10, 1940, the Germans invaded France, Belgium, Luxembourg, and the Netherlands. History was repeating itself, but this time with a lunatic at the helm.

Jean was nearing the end of his four-year prison term, with just a couple of months to go. But instead of being set free at the end of November, upon the declaration of war in September 1939 by the French, the government traded his prison garb for a soldier's uniform. Jean found himself once again an infantryman with rifle in hand. It wasn't long though before he would develop stomach ulcers. Call it a build up from years of drinking while he traversed the French countryside, or the humiliation, separation, and guilt of the scandal that pierced his life. Quit possibly too, the enormous punishment his body endured from all of the above plus his dilapidated years behind bars. Whatever the case, his ulcer erupted into a bleeding mess and he was transported to a French hospital. Surgery was imminent and successful, leaving a ten inch scar, and requiring him to get some much needed bed rest.

The very next month after Hitler's invasion, on June 22, 1940 France would sign an armistice with Germany. It was the beginning of the Vichy Regime as Marshal Pétain made a pact with the devil in exchange for a cease fire on France. Without even knowing it, Simone had moved her family from Vichy to Nice just in time. My aunt said Hitler wanted to burn Paris to the ground, and Pétain had saved France that day. But she also admitted it was at the expense of the Jewish people, and he would have been criticized no matter what decision he made. As for Jean, he had a long recovery ahead, but soon Papa would be going home.

Chapter 7

LIFE AS AN ALECK – NICK ENLISTS

By 1937-38 the US still hadn't fully recovered from the effects of the market bust. Gus and his family managed through the brunt of the crash, and with my grandpa's business savvy, they fared better than most. It didn't take long for the Liberty Club to become well established, allowing the family to get reacquainted with their home near the high school. It must have seemed like a palace compared to the past five years spent living in tents or a one-bedroom throw-together home. Business at the Oro Vista Rooming House was steady, with both Gus and Angelica now managing the rooms after the passing of her father. Upon coming to America my grandmother was able to spend another sixteen years with her dad, which I'm sure she treasured.

Much of the surrounding acres near the Oroville high school had both orange and olive orchards. The orchard owners were not immune to the disparity of the times. With no funds to pay a crew, one man can pick only so much fruit. The farmers agonized as they were forced to watch the ground turn to black with decayed crops. Likewise, Gus's boarders and friends were in need of work, desperate just to have something to do. So Grandpa, according to one of my dad's stories, came up with an idea to help all involved. He approached the owner of the olive orchard and offered to pay a crew to pick all his olives. In return the two agreed on terms which included Gus having an ample supply of the olives for his own use.

With an agreement reached, long tables were set in the yard at the house on Linden as my grandmother, with the help of her young daughters, cooked for the entire bunch both breakfast and lunch. The men were more than appreciative to have two square meals with the flavor from their homeland. As agreed, my grandpa got to keep as much of the picked fruit as he could handle. Even grandma got in on the action and cured batch after batch of mission olives in her own brine recipe. In those days you couldn't just go to the store to purchase real Greek olives, and fortunately for all, she continued the family tradition handed down through generations. In the basement, Gus had an olive press and his friends pitched in, grinding the fruit down to a liquid, then filling rows of five gallon pails with the savory oil. It was a collective undertaking where all benefited. They pressed enough that year that Gus was able to give a few pails away to friends and kept plenty for their own use. The rest was sold, and with the extra money, Grandpa was able to recoup the money he had fronted to pay the crew while still turning a profit. In fact, the results were so favorable this practice continued for the next two to three years until the economy righted itself again.

Angelica with daughters Bess and Joy on front steps of Linden house. About 1937 or 38.

The basement was the production arena. Not only did Gus press olives, but all the laundry for the rooming house was washed in the old ringer washer then hung to dry in rows that crisscrossed from one end to the other. Even when I was a wee one in the 60's, I recall seeing white sheets hanging everywhere while the old ringer had been left covered in dust replaced by a newer electric washer.

The family had chickens, hordes of rabbits, and even the old goat from C Street. Across the street the high school provided plenty of grassy areas where the goat still munched in circles. But this wasn't C Street anymore and the neighbors complained about the smell and the crow of the rooster. A city employee came by and Grandma was forced to give away their farm critters, including her pet goat. Gus found a Greek family that lived outside the city limits who would now benefit from getting a gallon of milk a day plus fresh eggs. My dad recalled of his mother, *"Oh, she was mad, mad at everyone and cried like a baby for days."* That goat had become a part of the family, and for months Grandma grieved her loss.

Wine making more often than not would become an event within their wide circle of friends. The wine in America was very different in flavor from what they were accustomed to. Outside and just off the back screened-in porch, Gus had built a good sized over-hang out of 4x4's, with thin narrow boards crisscrossed over the top. It was thick with grapes and leaves that provided full shade in the hot summer months. These grapes along with the harvest from friends' vineyards were used in their small operation.

My dad recalls one season when his mother took it upon herself to give her husband a lesson in vinification. They made a blend referred to as Retsina, made with the resin from pine trees that gave the wine a pine flavor. The thick goo would be added and depending on the desired palette of the connoisseur either more or less would be mixed with the crushed grape juices and left to ferment in the wooden barrels. As a result, some wine would be stronger while others weaker. Well, Angelica had her idea on the strength while Gus had his. As my dad exaggerated, *It came to blows! They had a knock-down-drag-out.* Apparently, wine making is serious business. In the end it was decided Gus would make his batch his way, and she would do hers her way, and with that, peace was restored in the Aleck home.

When I was young, maybe eight to ten years of age, I used to play in the basement. Once inside, the cool air immediately sent relief through my hot, sweaty body from the intense summer heat. Just as quickly, my senses were instantly struck with an overwhelming smell of fermentation. The old olive press sat just feet from the door, and in hindsight, it must have housed the pungent odor I can still recall decades later. Off to the left were ten 55-gallon wooden barrels laid on their sides, raised off the concrete floor on racks. Unfortunately, I never had the privilege of actually watching them make the wine. I do recall however, a small group of us standing around the barrels with glasses in hand. I'm unclear as to the occasion; it could have been Easter or Grandpa just wanting to share a glass of the good stuff. At any rate, he poured a small amount of Retsina straight from the barrel spigot for each of us. I remember very clearly taking a small sip then freezing in my tracks. I knew instantly that the foul liquid in my mouth, that tasted more like paint thinner, would never touch the bottom of my stomach. The unfamiliar flavor lay on my tongue and without warning, gag reflexes kicked in. Thankfully it forced my mouth to spew the poison back into the glass from whence it came. I'm sure my face resembled someone who had just sucked on a lemon. Everyone thought this was quite comical, and I too joined in the laughter. The tasting resumed, although after seeing my reaction, I don't think my brothers sampled theirs. Retsina is definitely an acquired taste, and in hindsight, my tongue was far too immature for such a bold flavor. My mother, who favored a good French Bordeaux, politely pretended to sip the inferior wine with a nod and a smile.

As with the soirees held where the large outdoor oven once stood, there was always an excuse to throw a party. With many of the Greeks making their own spirits it was expected that they would bring a few bottles when attending one of the festive gatherings at friends' houses. The proud men spent a good portion of their evening sampling the homemade brews of their friends, swearing their own was the best until bragging rights were in order. The women would each bring their specialty dishes as Greeks of all ages looked forward to swapping stories and catching up with close friends. This was also the time when future arranged-marriages were discussed as my dad recalled many of the women were much younger than their husbands. When one of these old gents had one foot in the grave the women played matchmaker, deciding which eligible young bachelor would fill his shoes. In many cases the poor old guy was within ear shot as the replacement was chosen. Considering himself Americanized, Johnny swore right then and there he wasn't going to marry a Greek gal, knowing how the game was played.

As dinner dishes cleared so went most of the furniture carried to the outside front porch, leaving just chairs and the long table pushed to one side. The fun had only just begun as the Greeks danced the traditional steps of Hasapiko and Syrtos. Melodic music played as the dancers held handkerchiefs along with each other's hands. The men draped their arms across the shoulders of the others in brotherly fashion as they moved with grace and dignity, encouraged with shouts of *"opa"* and clapping. Ouzo flowed as the dancers were cheered. Even an occasional plate crashed to the floor in true Greek tradition. Angelica and the other women and children joined in the dancing as my father declared, *"Every Greek was a great dancer."* Even through hard times the fellowship never stopped. They never gave up hope, living a simple yet profoundly enriched life.

As a convenience the family garden was moved from C Street to Gus's vacant lot across the street. Every night after supper Gus and some of the kids would merely walk across the road to tend to its needs. Long summer days provided sunlight that transcended into beautiful sunsets. The evening air was a bit cooler, which made for better watering, staking, and picking the bounty of their labor. It was Grandpa's way to unwind after a day filled with chatter from customers, clinking of glasses, and basically being "on" for the public. In short, it was his personal oasis where thoughts wandered with the mindless act of pulling weeds. Body and soul were rejuvenated in preparation for yet another day.

There was another way I was to learn that Grandpa re-energized his body and soul. The women loved him. He was very handsome, successful, and had a gregarious personality. Grandpa, as it turns out, enjoyed the intimate company of certain women who swooned over him. It is a fact that one particular young mistress found herself with child, and Gus was the father. Now Grandpa found himself in an entirely new predicament. Already having a family, he had to come up with a workable solution. The proverbial cat was out of the bag and if my grandma had any doubts before, she now knew for certain that her husband was a cheating man. His wife was tough and she wasn't afraid to speak her mind. Grandpa undoubtedly had to apologize profusely and swear never to see the trollop again. Did he keep his word? In a small town it would have been difficult to continue the secret rendezvous. Regardless, there was a baby on the way in need of a loving home as his mistress made it clear she had no intention of raising a child.

Back during the lean years when money was extremely tight my dad's godparents, who lived in Willows, had wanted to adopt him. The couple, unable to have children of their own just loved little Johnny and thought they could provide a more stable environment than his own parents. It's possible they even thought they would be doing Gus and Angelica a favor with one less mouth to feed. Obviously, Grandma and Grandpa were just fine raising their first born son and had no intention of adopting him out.

With that in mind Gus approached the only reliable Greek couple he knew who would be both willing and financially able to take on such an enormous responsibility. Just after the healthy baby was born my dad's godparents' wish finally came true. They were blessed with the joy of raising a son and named him Takie. Soon after the adoption the small family moved to Sacramento, making frequent visits less feasible. Even though Johnny's sisters always knew about the affair and baby, the fact is, my father didn't even know he had a half-brother until later in life. Both my parents mentioned meeting him one day. Dad said he could see his father in Takie, but a friendship or brother-to-brother relationship never came to pass. I imagine Takie's presence was an unwelcome reminder for Grandma and awkward for Grandpa. From what I have learned, I believe Gus still would have loved his son and kept in contact through letters, pictures, and occasional visits on his own. There was a silver lining for dad's godparents after all, as life has a funny way of delivering what we ask for.

Years later, my mother was in the basement with Angelica and noticed some old suitcases. My grandmother snatched one of the cases and pulled out a black and white photograph of a very pretty woman. *"Look. Look at this woman. She's not even Greek, she's German."* My mother, puzzled, asked who the woman was. With a sternness in her voice as if the affair was just yesterday, Grandma replied, *"She was my husband's mistress, Takie's mother."* I guess she had to get it off her chest and probably didn't feel comfortable sharing this story with just anyone, but I had to wonder why the picture hadn't been torn to bits. Grandpa, on the other hand, hadn't learned his lesson and upon the early death of his partner Andy, Gus continued with his infidelity. My mother recounted how one evening on a dimly lit street, intoxicated Andy had inadvertently stepped into the path of a car, was hit, and died. His widow June found comfort in Gus's arms and the romance began. Learning from prior mistakes, he kept an apartment for his new mistress in neighboring Chico. An out of town rendezvous was probably a good idea.

Years passed, and with the changing seasons the four Aleck teenagers were enrolled one by one at the convenient high school across the street. The Oroville Union High School back then was primarily a very large, square three-story building that included a basement. It was a great architectural achievement during it's time. The classrooms, library, and other rooms looped around the building leaving an open uncovered quad area in the center. I remember this building from my early childhood. It had massive steps with an entryway that lead straight up then split off going left and right to the second floor landing. My dad, aunt Bess, Joy,

126

and uncle Nick, were all in attendance together during the '41-'42 school year. Pops was the class president during his freshman and junior years, and Uncle Nick was during his freshman year. All belonged to various school organizations and were very popular.

Uncle Nick second from left, class president, freshman year. Oroville High School year book, 1941-42

Johnny had many interests in school, one of which was his musical talent. They had a high school sixteen-piece dance band back in those days called the Royal Tigers that traveled all over northern California playing at various venues. This was during the swing era of big bands with such legends as Benny Goodman and Mitch Miller. Dad was very talented, playing the piano and trumpet. In his later years, Johnny gave his grandson Jordan a pocket trumpet still in its original case from those musical days of his youth.

One day during his junior year Johnny had the creative idea to gather a few of the members of the Royal Tigers, maybe five or six, and entertain the students during their lunch hour. Many of the band members stored their instruments on the school grounds, including drums, horns, and the school piano which was on wheels. The very next day, a group of guys, without asking permission from the teachers, rolled out the piano, muscled up the drum set, and grabbed horns and instruments. To the delight of many they played a live concert for all to enjoy. Mind you, this was an outdoor quad surrounded on four sides by three-story walls.

Oroville High School Band. Johnny, 3rd row from bottom, 5th from right, (including teacher) with black hair. Table Mountain is in the background. 1941-42 OHS yearbook photo.

The acoustics were phenomenal and the energy of the crowd electrifying! Even the teachers tapped their toes and were in awe at the local talent in their midst. The sixteen-piece band rotated the musicians so everyone got their turn. In the winter months the mini concerts were held inside the packed library, so not a day went by without an afternoon "pick me up." The noon concerts became an instant hit as all this came from a simple idea my dad suggested to his buddies. The tradition continued for many years after that first day in the quad.

In addition to being a member of the Royal Tigers, playing the afternoon gigs, my dad continued the exhausting schedule of also running track and playing football where he excelled, even at his height of just 5' 7".

Johnny Aleck, freshman year. Courtesy of Butte County Historical Society.

Johnny held different jobs as an adolescent, one of which was delivering dairy products for M&M Dairy out of Biggs. Since he didn't have a car his father left his 1934 Ford convertible at the house so he could get to work every day. Johnny would get up at 3:00 am each morning and drive the thirty minute commute from their house to the dairy. Upon arriving he'd jump into the old butane fueled GMC delivery pickup and run his route, delivering to homes and businesses alike. When finished, he'd get back in the convertible, drive home and be ready to start school well before the first bell rang.

The Aleck siblings - Johnny, Bess, and twins Joy and Nick.

With all these activities, his general disinterest in studying, plus a strong ambition toward entertaining the ladies, my dad continued being a C average student. His brother Nick had even less interest in school, and by his junior year, quit to join the Navy. But while in school he too went out for football and made the cut. Dad says he was a good ball player, but one day he got real mad at the coach. A yelling match ensued and Nick was seen marching off with swear words flying. A couple of days afterward someone slashed all four tires on Principal Nesbit's car. Tire rationing had already begun due to America's involvement in the war after the bombing of Pearl Harbor. Uncle Nick and his buddy were accused of slashing the tires and the principal pressed charges. The pair was promptly arrested and hauled off to jail. They were still minors, but I guess back in those days it didn't matter. My dad summed it up:

"Mama was running the rooming house and she cooked up a great big steak for him and walked over to the jail. It was still downtown back then, just a couple of blocks away. She told the jailer, 'I've come here to feed my boy.' The jailer, looking down at the plate and seeing an over-sized knife laying across the top said, 'I can't let you in here with that.' She pulled that goddamn butcher knife off the top and said, 'You open that goddamn thing – I want to feed my son.' He looked at that knife, and from then on, when Mama wanted to feed her son, butcher knife and all went in that cell."

"Nick was behind bars a week or so but they never were able to prove if he did it or not. The principal had figured that since he had gotten kicked off the team for not studying he might have done it. I don't know if he did or not, but he could have, he was real mad! He never did tell me. Even years later he never confessed."

A few weeks into the school year and after the incident with coach Nesbit, on Sept. 21, 1942 he and his dad drove to Redding, California to the US Navy recruiting office. Since Nick was 17 1/2 at the time, he needed his dad's signature to join. Nick's official entry date was October 10, 1942 when he was bused to his basic training at the newly constructed Farragut Naval Training Center near Lake Pend Oreille in Bayview, Idaho. As a S2c, or seaman 2nd class, he was assigned to the USS Block Island CVE 21 which served in the Atlantic Ocean. The Block Island was commissioned and ready for deployment on March 8th, 1943. Likewise, Uncle Nick was transferred on that same day from Bremerton Navy Base in Bremerton, Washington to serve on the carrier. His name can be found on the Navy muster roll. His job was to hook-up the "hold-back release" on the catapult which assisted the planes on take-off from the flight deck. Like all deck jobs, take-off and landing duties required complete attention to ensure everyone's safety, especially his own.

The U.S.S. Block Island CVE-21 that Nick served on in the Atlantic. Picture courtesy Jack Sprague – webmaster of U.S.S. Block Island website.

The Block, with Nick on board, made two Atlantic crossings in '43 delivering much needed warplanes, P-47 Thunderbolts, and parts to ports in Ireland and England, hauling back badly damaged aircraft for repairs. The days were long as the men came up with ways to bide their time. Boxing was a favorite for many of these testosterone filled young men, and Nick shined at the sport despite his small stature. At just 5' 5" and 120 pounds he was quick on his feet and threw a tenacious punch, eventually landing him fleet champion.

Uncle Nick moved up in rank to AMM3c, or aviation machinist 3rd class. His new classification had him wrenching on fighter planes; a much safer job. The CVE 21 and her crew were given a new assignment as part of a task force accompanied by US destroyer escorts to seek and eliminate German submarines. Widespread destruction was rained on US convoys by the enemy subs which Allied aircraft were unable to reach by land. The planes didn't carry near enough fuel to make the round trip hundreds of miles off the coast while still allowing them a safe return. For that reason the escort carriers loaded with warplanes were put into operation to disrupt the success rate of the German submarines known as U-boats. The smaller escort carriers were also known as "baby flat-tops" and could carry about twenty fighter planes with a crew of some 900 sailors. During four combat cruises with Nick on board, the Block Island Task Group sank two submarines and shared credit for the sinking of two additional subs. This earned her the nickname of "FBI" for Fighting Block Island.

After resupplying and refueling the task force fleet at Casablanca, the ships continued to patrol the known infested area of U-boats. Nicknamed "The Black Pit of the Atlantic," it was located just off the coast of Africa in the vicinity of the Cape Verde Islands. This trip would be different as the cat and mouse game would prove unfavorable for Nick and the other crew members. A periscope had been spotted earlier in the day of 29 March, 1944 which prompted the Block crew to search for hours for the U-boat which ended in vain. Then on that same evening the periscope reared its ugly head once more, this time with the CVE 21 right in its sights. At 2013 hours, or 8:13 pm, a torpedo careened into the bow and about

4 seconds later a second torpedo hit the stern of the Block, penetrating the oil tank. As sailors were scrambling from below to get on deck, yet a third torpedo hit ten minutes later and the captain gave orders to abandon ship.

I was amazed to learn my uncle had been through such an ordeal. Even though I was never able to hear his tale of that horrific day, I have read many of the accounts from fellow sailors who survived. In all, six men lost their lives, some due to the fact that they were in their fighter plane at the time, and not having a place to land, were never heard from again. On board, a sailor had his leg wedged, unable to free himself. After sustained attempts to dislodge him they finally amputated it on the spot, but with much blood loss he died a short time later. As the ship was sinking the men slid down ropes into the ocean thick with oil from the freshly refueled carrier. The toxic fumes made breathing difficult and it was like swimming through mud. Some sailors drifted in life rafts as others took turns treading water and holding onto the sides for hours as nearby destroyers came to their rescue. Uncle Nick was fortunate to end up in a dingy with a couple of brothers who also hailed from Oroville.

While the CVE 21 was sinking, what the crew had not known was that four torpedoes had actually been fired, with the third hitting the US destroyer, the *Barr* near the stern. That resulted in twenty-eight deaths and many injuries. In the end though, the German submarine was spotted and taken out by the destroyer, the *DE 686 Eugene E. Elmore*. The entire crew of the German U-549 perished. Fortunately, all who scrambled over the sinking CVE 21 survived as 674 sailors filled the *Ahrens* and the remaining 277 stuffed themselves onto the *Paine*.

Uncle Nick sitting - bottom row - far left with big smile. Picture taken after the CVE-21 was sunk. Picture courtesy Jack Sprague.

The destroyers returned to Casablanca where the men washed up and were given clean khakis and some R&R time after their ordeal. On the website www.ussblockisland.org where I derived the aforementioned information, I found a picture of many of the surviving men. Low and behold, in one of them, seated in the front row, I found my Uncle Nick with a great big smile. I could hardly believe my eyes! After the dust settled, the sailors were gathered and given a mandatory thirty- day leave back to the states. In June/July of '44 Nick was able to go back to Oroville and retell the harrowing story to all. What a "welcome home" that must have been!

AMM3c Aleck finished out his Navy stint as a 20mm tail gunner with the Bomber Fighter Squadron ninety-eight, one of the most dangerous jobs in the Navy. Fortunately the war was coming to an end as he held the position from February of 1945 until November of '45 when he was honorably discharged.

Uncle Nick in his Navy uniform.

Chapter 8

PAPA'S HOME AND SO IS THE WAR

Mother and daughter rode silently on the train, enjoying the mountainous beauty of the French Alps. It was the winter of 1939-40 and an endless blanket of snow draped clusters of tall pines in the distance. Frigid outdoor temperatures frosted the glass window, but inside with blankets laid across their laps, the pair was warm and cozy. With chin nestled in her palm, young Monique sat in quiet anticipation, knowing soon she would be reunited with her father again. It had been a little more than four years and even Simone's heart had softened for the man who had betrayed them. The military had sent word that Jean had recovered from surgery, and was now strong enough to make the journey home. Fear of the unknown caused Mame' to feel anxious, which she did her best to hide from her daughter.

Finally reaching their destination, blankets were folded and set aside for the next passengers. They made their way to the hospital where Jean eagerly awaited their arrival. My mother was now twelve years old; her father just shy of forty. As their eyes met, young Monique ran to greet him, throwing her arms around his neck, and repeating over and over, *"Papa, Papa."* Tears rolled down their faces and soon Simone joined, embracing the man she never loved. He had aged and was noticeably thinner, but he was there in the flesh, and for this moment at least, there was happiness. The three found accommodations for the night and started the return leg of their journey back home the following day. Father and daughter sat close on the train as she held his hand and smiled and smiled until her rosy cheeks hurt, then she smiled some more.

Louise and Colette had stayed behind at the apartment, and upon seeing him, Colette could hardly contain her excitement at her father's return. For she was but six years of age the day she was told her father had left for Africa in search of gold. Now at ten, the stories didn't matter anymore. Even though the children remained puzzled, they were accustomed to locking questions deep within the confines of their minds. It was a wonderful reunion with not a hug nor tear held back.

Louise took notice of the man who stood before her; a man who once held his head high with broad shoulders and the smell of money on his hands. With a warm smile her son-in-law approached as she realized this wasn't the same person at all. Wrapping her arms around his thin frame, Louise cried in pity more so than joy.

It was still early in the war with the south of France occupied by the Italian army and thankfully not by the murderous Vichy Regime. Nice is just minutes from the Italian border, and at one time in history was a part of Italy. Many Italians had made Nice and neighboring towns and villages their home. As with Alsace Lorraine, where they spoke both French and German, in this region French and Italian dialects were prevalent. Much of the population was of Italian decent, and now found themselves under the rule of the Fascist dictator Benito Mussolini. Encouraged by Angelo Donati, a prominent Italian Jewish banker, the Jews living in the demilitarized zone were for the most part left unharmed. Because of this, thousands migrated to the south, escaping persecution from the Germans in occupied territories to the north. Jews from other countries as well, especially Germany, fled for their lives to live amongst the

Nicoise, the people of Nice, France. Everyone knew this could very well be a false sense of security, but to stay in Germany or the French regions ruled by Pétain's Vichy regime, was to write one's own death sentence.

The effects of war were already paralyzing the economy. With food becoming a scarcity, it was difficult for Jean to put on weight and regain his strength. Prescribed medication was a constant part of his daily regimen which he was lucky to get, attesting to the illness that still prevailed. Simone continued to work her usual 7am to 6pm schedule, including commute time. Someone had to keep the family fed. The children did their part as well. My mother, who at times was accompanied by her younger sister, arose early each morning and at least three days a week walked to the nearby market. The later in the day, the longer the line, so, as tired as she was, Monique would do her best to be first in and first out, rushing back home to drop off the meager morsels before heading to school. A head of cabbage, a few potatoes, maybe some fruit, but meat was always noticeably infrequent at meal time. Fortunately, dried beans were sometimes available for the family to get much needed protein in their diet. Continuing on to class, every day started the same with an hour mass spoken in Latin, followed by classroom studies. Later in the day, Vespers for another hour where my mother would daydream the time away in a fantasy world. It was a welcome escape from the mundane reality of her new life.

It is well known that the French are fond of their escargot, or snails in English. Occasionally my mother and aunt collected mollusks in the neighborhood for special occasion meals. It is necessary to purge the snails to rid them of their grit before cooking which involved having them fast for a few days. To do this, all the *escargot* where put into a large pot with a lid atop and left on the balcony. On one occasion the unattended slugs were able to force the lid open just enough for them to make their escape. In search of food they slithered up the walls to the apartment above and proceeded to devour the potted plants. The upstairs neighbor, obviously upset, easily followed the snail trails to the apartment below, to which the woman leaned over her balcony rails, and with raised fists, ranted a piece of her mind. The young sisters found this to be quite comical, but made sure to place a heavy brick on the lid in the future. With Germans in control, this French delicacy was seen as a decadent escape. When my grandmother placed the platter of escargot on the table the family started clapping in anticipation of the flavors that awaited them. The sisters shouted *mervilleux*, or marvelous, with huge smiles of excitement as if applauding an encore at the theatre. It was the simple things in life that helped get them through this war. When my mother told this story decades later, she still had a big smile. She couldn't help herself from describing the recipe of garlic and herbs, adding that they tasted like chicken gizzards.

The Poulains were fortunate in that Louise had a friend whose home was in the hills just outside of Nice. She was a sweet little Italian lady who lived with her husband and thirteen children on a small patch of land littered with chickens and a vegetable garden. On many a Sunday my mother and her family would visit this unusual slice of paradise. There was a small chapel on the lot next door where they attended mass when in the area. Heavenly voices of the choir comprised of a small group of nuns erased all thoughts of the atrocities of this world. My mother recalls this was a wonderful escape, and many times they were invited to a deliciously prepared Italian meal. In the summer months, the family was sent home with vegetables, and sometimes, even fresh eggs. It was a godsend, indeed.

The Poulains enjoying the hills with friends. Monique, Simone, and Colette to the right.

Colette too, had her own little farm in the form of two pet rabbits. They provided a playful element during wartime, calming the nerves. Cuddling with the soft furry bunnies helped the family to heal quicker when someone had a cold or the blues.

After months of recovery Jean was finally able to find occasional work, although nothing permanent. His ulcers would plague him for the rest of his life, making him rely on pain shots during severe flare-ups. This of course made work even more difficult. My mother recalls a job he had at a winery as a laborer pruning and helping in the harvest, as well as overseeing the burn piles. Much of the charcoal that remained from the burned branches in the piles was used for generators that had been converted from gas to charcoal burning. Since gasoline was unavailable, these converted charcoal generators were used to power the few cars and trucks that still roamed the streets.

One time when my mother went to work with him, the temptation of the sweet tasting Muscatel grapes had taken hold. She plucked one after another until a hidden snake poked its head out and hissed a warning. Young Monique screamed and raced to her father. To this day she is deathly afraid of snakes and even glued the pages of a school biology book together so she wouldn't have to look into their eyes.

Adjusting to his new life would prove more difficult than Jean would have liked to admit. He was a beaten man on all counts. To pity your husband is not love, and it was obvious Simone and the rest of the family had been managing just fine without him. His own children never really knew their father and both felt sorry for Papa. Now that they were a little older the dynamics between their parents was more evident and their marriage was seen as being less about love, and more about survival. They still didn't know why their parents' relationship was so difficult though. Young teenagers are not privy to the intimate details between husband and wife. They were not aware until years later that their mother had never really loved this man. They were forbidden from asking personal questions and so they could only form their own conclusions at the time. What they saw was a man who had been very sick and now needed the support of his family. What they still didn't know was that he had an affair with Mrs. Pedoite, and worse, had been found guilty of fraud, losing the family's ill-gotten fortune, and had been living the past four years behind bars. Their former lives lay in ruin, but Mame reinvented herself, found a career, and never looked back. Having her husband in their lives once again stirred the memories that had been pushed to the furthest recesses of her mind. Her pity turned once again to anger, resentment, and bitterness.

In prison, depression gnawed on his soul, and now Jean saw himself through the eyes of his wife. It wasn't long before Papa had a new best friend; one in the form of a bottomless glass of wine. Even with his ulcer and pills, Jean sought to obliterate this loveless, penniless existence through a distorted mind, soaked in alcohol. When he was at home, the temperature of the room was regulated by his mood.

Simone and Jean on a small family outing. My grandmother's body language tells all.

It didn't help matters that Europe was now waist deep in one of the worst wars in history. Italy's army was weak and poorly equipped; so on September 3, 1943, an Armistice with the Allies was signed. The worst fears of the Jewish people were realized just days later when the German S.S. stepped in to the formerly Italian occupied zone and initiated raids on Jewish homes and businesses. Within just five months over 5,000 Jews were rounded up like cattle and taken by rail to concentration camps.

This was a very unnerving time for all, and it made small heroes out of ordinary people. By now all the schools were closed and Simone was able to find work for Colette at the dress shop where she worked. Mr. and Mrs. Cohen, friends of the owners had gone into hiding and were living in a basement of a friend's house. In their haste to hide from the S.S., they had left important documents in their home. Colette was asked if she could go quickly to retrieve the papers, such as birth certificates, marriage license, pictures, and anything that would reveal their Jewish identity. It wasn't uncommon for the Nazis to do house to house searches as they continued in their extermination of the Jews. The next day, without a thought for her own safety, my aunt at the age of fifteen took a small flashlight and rode her bike to the address she was given. She had been told where the papers could be found and crept quietly through the rooms. It was an eerie feeling as she realized the magnitude of what the consequences of her actions would entail. But Colette wouldn't abandon the lives of innocent, decent people, and continued slinking through the house, tucking papers into the satchel she wore across her shoulder. When she was confident all references to their identity were in hand she rode as fast as she could to the safety of her apartment. The next morning Colette hastily returned to the people who were in hiding and hand delivered the papers to them. To say the least, Mr. and Mrs. Cohen were greatly indebted for this courageous act that may very well have saved their lives.

Another request was made where there was a situation involving two Jewish sisters who needed to go by tram back to their home. The girls' parents asked Simone if they could use her daughters' identification papers to make the necessary trip and to retrieve some important items. Without hesitation Monique and Colette gave up their papers which in turn were given to the very scared teens. Before boarding the tram German soldiers checked each ID which included a picture of the bearer, to the person boarding. Colette said it was a blessing that the pictures were not of the best quality. Fortunately for all, the teenagers were able to make their journey undetected and return back to Nice safely. The identification cards were later given back to Simone with a heartfelt, thank you. But had there been suspicion, the German soldiers could have easily traced the ID's back to the Poulain family since their home address was listed. If caught in either situation, it would have been certain death for all involved, and yet, as my aunt put it, *"We had to save those people."*

Jewish sympathizers *were just as much* a target of the Gestapo as were the Jews themselves. The French resistance was instrumental in undermining the German ambitions for the Aryan race. These were brave men and women who made it their highest priority to covertly dismantle the infrastructure of German intelligence. Their numbers grew by the hundreds of thousands after the allied invasion in Normandy. Invaluable information was delivered to American and British forces and used in their strategic attacks on the Axis powers. A great many of these selfless men and women were armed and fought in the streets against their oppressors. The FFI members, or French Forces of the Interior, as they were officially known, drew many teenage boys to the cause, banding together and carrying with them the seeming invincibility of youth. But the sad truth is, war knows not gender nor age, race nor religion, rich or poor, for all are potential casualties in her wake.

Colette Poulain at about the age when she did her heroic deeds.

And the day came when a group of these young determined boys were discovered by German soldiers. It is obvious my mother's recollections of the days to follow were somewhat blocked from her memory. She had very little to share on this subject, and it was clear she did not want to relive the feelings from so long ago. In order to make an example of these freedom fighters, a public hanging was ordered in *Place Massena*, a public square in Nice. My mother personally knew many of these brave young men, having gone to school with them. The Germans rousted the *Nicoise* through fear and intimidation, corralling them into the square. My mother and her family, unfortunately, were among the masses that turned their heads and wept when the bodies swayed.

It was never known for certain if the German soldiers would harm non-Jews whose main objective was simply to survive. Fear and anxiety kept the majority complacent in their daily routines. As the youngest of the workers at the clothier store, my aunt was given errand jobs as well as her usual duties. One day she was sent to fetch some fabric needed for the dress shop. Upon her return she carried a large suitcase filled with textiles. She was stopped at a corner just a couple of blocks from home by a young German soldier wanting to know what she had in such a heavy case. Even though she had nothing to hide, being stopped and standing face to face with this Nazi soldier sent unparalleled fear throughout her body. The soldier examined her papers and the contents in the case. Finding nothing unusual, he offered to carry the awkward bundle for Colette to her home. A thousand thoughts raced through her panic-stricken mind. He would know where she lived, the neighbors would see her as a German sympathizer, or worse, maybe his girlfriend. She would be seen as a traitor and her head would be shaved or she would be tortured, probably even killed. Trembling to her core, she waved her hand back and forth and repeated, *"No, no, no."* She leaned down and clutched the handle of the suitcase tightly, forced a smile so as not to seem unappreciative, and turned quickly, walking as fast as her thin legs would carry her. Upon telling me this story decades later, she had to take a breath to calm her nerves. The German soldier was still present and very much alive in her mind. As she closed her old eyes, Colette waved a hand in front of her face trying to rid him from her view.

The Palais Saluzzo apartments in Nice where my mother and her family lived on the 2nd floor, far left, during the war. Built in 1934, it was practically brand new when the Poulains moved in. Picture is how it looks today.

Feeling safe in their upstairs apartment, my mother and Coco, (my aunt's nickname,) heard men's voices one day coming through the open bedroom window. Being bored, they spied on some German soldiers who were talking loudly at the outdoor cafe across the street. To their horror, one of them looked up and saw the two pretty young French girls and whistled loudly. The other motioned with his hand for the pair to come down and join them. My mother and aunt instantly closed the window and pulled the curtains tight. They held each other in fear and never attempted to spy on any soldiers again.

There was no avoiding the occupation as even right in front of their apartment building the Germans had set up a bunker equipped with heavily-armed soldiers and a machine gun. Anytime they entered or left the apartments they had to walk past the Nazis. Even though they never bothered any of the tenants, their presence was a constant reminder of this awful war. Swimming in the Mediterranean or walking along the sandy shores was off limits. The beaches were riddled with mines to detonate upon any amphibious attack by the Allied forces, and barbed wire barricades acted as deterrents on the walking paths. There were very few vehicles as the new regime claimed all the rubber for itself. Even leather was nowhere to be found, having been confiscated for the boots of the growing number of German soldiers. Many of the French instead had wooden soles attached to their shoes. My mom and aunt said it took a little while to get used to the inflexibility.

Strict curfews, total darkness in homes after dusk, and rationing of some food products such as bread, meat, and oils, was also enforced. My aunt retold a story of her grandmother who was coming home one day after getting a bottle of goat's milk for the family. It was only about a pint, but no one was supposed to get milk on that day. She was alone when she was stopped by the German patrols and detained for hours for her crime. Finally, they released her unharmed, but most certainly not unnerved. I found it interesting that after all that trouble they let her keep the warm bottle of milk. After that harrowing incident Louise paid heed to their inconvenient rationing rules. For the most part, the war was an inconvenience for some, and brutality followed by death for others.

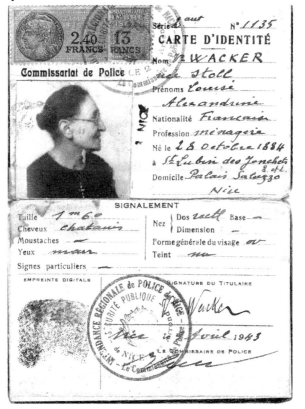

The document my great grandmother Louise had on her at all times.

Even in wartime life still needed to be lived. My mother finished school at the age of fifteen just before the schools closed. Her first job was at Mumm Champagne and she recalled they had a break every day at 3:00pm when everyone had a small glass of champagne with *fromage* and bread. Saturdays were only half days, with the employees sent home with an open bottle of the bubbly for their families to enjoy. After that she took a job at a concrete supply company where she was the sole office employee. Most of the contracts were with the government, although I'm not sure which one. As time went on and the weariness of war continued to stifle the nation my mother grew tired of her monotonous work.

I was surprised to learn that even living in an occupied country during one of the greatest wars in history, my mother, now sixteen, was a bored teenager with many of the same issues and concerns of today's youth. She obsessed about being overweight yet loved baking cakes and pastries. She had two best friends, Gabby and Ester, with Ester's nickname being Deedee. Gabby's parents owned a small shop with candies, cakes, and pies. On occasion, my mother was able to get ingredients for her own pastries, and unfortunately or fortunately for her, the sweet temptation was always present when she entered the store.

Monique bottom row far right, looking left, having some fun with classmates before the schools were closed. Taken about 1943 while under the less restrictive Italian occupation.

Monique was the youngest of the three friends by two years, but all shared the same ambition. To find and marry the men of their dreams. It was a constant topic along with having the blues and an overwhelming feeling of disparity. My mother spoke often of the dysfunctional home-life her and her sister faced daily, with a father who came and went, and a mother who was hardly ever home. The pair had thought that having their father back home again would mean a house filled with happiness, love, and joy. It didn't take long for the elation they'd felt after his return to dissipate into the air they breathed. The young teenagers wanted to burst free from the life they lived, but had no idea how or when this would happen as the war drudged on.

Chapter 9

FROM AFRICA TO ANZIO

Two months after Uncle Nick joined the Navy his brother marched over to the Veterans Memorial Hall in downtown Oroville and signed up to be a soldier in the United States Army. Johnny gave up his job as a gas station attendant and like so many young men at that time he never finished his senior year in high school. The induction was made official on January 3, 1943 as America's war effort was growing strong. Johnny completed his basic training at Camp Roberts in California, and being a natural athlete, he excelled. My dad's sharpshooting abilities from his youth would carry over into his military experience. With 20/15 vision and a steady aim, he consistently hit the target at a thousand yards with a British 303 rifle the Americans trained with. He complained that the recoil was so stout, that while shooting in the prone position, it would drive him back almost two feet after ten rounds.

Still a teenage kid at heart, he and his buddies decided one night to do their target practice with tracer bullets. The straw supporting the target caught fire which prompted a good tongue lashing, but in wartime was quickly overlooked. From there Johnny was shipped to Fort Benning, Georgia to continue his training, where he was assigned the dangerous job as a parachutist. After four weeks and five jumps he was fully qualified. Dad got his radio training and learned Morse code, how to string lines, and all the nuts and bolts of what would be his new position. He mentioned that he thought they assigned him as a radio man because of his bilingual skills. Classroom settings didn't teach the difficulties these young men would find themselves in while trying to relay messages under constant enemy fire. Most would be learned through gut instincts.

Within the first few weeks Pvt. Aleck was assigned and reassigned to different units until finally becoming a part of the elite HHC 509th PIB which is short for Headquarters, Headquarters Company, Parachute Infantry Battalion. Prior to my dad's enlistment this battalion had its origins with the 504 PB where the nickname *"Geronimo"* stuck as a member of the Parachute Test Platoon yelled the famous expression as he jumped from his plane.

To distinguish an identity for his men, Lieutenant Colonel William Yarborough had a patch designed with characteristics of a Native American stick figure. The paratroopers jokingly said it resembled a gingerbread man, thus the new 509 became known as the "Gingerbread Men." Yarborough was instrumental in the creation of the paratroopers' uniforms as well. He designed jackets with pockets at a slant for easy access. Because these brave young men were dropped behind enemy lines it was important for them to carry as much gear as possible. This time Yarborough perfected the British Armed Forces version of pockets sewn on the outside pant legs with oversized pouches to stuff whatever small items would fit. In fact, this style would be copied years later to make a statement in today's fashion world, becoming known as cargo pants.

During a jump, in order to keep air from rising up their pant legs, the men wore them tucked into calf high special boots. These boots had reinforced heals and the extra length up the calf provided stability to their ankles upon landing. The pant legs billowed slightly over the boot tops and became a distinguishing trademark to this day of the airborne units. Due to the nature of this new look and the destruction the paratroopers rained on the enemy, the Germans of WWII dubbed any soldier wearing this uniform the "Devil in Baggy Pants." It was an honor to be branded with such a distinctive name.

Picture of an original 509 PIB "Geronimo" patch. Colors: yellow on black.

When young Johnny first came to Africa he had missed the first mission of the 509 in November of '42 named Operation Torch, since he was still a junior in high school, but other waves of replacements followed throughout '43. Thankfully, by the time he arrived, his plane was able to land on a makeshift airstrip. Dad's parachute training would wait for another day.

"I was a last minute replacement for a soldier who had been killed during a practice jump in England. I wasn't supposed to go on the first flight. On the flight to Africa it was so dark in the plane you couldn't see your hand in front of your face. It was real quiet except for the sound of the C-47's engines. Everyone was silent, deep in thought. Someone might bump you, or somebody would vomit. Other than that, no one said anything."

Touching down on September 25, 1943, it had been only nine months since leaving boot camp as my father, at nineteen, set foot on foreign soil a lifetime away from football, school bands, and his mama's home cooking. As with the other green-horns he had no idea of the horrors that lie ahead. Many of these brave young men would never make it home, and as aware of this fact as they were in their hearts they always believed it would be the other guy. How else could one face death's door?

He was stationed at the replacement training center in Oujda, Morocco, where Johnny continued to perfect his combat skills and learned to shoot short bursts from his Tommy gun at hip level. My brother Gregg shares one of Dad's stories:

"Had a piece of steel welded to my Thompson machine gun. I had it put on at a right angle on the left side so I could hold it palm down and help control the recoil. I'd practice shooting it one-handed and got to where I could shoot accurately in three round bursts. Wanted to conserve ammo." It was important to learn to

shoot in this manner since on the battlefield the other hand could be busy calling for artillery support.

The North African campaign had officially ended in May of '43, so by the time Johnny landed, the battle plans had shifted to Avellino, Italy with the 509th Parachute Infantry Regiment parachuting behind enemy lines on September 14. My dad missed that jump as well, but other matters needed to be addressed, providing for an excellent training opportunity. Nomadic bandits had been pilfering US supplies to sell on the black market. These much needed stockpiles required protection. I don't know for certain but my father had mentioned he either fought or trained alongside an outfit known as the Moroccan Goumiers and may have been involved in protecting these stockpiles. Earlier in the year when the North African campaign was in full swing these tall dark-skinned stealth fighters were feared by German and Italian soldiers alike. Particularly effective in night raids, these men were able to move silently past enemy lines. If they found two Germans sleeping, they would kill one of them. If they came across three of the enemy asleep, they would kill the one in the middle. The Goums, for short, always cut off and took an ear of any enemy they killed, keeping them as souvenirs. Their gruesome tactics created terror for the enemy, with many German and Italian soldiers surrendering just to stay alive.

"Of the different outfits and allies I trained alongside, I think the best fighters were the Moroccan Goumiers. Man, they were good at what they did. Being a radio man and having an ability to pick up other languages quickly enough to get an idea of what was being said, I was sent out on patrols with them on different occasions."

The soldiers also enjoyed some personal freedom. My brother John shared this story our father had told him: *"One of the hardships of war is not getting to go to a barber. In North Africa, Dad didn't say where, but between breaks in patrolling, he and his buddies were looking to get decent haircuts. When there wasn't a barber around they'd use razors or scissors to crop and chop each other's hair. Anyway, this was in an Arab market, and Dad saw one of his buddies pass by with a great haircut. He told Dad he had his hair cut a short distance away and led him to the shop. Dad said he was shocked when he saw the Arab barber burning another G.I.'s hair and shaping it. He said the Arab had a steel comb with a wooden handle wrapped in leather in one hand, and an assortment of small pokers. There was also a number of long-burning incense like sticks burning. Dad said the guy was a wizard and gave him the best haircut he had during the entire war. He said it smelled terrible, but was worth it"*

It took just a few months in North Africa before the replacements were deemed ready for the next big battle. All the while plans were being finalized for a full-scale attack in Italy as the troops geared up to save the *boot*. Three months after Johnny's initiation into this strange new world he boarded a ship headed toward the sandy shores in what would be known as Operation Shingle, but universally famous as just Anzio. Another re-designation of the 509th PIR would come just prior to the Allied invasion on December 10, 1943 when his unit changed names for a final time from a Regiment to a Battalion, thus the name 509th PIB.

The Anzio beachhead invasion began at 0200 hours, on the early morning of January 22, 1944 along a lone stretch of beach in western Italy. By the time the Allied forces arrived the Germans had been caught flat-footed, having sent all but one unit to other regions. Barge after barge unloaded thousands of men and equipment from the deep blue waters of the Mediterranean Sea. My dad, who was in the first wave, recalled, *"We got along fairly easy. There had been two battalions of German paratroopers, but their intelligence had told us they were transferred to the front that was 100 miles south of Rome. That's why we went in at Anzio."* The Allied forces consisted of a mix of British and American units. My dad's battalion, which was some 675 strong, made an easy push onward to take Nettuno, while Darby's Rangers conquered Anzio. By midnight of the D-day landing over 36,000 men and 3,200 vehicles had unloaded onto the Italian coast.

While my dad was fighting in the Nettuno/Anzio area, a crisis was developing, resulting in the likelihood of a breach in the American line. Intelligence had disclosed a company of German paratroopers had deployed in a defensive position against my dad's battalion headquarters' left flank. The Americans were about to face an attempted breakout by the Krauts.

Because communication lines were down, HQ was unable to notify the company in this vulnerable position. Dad was given orders to get the message to them, stat, so Private Aleck decided the quickest way to get there was on a military motorcycle. Without hesitation, Johnny rode pony express style, weaving through the slippery sludge left from the wet weather, when suddenly, snipers opened fire. With the sound of the screaming engine between his legs, the only knowledge he had of being a moving target was the splattering with each missed shot. With head down and throttle wide open, Aleck miraculously made it to his destination. I'm not privy as to what took place after relaying the information. I only know he made it back unharmed and the Jerry attack was unsuccessful.

Over the next few days Allied forces would gain as much as seven miles past the beachhead. The area just past the shoreline was littered with small farm houses and rolling hills. Small units would scout the area as my dad strung his communication lines. It was during these early days Johnny came in contact with the enemy and wounded his first German soldier. My dad's words, again paraphrased by my brother Gregg:

"I remember the first German soldier I shot. We both came around the corner of a high row of brush, me on one side, him on the other. We saw each other at the same time and both brought our guns up. I got the first shot off and hit him in the stomach. "Took him back to our medics. I caught hell for doing it, but it seemed like the thing to do."

At Anzio, Dad and fellow 509er James Batton were sent out on reconnaissance and stayed for a few days in an old dirt-floored farmhouse, keeping an eye on things. A pig was living there and James and my Dad threw it scraps of C-rations from time to time. When the Germans advanced, they beat it back to their own line and the unknowing swine followed. Mind you, these men were hungry for a hot meal and this four legged creature had ham written all over it. They hadn't had fresh meat in a very long time. One of the guys killed the poor thing. It was gutted and cooked, feeding quite a few soldiers that day. Not sure if Johnny had some too, but it is a well-known fact in our family that Dad never really cared for pork chops.

Just a few days after landing, the units were making rapid progress until opposing resistance strengthened. *"Soon after we got there the Germans ringed us all around."* But then on orders from the corps commanders, Maj. Gen. Lucian K. Truscott, Jr. put a halt to the assault, and for the Allies to regroup. The command as it turns out, would be a costly error as this gave the Germans under orders of Hitler himself, time to seize upon the moment. Even with that, Allied forces by February 1st increased to just over 61,000 men with over six tons of material stacked at the Anzio port in preparation to overtake the German foe. Within the next week, fierce fighting erupted by land and by air. Key targets were destroyed with airstrikes, but the Germans kept coming like a swarm of army ants attacking their prey. Hundreds of lives were lost as British and American ships anchored at sea were sunk, including a U.S. hospital ship full of wounded soldiers. Many dogfights ended with black clouds of smoke spiraling downward as the losing pilots fell to their watery graves. The rains continued, leaving the terrain soggy and slippery; just one more nuisance to have to deal with as the battle raged on.

By February 7th, two weeks after the landing, the British 1st Division was weakened from two days of bitter fighting. Reinforcements were called in from several divisions, and regiments including the 509th PIB who were directed to take back what was known as the Factory at Carroceto from a multitude of fighting Krauts. And there was my dad in the midst of it all, doing double duty, fighting the bad guys and stringing his lines.

"My main job was to make sure every unit had a telephone hooked up during the battle. The Colonel insisted on being able to talk to everyone on the battlefield. What happened is you're up walking around when you should be in a foxhole. All we wanted to do was get back alive."

Being a communications man, Dad became a jack rabbit in the open terrain. Snipers loved taking pot shots at him and his buddy Batton. It wasn't safe to go out alone so they always partnered up. It soon became apparent that day work was too risky, so running, splicing, and fixing lines was done under the cover of night. Even then, many times the soldiers opted to crawl through the marsh. Finding a damaged line meant recovering the other end then splicing the two back together. It was important to work as quietly and quickly as possible, and then make it back to camp alive.

My brother Gregg had located our dad's 509th brother, Mr. James Batton who recalled a close call our dad had one night as retold by Gregg. *"He mentioned Dad and him getting separated one night heading back to CP at Anzio. James made it back alright but dad was brought back a couple of hours later by a couple of soldiers who had found him in a ditch full of water hiding from a German machine gun emplacement. Dad had got turned around in the dark and had wandered to within 30 yards of the enemy position."*

John, my older brother, reinforced the idea of our father having nine lives. *"Another time at Anzio, Dad was knocked unconscious while in his foxhole. He said he was told three 88mm shells landed around his foxhole and he was knocked out of the hole. Buddies found him, and Dad came to while they drug him to a makeshift treatment area. He was out of action for a couple days."*

A tug of war began as forces on both sides weakened then strengthened, with men and equipment being replenished from the rears. *"When it got real foggy they tried to push us back into the ocean. They did push us back about 500 yards, but then we held. We stayed dug in there for four or five months."* This stalemate, such as it was, found the weary soldiers living a miserable existence in foxholes made by exploding mortar shells. There was no escaping the smell of gunpowder and death that filled the moist air. On one of those overcast nights, Johnny was laying low in his own mud hole, tired, hungry, and cold.

"I remember at Anzio hiding in a shell hole half full of water and mud for a long time. My Lieutenant, Sol Weber came to look for me. It was night and he jumped into the hole I was in. My knife was out and at his throat when he said my name. Scared the hell out of both of us."

Needless to say, nerves were on edge as horrific German bombardments with hundreds of thousands of mortar rounds, air strikes, and machine gun fire severely crippling the Allied armies. Likewise, our fighting G.I.'s played havoc on the German muscle machine keeping their advances in check through courageous battles. Battles in which our guys were outnumbered, but would still gain the upper hand. And to make matters worse the Germans had two mounted guns nicknamed Anzio Annie and Anzio Express by the Americans. Paul Bunyan cannons is what they were, nicknamed Robert and Leopold by the Germans. Each weighed over 200 tons with 71 foot long barrels. Krupp K5's (or K5's for short) crept slowly along tracks laid in the distance above Anzio. They fired 280 mm shells on the beachhead day and night after night and day at a rate of fifteen rounds per hour.

"There was not one place in a 10 square mile area where you could look and not see shell holes and shell holes inside of shell holes. It sounded like the end of the world and felt like an earthquake when they hit. I would watch the shells hit as the Germans would sweep the beach with their artillery. I figured they wouldn't hit the same spot twice so I'd crawl into a fresh shell hole. Guess it worked because I made it through okay. I could never figure out how I survived with so many around me getting killed.

They overran us, but we counter-attacked right back. We didn't even wait to regroup. Then the white flags came out from both sides so we could pick up the dead and wounded. It took us about a half a day to get that done. Then it was business as usual".

John had this to add: *"I do remember Dad telling me about his unit being pinned down and the black pilots coming in and bombing and strafing the area until they were able to get reinforcements and supplies up to really secure the area. He said they flew so low you could see their faces. He expressed that his unit was really happy to see them."* Gregg followed with, *"That was the all-Negro squadron at Anzio where the Americans were pinned to the beach for seventy days by the Germans on the high ground. They were called the 99th Pursuit Squadron, before they were known as the Tuskegee Airmen."*

During intense fighting my dad described a scene no one in their lifetime should witness. With the battle raging, a soldier he described as a *"big blond Swede,"* attempted to move from his position, and as he stood up, was cut down by enemy machine gun fire. When he got hit, one of the bullets ripped through the WP (white phosphorus) grenade he carried and exploded, sending his body parts flying. The WP had attached itself to his clothing causing an incendiary effect. With the phosphorus creating extremely high heat, it ignited, producing a dense, white, choking smoke. The sight of his smoldering body parts, along with the overwhelming reek of burning flesh was almost unbearable.

The drama of battle continued, as one night while my dad and the other fighting men were getting plummeted, a band of US soldiers with B Company 509th PIB were being hit hard during a night raid. Private Milo P. Peck, one of the soldiers of that reinforced platoon, was dug in behind a sandy mound. At least a company or more of Germans were advancing quickly on their position. My dad, who was just behind Milo's platoon, was keenly aware of the dangerous predicament his fellow paratroopers found themselves in. Equipped with an EE-8 military field phone he didn't have time to get the "okay" from his superiors. Time was of the essence, and without a second thought Johnny ordered flares shot into the blackness of the night. With the skies lit up, suddenly the German position was exposed and Milo and the other soldiers were able to take advantage of the moment. They gave them both barrels, so to speak, and the Germans were beaten back by intense mortar and artillery rounds. The Nazis took heavy casualties while Peck and most of the other men survived the ordeal. For his bravery and take-charge attitude Milo would later receive the Silver Star.

Johnny, on the other hand, got his butt chewed by his senior officer for giving away the Americans position, to which my dad replied, *"Hell, they knew our position. Why do you think they were there"?* Milo and my dad became good friends after that, and years later he showed up in Oroville at the Liberty Club. My oldest brother John recalled: *"When I met Milo, he was pretty down. Dad let him stay with us for a couple or three days. Fed him and gave him some money to help him get back on his feet. Wasn't privy to what his problems were. I was 13 or 14 I think. Milo really said Dad deserved the Silver Star not him. He said Dad flat saved his life and many others by ordering the flares to be shot as the Germans were trying to take Milo's position."*

My dad kept a picture after all those years of Milo dressed in his uniform, which I have to this day. He looks like a real nice guy and on the back it reads, *"Your pal 'til Hell freezes over and the devil skates across."* As B4, Milo Peck, Barre, Mass.

Milo P. Peck

In another fierce night of fighting, C Company 509th PIB earned one of two presidential citations at Anzio; the other being awarded to the entire battalion. Johnny was assigned to fight alongside Company C and was involved in the two day conflict. On his DD-214, or Honorable Discharge papers, where it reads "wounds received in action" it states, ANZIO 15 Mar. 44 (not auth). He had been hit by a small chunk of shrapnel from an 88mm mortar shell. Fortunately, it hit his code books which were in his chest pocket and ricocheted down to his side where it punctured the skin. Not enough, in my dad's opinion, to take him out of the game as it was patched up soon thereafter by a field medic. As a kid I remember the jagged three inch scar just above his right hip but only knew it had come from the war. John, thankfully, was able to fill in the rest of the story.

The following is an account by the commanding officer, Lieutenant General Clark for Company C of the 509th PIB Presidential Unit Citation awarded during the two day battle at Carano, also known as houses 5 and 6. My dad and the other survivors definitely had lady luck on their side.

COMPANY C, 509th PARACHUTE INFANTRY BATTALION is cited for outstanding performance of duty in action, on 15 and 16 March 1944, near Carano, Italy. Company C was given the mission of securing two heavily fortified houses vitally needed for use as a line of departure for a large-scale attack. These buildings were organized into a strongpoint, well wired in, heavily mined, and with mutually supporting machine gun fire. The attack took place under a full moon, across open, flat marshy land. The leading platoons of Company C approached to a point within two hundred yards of the objective before contacting the enemy. At this point the attacking force encountered withering fire from ten enemy machine guns, in addition to heavy rifle fire. The fire momentarily halted the company and intense artillery and mortar fire fell on its position. Company C continued to push forward. About seventy-five yards from the houses, they drew still more intense machine gun fire and encountered wire and mine fields. In spite of heavy casualties, this small group of men moved forward across the obstacles and rushed the houses to engage the enemy in close-in fighting with hand grenades. All but four machine guns were finally eliminated, but the opposition provided by these weapons and continual rifle and hand grenade assaults made the positions almost untenable. The area around the house was subjected to heavy mortar barrage, and the enemy launched a fierce counter-attack with an estimated strength of two platoons, but the attack was halted by artillery, and small arms fire from Company C forced the enemy to withdraw. The objective was finally consolidated at daybreak, and throughout the day under heavy periodic artillery fire the position was held. Members of Company C continued to snipe at the enemy, adjusted artillery fire on enemy targets to the front, and surprised an enemy patrol, inflicting heavy casualties and capturing four prisoners. The courage and determination displayed by members of Company C against overwhelming odds reflect the finest traditions of the Armed Forces.

Gregg had this to add, *"This is the farm houses Dad talked about when he was attached to Company C. Dad was hunkered down next to one of his Lieutenants when the Lieutenant looked over a wall and took a bullet to the head, tearing off his helmet. He sat there stunned a second then started cussing. The helmet had deflected the bullet and he wasn't injured. Dad said they were pinned down by heavy German machine gun fire, but despite that were laughing out loud at the Lieutenant. Dad is the one that called in the adjusted artillery fire on the German position."*

Even though our side won it was at a very high and somber cost. Casualties included 43,000 for the Allies, of which 7,000 were killed, and 36,000 wounded or missing.

Half of my dad's battalion were killed in action, wounded, or taken prisoner. *"We became a force there,"* my dad said as he recalled the hand to hand combat against greater numbers of German soldiers. But the time had come and Johnny and the other exhausted "gingerbread men" were finally retired from the campaign on 31, March 1944, being replaced with fresh young faces to continue the fight. The next day, what remained of the battalion was sent south to Baia Bay in Naples, Italy.

Johnny carrying the comm pack, with Edward Blass to his right and John W. Casey in the shadows to his left. January 22, 1944 - Nettuno, Italy.

Decades came and went after my dad's amazing survival at Anzio. Then one day a letter from the Museum of Allied Landing in Rome showed up in the mailbox. Along with that letter was a picture of him in Nettuno carrying a ship to shore communications flasher. Dad said the pack weighed some ninety pounds, and it was obvious from the photo it required both hands to carry. Being in an unarmed position, Johnny was flanked by two armed buddies, John W. Casey and Edward Blass. The picture and letter came as a huge surprise since it was sent some forty-seven years later. Our local small town newspaper wrote a front page article about Johnny, inserting the picture of him in the famous Anzio battle. He was pretty darn proud that day, as was our entire family.

Chapter 10

PERFECTION IS NOT FOR THIS WORLD

With mom's journal, video camera, and tripod I drove to my Aunt Colette's house to finally unlock the treasures of my mother's diary. She was more than happy to oblige me in reading the eighty handwritten private thoughts of her older sibling. What sister wouldn't? I was fortunate to have someone who had lived in the same household to interpret my mother's words. My aunt was able to enhance the events in a way that I never would have learned from a stranger. As she got comfortable I could hardly contain my excitement as I had waited three long years from the time I placed the small brown book in my truck.

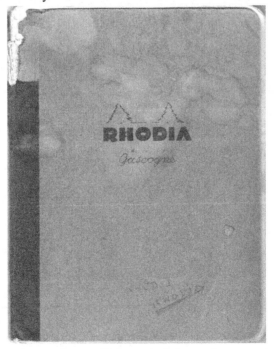

Cover of my mother's journal

My mother had cut slits into the first page and tucked a picture of herself into the corners. It was great to see what she looked like when she first started to write down her thoughts. The journal begins two months before her seventeenth birthday as she was both consumed with the teenage blues and preoccupied with the romantic notion of young love.

15/12/43.

Journal picture of Monique Poulain, two months shy of her 17th birthday.

December 17, 1943: *"Calm, overcast and rainy at 5:30. My life is so monotone and boring and this incessant rainy, humid and gray weather, I've had enough of it. I met up with Gabby, still as nice as ever. We returned home together, she isn't having much fun either. Dedee and Ginette are bored too. In 1943 young ladies who have fun go crazy and give surprise parties, that's not us. Our big outing the movies, we are kept on a tight rein, but I'm not having fun right now. I sometimes feel like getting married, like tonight I would like to marry a man that I can lean on and trust, warm and secure protection. I want a marriage of love, to love my husband a lot and to have a beautiful little family. Oh God, make this happen for me. I don't want a husband who's too young. I want a husband who is at least three years older than myself. I want to be loved a lot."*

It was evident my teenage mother wanted the complete opposite of her parents' marriage that she witnessed daily. As was the norm for those days, young Monique and her girlfriends were waiting for their knights in shining armor to sweep them from their dreadfully boring youth.

My mother continued page after page of how dull her life was as she described the rainy weather as it approached, *"Here once again, gray dreary weather with its parade of wind, rain, and black butterflies."* She hated working at the concrete supply company, and the fact that it was expected of her by her mother. Monique had to hand over most of her earnings to Simone who used it for the necessities of life. For Colette, being the youngest, it was worse as she never saw a dime the entire time she worked since her boss handed her wages straight to her mother. I suppose this was typical for struggling families. Monique went on to complain that she would never meet a man working all day and having such strict rules tied about her waist.

On Christmas Eve of '43, she made a single entry, *"I went to see Esther and she is bored to death. Saturday, Var Porte was bombed and it was blown up. There were some deaths and injuries."* The war was getting closer, as she would casually mention, *"We are on alert but nothing serious in Nice."* Midnight mass was cancelled due to the curfews, so the family went to an earlier service. The train tracks had also been destroyed that day while all worried about Papa who had been out. But by 8:30 that evening the familiar squeak of the door was heard along with sighs of relief.

The family was very grateful as now all could celebrate Christmas Eve together. My mother wrote of the wonderful gifts she received. *"I got a bottle of Jasmine perfume, a pair of stockings, and a pretty slip, a tube of red lipstick, my first, a pocket comb, and a bottle of hair product from Coco. The last two items are very rare to find. I am very blessed. And I received candy and a book."* Christmas morning the family slept in. Jean had been able to find some meat on the black market and they feasted on the delicious meal as if they hadn't eaten in years. Later that day all took part in their favorite French card game, *Belotte*, and by bed time fell fast asleep. If not for the over-bearing uncertainty of the war one would think it had been the perfect family Christmas, and in many ways it was.

Alerts were almost daily with as many as four or more loud obnoxious sirens filling the air in a single day. They were so frequent in one entry my mother wrote she wasn't going to mention them anymore, although she did. They became a part of the natural sounds of the city along with the explosions heard in the distance as plumes of smoke revealed their nearing positions. On another occasion she writes that she and Ester were on their way to see a movie when someone shot and killed some German soldiers. Resistance fighters, I'm sure. They had to return home as everyone was instructed to stay indoors. To my mother it was just another inconvenience for two bored teenage girls.

Rumors whispered across Europe, finding their way to the ears of the citizens of Nice. There was talk that Rommel and his army was coming to invade their region. Evacuations were called in anticipation of fighting in the streets. *"Many people are leaving, but we did not. We are going to wait and see."* She talks about planes being shot down over the skies and hearing their fiery crash in the outskirts of town. On January 24, 1944 there is more serious talk of evacuation as she writes, *"It would be so hard to leave Coco's little rabbits and our apartment my mother works so hard to keep."* Colette's rabbits had five babies. *"It is hard to think about leaving everything you have. Alas in 1939 and 1940 all those poor people who left everything during the exodus. And we were living selfishly. My God I would be really sorry if we have to leave Nice. Its blue skies, its nice sun, and its beautiful sights. And yet it is not just Nice, but the surrounding area with beautiful flowers, and cactus, and palm trees, it's so marvelous! We will have to see what happens."* Other lines reflect her concerns. *"Oh I love the sun, the blue skies, light and bright. How can man want to fight? Everybody could be so happy. Perfection is not for this world."*

With the continuous barrage of death and destruction there was at last one silver lining as my mother on January 26 writes, *"Mama might be pregnant."* Simone would go with Colette to the doctor in Monte Carlo to find out why she was feeling so sick in the mornings. And four days later my mother logged again, *"I'm so happy Mama is certainly pregnant and I can learn how to raise a child and I will be the Godmother. I hope everything will go well. My grandmother is not happy and says I am not aware that at this time in her life it is not good for her to be pregnant. If everyone thought like that France wouldn't have any more babies. I understand why my grandmother only had one. I myself want to have more than one."*

It was true, Simone was thirty-eight, not a desirable age to bear a child in those times, especially during a war. But my mother was just seventeen and a very naive, sheltered seventeen year old at that. She yearned for something new in their lives; a distraction, and yes, practice for when she would have children of her own. She even started crocheting a small sweater for what she prayed would be a healthy baby boy.

Day by day the war was drawing near as air raid sirens continued. German and British planes engaged in dogfights within three hundred meters of their home. A convoy of German soldiers was just a kilometer away. Bombardments were all around, as my mother wrote, *"I'm not even afraid. Ester and I are going to go to the movies."* It's not as though they could do anything about it anyway. Why not enjoy the days you have? Some of the bombs hit very close to their own apartment. Colette, being very curious, hopped on her bike and rode just a couple of blocks away to see the war close up and personal. What she found was more than she was able to digest. The building lay in ruin with rubble closing off part of the street. The wounded covered in blood were still being attended to by local good Samaritans. And then she saw with her own impressionable young eyes the body of a woman who had died in the blast. She was still half buried under the concrete chunks, covered in a powder of gray dust. With eyes still open, her empty stare met with my aunt's. It was a nightmarish site; one Colette would never forget.

My mother recalled a battle that took place on the streets that saw another innocent bystander killed. Except this time it wasn't a person but an unfortunate horse that due to the shortage of fuel and tires had been used as a beast of burden. After the exchange of gunfire had come to a halt and the streets deemed safe, it was obvious something had to be done with this magnificent yet deceased animal. Food rations and a protein shortage made for an easy decision. The local men joined together and started carving up the dead horse right there where it lay. Word spread quickly that there was fresh horse meat as the neighborhood showed up with pans and plates to get their share. The Poulain family was able to get enough to feed themselves for a week. Simone cooked it with onions and my mother said it was delicious; tasted like beef but sweeter, and in her opinion, even better. Makes one wonder about the expression, *"I'm so hungry I could eat a horse."*

February 20, 1944, *"Tomorrow I have to take courage between my two hands. Now they are talking about occupation. I am so tired of my life, tomorrow if I could I would get married with anybody to change my life."* Clearly my mother was at her wits end and still had high hopes that Mr. Right, or in this case, Mr. Anybody would magically appear.

On February 21st my mother's entry mentions a German SS trooper that came to the small dress shop where Simone and Colette worked. He naturally asked to see both their papers and asked the whereabouts of the store owner. Simone acted like she didn't know what he was talking about. Colette was not able to recall the conversation, but assured me they were both deathly afraid. Mame, having her own issues with morning sickness now stood face to face with a man who had the power to have both of them hung. There was no pity for women or children. Colette stood sheepishly off to one side as all attention was on her mother. Somehow my grandmother was able to remain calm and persuade the high ranking Nazi that she knew nothing.

Upon coming home, both Mama and Coco were noticeably shaken by the experience, with Mama taking the brunt of the interrogation.

After that incident my grandmother and aunt went to Monte Carlo where they had previously sought employment with Mr. Cohen of the family Colette had risked her own life for when she gathered their documents. Even though his family was still in hiding, the pair knew where to find them. She warned him not to go back to Nice, as it wasn't safe and to send word to her boss as well. Fearful to return to the dress shop where the SS had questioned them, Mr. Cohen in his gratitude hired both women to work at his shop, which they accepted. My grandmother had developed many skills in the dress making trade, and became a valuable asset to his business. He already had hired a non-Jewish manager to run the business while remaining underground, but soon that position was given to Simone, as she had earned it. My mother wrote at the end of the entry, *"Lots of people are evacuating in Nice and it is very dangerous. We are waiting to be obligated to leave."* Fortunately, they did not have to go this time.

A partial entry for March 5th 1944 reveals, *"Papa is always ready to have a big job but finishes nothing. He is not very nice lately and my mother is very worried since she is pregnant. He is not here naturally neither was he here for my birthday, or Coco's name day."* (In some European countries, a day that is associated with one's first name is celebrated, similar to a birthday.) My mother goes on to list the gifts the two sisters received but I am sure the gift that would have brought the most joy would have been for their father to have remembered his daughters special days. How sad for my mother, I thought. How sad for all. Her journal continued, *"Tuesday the Germans are going to do some maneuvers so we can't go to work or outside."* Curious, I asked my aunt how the Germans communicated with everyone and she said it was by loud speaker and that they spoke in French.

The very next day would bring much heartache. March 6, 1944. *"My, what an event we had. I have a good one but not one I like to speak about. My mother had a miscarriage and I was very sad. Not just because I won't have a brother, but my mother had so much pain, and was so sad because she wanted to have another baby. I think it's terrible and I'm sure it is from her travel from Nice to Monte Carlo because she was passing blood on Saturday and Sunday. She had a lot of pain and was passing more blood so the doctor came at midnight and he came back the next morning, but the fetus didn't come out yet. So he was talking about having to take it out. I went back to sleep and woke at 2am the next morning and Coco woke up and we were both crying because we want a baby so bad. We were making so much progress and then in one night it all changed. Oh my God why didn't you make this baby alright, and why all the complications? My poor little mother I adore her. Not like I love God naturally, only God we are supposed to adore, but I love her so much."*

After my aunt read this passage, I could tell she had more to say about that un-expected night. She explained that she didn't think it was from the bus ride back and forth to Monte Carlo, because she rode the bus as well and it was always a smooth ride. I asked if maybe it had been from the SS troops visit not even two weeks earlier. She didn't think so, but I know the confrontation had to have left an undue amount of stress on my grandmother's already taxed body. It was a very unfortunate situation and I believe it just wasn't the right time for this baby to enter into the world.

What remained of the fetus had been put in a pot, having nothing else available. The doctor had set it in the bathtub while he and Louise tended to Simone's needs. Both my mother and aunt saw what was left, a fleshy bloody mass about the size of a baseball. What an awful and depressing thing to have to witness for these two young teenage girls. To this day, my mother swears it was a boy, but my aunt says it was too early to tell. Both agreed their mother was extremely depressed afterward, and took some time to recover.

Simone Poulain at about the age when she lost her baby.

To add to the mounting stress for the family and the community of Nice, during a two week span, every night a German plane would fly haplessly overhead. It was as though the pilot was drunk as he'd weave this way, then that. It was well after curfew with curtains closed and lights extinguished per the strict orders of the oppressors. This plane with its roaring engines could be heard in the distance as it flew closer and closer. It would drop bombs at random as the French lay in their beds ducking under covers and burying their heads in pillows trying to escape the terror of the moment. Entire neighborhoods cringed in the privacy of their own bedrooms as their windows rattled with each explosion. The ear of God overflowed with prayers on those nights. After a few minutes, which seemed like hours of sheer panic, the plane could be heard flying back from whence it came. The townspeople breathed a collective heavy sigh of relief knowing this night they had been spared, and at the same time wondered who had not. This *"War of Nerves"* as my mother referred to it ended as quickly as it had started. My guess is that a British fighter pilot must have finally shot the plane from the sky, but I like to think the Marquis, the guerrilla fighters of the French resistance played a role as well.

Clearly my mother's nerves had been severely tested as she wrote on May 3, 1944, *"Two months have passed since I wrote in my little journal, but I am at the end of my rope, and I want to write as therapy for myself. Nothing really new, but if I could I would put a rope around my neck. I cannot stand it anymore I am over my head. My work is really bothering me and monotonous. The family life here is terrible, three months now my father doesn't bring in any money. He has outbursts and my parents are talking about separation. But now he says he has a good place for employment. My Grandmother has a bad temper. She doesn't want to go to Normandy. She'd rather bother me. And I have to live the existence God has given to me. And at seventeen years old all the poems say it's the best age for celebration. If this is life it does not please my existence. I worry about my job, but what did I do wrong to deserve this. I don't have any more passion and I am thinking I am wasting my youth.*

I hardly see my friends anymore because they are all busy. I have been making baby clothes for Madame Oseti because she is pregnant. She cannot pay me because she has no money, and she is very sad. Naturally for me I cannot find a man, and I will not have any babies, and I will be an old maid. Oh my God listen to me, I am depressed. I have to change my attitude. Give me some ideas I am so depressed! The events for the war are always the same. We have some terrible bombardments all over France and hundreds of people die and the dirty Germans make us work for them."

As the daughter of the young woman writing these words, I had great empathy for her plight. It was impossible for me to put myself in her position. Even trying to imagine the utter frustration that boiled through her veins left me coming up terribly short. In regards to her grandmother, my mom told me she had a way of seeking attention through outburst. She said Louise would yell and scream for no apparent reason, and one day acted like she was falling down the stairs. When my mother and sister were still pre-teens, she said her grandmother took a switch to her for talking at the bottom of the stairs too long with one of her friends. It sounded as though there had been friction for some time. And yet my aunt maintained that her grandmother was cheerful and loving, but I recalled Colette was also Louise's favorite. My great-grandmother's sisters still lived in Nonancourt during the war, which is why there was talk of her going to Normandy. She did however travel back to the

Alsace region for a short time, returning well before the Battle of the Bulge. I'm sure while she was gone, my mother was very happy.

It was true the German soldiers forced the French into manual labor for their cause. Many of these brave young men escaped into the surrounding mountains to avoid the compulsory enlistment of the Vichy, France *Service du Travail Obligatoire,* or STO to the German labor camps. These escaped Free Frenchmen soon banded together eventually forming the Marquis, or French Resistance. Many of the young men from Nice were forcibly taken from their homes to be a part of the STO, and the people of France were keenly aware and adamantly opposed. Resistance was met with death.

It became evident to my mother her depression had gotten out of hand. She sought the help of a doctor who said she had to change her life and have some distractions. He also prescribed medication as I'm sure he realized the depth of her disparity. With the war there was only one thing Monique really had control over, and so informed her mother that at the end of June she would be quitting her monotonous job.

July 1, 1944, *"Between May and this entry Nice had a big bombardment and that woke me up. Five hundred died, more people were hurt and thousands of people had someone in the family that died. Everyone around us was scared. At our office too, the house next to us was bombed and five people died while still in the house. In other towns in France they had the same. No one had a chance to get away. It's the war and now it's touching us. That completely woke me up! Since the invasion in Normandy we have been waiting for this terrible war to end. At the office there is not much work and both of them are just so nice to me."* My mother didn't quit her job after all.

What my mom and many other French nationals were unaware of is that much of the bombing was done by Allied forces in preparation for their next planned invasion. Key targets were taken out but without the technology for precision air-strikes bombs were released with a wish and a prayer. As a result there was extensive death and destruction for many of the innocent. It is a fact that there were thousands of civilian casualties during these preparations that were considered a by-product of war. My aunt turned to me, rubbing her hands up and down her arms. Almost in tears she said, *"It was awful, Marianne, it gives me goose bumps."*

Aunt Colette reading a copied page of my mothers' journal. 7-28-2012

There were no more vegetables to be found in Nice, so three times a week members of the family went to a neighboring village to gather what they could. *"It was the only way so we wouldn't have to eat bricks."* Even though there were no vegetables, somehow there was always ice cream.

The store fronts were closed but if a person had some extra money, they could go to the back of certain stores and make requests. My aunt referred to this as the black market, and the Poulains thoroughly enjoyed this decadent comfort food in the wake of complete misery. My mother's words, *"My obsessions, I am fat and I have to realize I am sick. I eat too much fruit and I have to stop eating sugar and things that are fattening."* Cakes, cookies, candy and ice cream were what my mother lived for and was mentioned consistently throughout her journal. It was food to heal her inner wounds. Comfort food for the un-comforted. With the daily uncertainty of whether your home would be bombed or not, I say why not enjoy.

Continuing her July 1st entry, *"In the meantime, two young men, idiots, wanted to flirt with me. But I did not like those idiots. They were really like glue around me, and were about seventeen years old. I had trouble getting rid of them. I see Gabby and Ester often and we get along good now. With Coco we get along very well. We don't fight which is very rare between sisters. And with my mother we eat plenty of ice cream."* With all that my grandmother had been through, the ice cream was a welcome bowl of unconditional love.

"At the house it's like the war between Italy and Russia. Papa and my grandmother are the fighters and probably with patience it will end up like the war. But now I am happy to be alive. All my morbid ideas are gone and I am happy to be seventeen. Even with my sad life I want to scream Vive Le Vie"!

Long Live the Life! I think the medicine worked!

Chapter 11

THE CHAMPAGNE CAMPAIGN & ROMANCE

While our brave young men were fighting for their lives at Anzio, the planning of Operation Dragoon, the Allied invasion into Southern France was well under way. Originally named Operation Anvil it was rumored to have been changed to Dragoon because British Prime Minister Winston Churchill felt dragooned into going along with an invasion he opposed. Referred to as the Forgotten Campaign, little mention is made of this operation even though it was the second largest invasion during WWII.

The 509th PIB had been relieved of their duties from Anzio's front to start their new training in Naples, Italy. Because the battalion had lost half their men, replacements slowly brought their total back to 675 strong. It was the job of the seasoned soldiers, including Johnny, to whip the newbies into shape. Meanwhile, the remaining Allies still battling it out in Anzio beat back the weary Germans, then pushed onward, reaching and liberating Rome on June 4, 1944. Careful planning had determined a list of nineteen units including Paratroopers and specialized forces that were assigned to the 1st ABTF, short for First Airborne Task Force. With Rome cleared by June of '44, all nineteen were dispatched to the Eternal City which became the Airborne Training Center for thousands of men.

The paratroopers soon learned their next mission would put their parachute practice to the test. According to Matt Anderson, WWII historian, of the 675 men, 569 Geronimos would enter the battle zone by air, with the balance of 106 arriving by ship as part of the rear echelon, driving vehicles and hauling equipment from Italy. My dad of course was just one in a sea of green preparing for what would be his only combat jump. The G.I's spent mornings and afternoons getting schooled in any and all foreseen battle scenarios, with their evenings free to relax. The troops learned about the terrain of the drop zone (or DZ) and their objectives once they had parachuted safely behind enemy lines. Maps became a problem in that there were few, and didn't show the Nazi obstacles set in place for the glider planes that would make an important contribution to the pre-dawn surprise.

Johnny on left with unidentified soldier in Italy. "The 509th was authorized to wear the 5th Army patch that the other soldier is wearing for only a short time in Italy. Some soldiers never got around to putting it on their uniforms." - Matt Anderson, Historian

There wasn't time for full scale jump rehearsals so the training was downscaled to drops of two to three men. The rest of the paratroopers were already on the ground and as the skeleton crew landed, the tactical procedures were experienced and tested. Likewise, the C-47 lead pilots flew practice flights in V formations of three planes each, with timing and altitude assimilating the actual day of the operation. This was going to be risky at best as the pilots would be flying blindly, guided only by radio and radar which was susceptible to malfunctions. The operation wouldn't just be confined to air, but would also be conducted by land and sea. Once again, hundreds of ships were dispatched to the Mediterranean.

My oldest brother informed me that our father had mentioned while in Rome he had gone to a couple of operas, one of which was *The Marriage of Figaro*. I thought this to be pretty amazing that while the war was not yet over, the Italian Opera was still performing, and even more dumbfounded that my dad and his buddies had the time to take in some local culture. Obviously having never been in war myself I had my own preconceived idea that WWII was a tumultuous, non-stop see-saw of muscle. It never dawned on me there would be downtime to regroup and re-energize the weary fighting machine. But the downtime would be short lived as the D-day invasion into Southern France was drawing near.

While my dad was mentally preparing for his parachute drop, my mother was still tiring of this bothersome war. She writes in her journal on July 24, 1944 of the monthly food rationing as it applied to her family. *"Bread 750 grams, meat 90 grams, oils 15 grams. I cannot get fat because I am starving. We went to Monte Carlo and the beautiful Promenade. When we got back I wanted a new dress, but my mother said I couldn't have one because it is too expensive. I'm getting tired of living with so little money. I understand why some women find a man to pay their bills. I can't wait until the end of the war."*

Less than a month after her journal entry the stage was being set for Operation Dragoon. Continuous air strikes and artillery fire from ships anchored at sea pummeled strategic targets. The relentless assault bombarded ports of enemy weaponry and knocked out bridges. Seizure and control of key southern harbors in Marseilles and Toulon would be necessary to funnel much needed supplies to the anticipated growing Allied force. In addition, the Resistance continued to gather German intelligence, as well as wreaking havoc on the Jerrys. They stayed busy cutting communication lines, seizing bridges, destroying railroad tracks, and a host of other methods to undermine the Nazis' efforts. Actions taken to cripple the German military strength were well-executed, and prepared the way for the massive amphibious assault on the southern seashore.

The airborne operation began with a deceptive DZ by dropping rubber parachute dummies into a selected area. Six aircraft were used to give the appearance of a much larger attack. In all, some 600 dummies attached to parachutes were dispersed north and west of Toulon. Gunfire simulators and other battle noises were attached to the dummies giving the decoys a sense of realism. The bait was a success as German radio reports indicated they had bought into the Allied trickery.

With the heavy losses from the turf war during Anzio, the Germans had their hands full. Two months prior, on June 6th, the massive D-day invasion into Normandy had been launched. The one-two punch had arrived. In the pre-dawn hours of August 15, 1944, Operation Dragoon officially began. In the thick of night, far off in the distance came a low roar as hundreds of C-47s flying in V formation approached the drop zone. Each configuration consisted of an average of 45 planes with five minute intervals between each grouping. Aboard my dad's plane, which included Lt. Col Yarborough, *"Most of our "stick'" slept or smoked, very little talking."*

Due to the mountainous terrain the paratroopers and gliders would have to be dropped or released at high altitudes of 1500 to 2000 feet. Speed for towing the gliders was set at 120mph and the paratroopers would jump at 110 mph. As they neared their targets the rumble became a steady hum of ominous proportions. The Nazis sensed it was only a matter of time before thousands of Allied troops descended upon them. Reaching their target, the 509th led the pack. At 0430 Johnny and the other paratroopers jumped in the Le Muy area of France about 80 kilometers east of Nice, and a dozen miles inland off the coast of the Mediterranean.

An idea of the scope of the operation shows the initial pre-dawn attack consisted of 396 planes with more than 5,000 paratroopers. As the morning progressed, the Provisional Troop Carrier Air Division had an approximate total of 987 aircraft that carried 9,000 airborne troops, 221 jeeps and 213 artillery pieces. The foray included 407 towed gliders that carried over two million pounds of equipment into the battle zone. Many of the bravest of the brave of these glider pilots crashed as they attempted to land. With no engines, pitch black skies, rough terrain, and anti-glider poles, it's a wonder that any survived at all.

HHC and A Company 509th PIB landed on Drop Zone C just south of Le Muy. My dad was fortunate to have been aboard one of those planes. Unfortunately, B and C Company 509th PIB, which totaled about half the 509th PIB, was miss-dropped at Saint Tropez, a seaside town a good dozen or so miles south of Le Muy. With the disadvantage of low clouds and possibly faulty equipment these gingerbread men mistakenly jumped onto the beach, with some landing chest high in the sea. Within a short time, French Resistance fighters from the *Brigade des Maures* who had decoded American transmissions and knew Operation Dragoon had begun, found the paratroopers. With their assistance, the 509ers were able to determine where they had landed and that they were about 12 miles from the DZ.

There were no straight roads that led back to Le Muy and the terrain was much too mountainous to advance by foot. So, instead of scrambling back, they teamed together with their French counterparts and began clearing the seaside town of enemy soldiers. When the Allied units from the amphibious assault arrived it was an unexpected relief to see fellow comrades and French combatants so far from the DZ who had survived and continued the fight. For these young men had no idea they had been the lucky ones. Seventeen fellow 509ers of B Company missed the beachhead altogether, and drifted into the Gulf of Saint-Tropez. None survived.

Today there is a monument to honor these brave young paratroopers listing their names, rank, and home state. The plaque reads simply: *"Here at dawn on August 15, 1944, on board one of the numerous C-47's, 17 parachutists of Company B of the 509th Battalion jumped into the waters of the Gulf of Saint-Tropez to liberate France. Not one of them was ever found."* There's a good chance my dad knew some, if not all of these fallen heroes. Five days into the surge, by August 20th, American soldiers that were listed as killed, captured, or missing in action totaled 434, including the seventeen young gingerbread men, gone but not forgotten.

After my father landed safely behind enemy lines he had a job to do. With a war going on Dad recalled some of the soldiers he fought alongside were convicts who exchanged a stint in the war for an early parole. They weren't part of 509th, but instead special groups of scouts or advanced recon. Their job was to go behind enemy lines to gather as much intel as possible and sometimes to disrupt enemy movement, like hitting a gas depot or ammo dump. Some of these men were street tough and played by their own rules. They'd go out on small patrols made up of six soldiers, including my dad carrying a radio on his his back. It was Johnny's job to relay information about the enemy they encountered to the brass waiting in the rears. Weaving through thick brush with visibility practically nil, my father recalled, *"It was dangerous as hell, not even the cons wanted to go first."*

Outside the prison walls these men were a breed unto themselves. Sometimes when they'd capture a Kraut they'd take him back to camp. Other times the German soldiers were forced to their knees. With a gun held to the prisoner's head, their captors demanded answers. There were occasions when, if the guy didn't talk, he was shot dead. Other times, if he did talk, he'd still be shot. It was always best if they captured at least two at the same time. One of the German soldiers would be shot right on the spot to invoke fear. Dad said, *"The other always sang like a canary."* But as soon as he was done singing he'd get a bullet too. Dad never approved of the convict-turned-soldiers' tactics. After witnessing this gruesome interrogation Johnny radioed back the information obtained but watching how they got it made him sick to the stomach. He added, *"The Germans did the same thing to our guys."* I guess he had to reason away the murderous acts he witnessed.

While out on another task, he and a buddy were positioned high on a hill with two other soldiers perched on an opposite hill about a 1/2 mile away overlooking a valley below. They were acting as look-outs for the reinforced company of some one hundred plus men crossing the dangerously exposed open terrain. I don't know what unit the company was, but I know it wasn't the 509th. If they spied enemy activity Dad's job was to radio it in. As he searched the area through his binoculars, seemingly from out of nowhere a German bomber came roaring over one of the hillsides. There wasn't even time to take cover. Johnny watched helplessly as about a quarter mile away a single percussion bomb was dropped. He said it must have weighed between one to two thousand pounds. Just a single bomb that was a direct hit on the company below. Johnny watched helplessly as at least ninety percent of the American soldiers were killed instantly. The others sustained serious injury. Even from his distance, the ground shook as my dad ducked and prayed for those poor souls in the valley. Aleck radioed back to his superiors the nightmare he'd just witnessed.

The continuous push of the Allied Forces heading east toward the Italian border was making an impact on the lives of the French citizens of Nice. My mother writes on August 28, *"What sensational news since I last wrote to you. After the appearance of the Americans and English to wonderfully transform France they are half way through France everywhere, and on the 15th of August they started coming from the Mediterranean. They came very close to Marseille and Toulon, and on Tuesday the 15th we had orders to evacuate our place. So we went with our neighbors and we found a place to stay at the Salvation Army. They were so nice and welcomed us. We went twice to get vegetables at St. Barthelemy and St. Augustine, 18 kilometers away."*

The Salvation Army had set up makeshift safe houses in the surrounding countryside a few miles away from the anticipated heavy fighting. It was actually the Germans who had ordered the evacuation, which again, I found odd. The only place to sleep was on the floor as families staked out small sections for themselves, making the best of their situation. I was to discover through my brothers recordings that my mother had left out an unpleasant incident in her journal. She revealed that one of the French workers at the Salvation Army was, as she put it, a pervert.

Every day many of the evacuees would gather for prayer, and this middle-aged deviant always managed to stand next to her. While everyone prayed with hands folded and eyes closed, this lecher found delight in pinching and pawing at my mother's breasts. Monique kept pulling away and glared into his eyes, but his abuse continued. This Catholic teenager had never experienced such intrusive behavior. Finally, without saying a word she reared her leg back and kicked him in the chin as hard as she could. Well, that put an end to his nonsense as she was now able to pray in peace. I asked if she had ever shared this story with her family, and her reply was a quick, *"No. You didn't talk about such matters."*

Colette on the other hand, was pre-occupied with the two rabbits she lugged around in a basket. Since they didn't know how long they'd be gone she was afraid the little bunnies would have starved if left at home. Roaming about from room to room she kept busy scavenging for food scraps for her furry friends. On one occasion Coco was standing by a window, and hearing voices, she peeked through the curtains. To her complete shock, there was a German soldier so close that had there not been glass between them she could have reached out and touched him. His back was to the building and she thought, *"If only I had a gun, I would shoot him."* She told me she had grown to hate the Nazis so much that she would have done it without an ounce of remorse. But within seconds shots were fired and she quickly closed the curtains and ducked. Knowing it wasn't safe, Colette was too scared to peek through the window again. A French resistance fighter had exchanged gunfire with the German soldier, only to be shot and killed. Later, when she heard the Frenchman had died, it enraged her even more as she had a clear shot at the enemy and could have saved the young patriot's life. Eventually though, other FFI fighters appeared, but this time the gunfire exchange was favorable and eliminated the German patrols.

Aug 28th, continues: *"This morning we went to Gairaut, ah but it's beautiful. It's in the country, but when we got back they told us there was fighting in the streets of Nice. The Patriots and the Germans are fighting and they don't know if we can go through Nice. We did arrive in Nice, but we heard constantly the guns and machine guns, even some revolvers. The Resistance is almost everywhere and they are winning. In the Vars, the apartment next door all the Germans are already gone and the Americans are there too. How happy I was when we arrived and the Resistance was in the neighborhood. The Liberation is here and I am very happy!"*

I cannot even imagine the elation that must have run through my mother, and all the citizens living in the South of France. It wasn't long before a military convoy made up of hundreds of vehicles wound through the Provence countryside. News spread that the Allies were coming as the streets flooded with onlookers. Soldiers heaped onto the slow moving tanks, jeeps, and trucks as they crawled through the streets of Cannes and Nice. Troops helped women aboard and were rewarded with generous kisses and embraces. Many walked in the impromptu parade as *femmes* blew kisses, threw flowers, and even themselves upon their liberators! The men cheered and clapped, with tears shed by all, and for the first time in years, smiles emerged from the depths of their souls.

FFI soldiers donned in black French berets absorbed the tremendous pride of having played a vital role in freeing fellow Frenchmen. All across France hundreds of thousands of everyday citizens, both male and female became small heroes, even after their own government had signed a pact with Hitler. Driven by passion and selflessness their tenacious spirit was unparalleled. So great was the bravery of these "Silent Heroes of WWII" it would take volumes to honor them properly.

Paratroopers of the 509 PIB being cheered as they ride through the streets of Nice, France - picture taken by an unknown French photographer - August 30, 1944

And so the valiant warriors American, Canadian, British, and French alike, weary from battle, hot, thirsty, and hungry, were greeted in true French style. Champagne and wine flowed abundantly as the liberation of the South of France became known as the Champagne Campaign. Viva La France!

But the war was not yet over, and despite the celebration there was still fear in their hearts. Although there would be no more looking over one's shoulder or hurrying home before curfew, it was easier said than believed. Years of living under the Nazis thumb meant the transformation had to be felt from the inside out. To be sure it was safe, many families chose to go back to the Salvation Army. The Poulains had returned to the hills, making short trips back and forth.

My mother wrote a more detailed seven page account of the events of the *Liberation de Nice* on September 12, 1944. I found the folded papers amongst my father's letters. What a wonderful gift my mom left for our family to share with the world. The first page is written on the back of a survey questionnaire from the concrete company where she worked, which tells me she wrote her thoughts while working that day. Anne Marie who had translated my grandfather's court documents transcribed my mother's narrative.

"Today I want to talk in detail about multiple events that happened since August 15th, but it is difficult to express all the feelings with simple words. Since the beginning of August, we were frequently in the state of alert, and often Allied planes were flying over. The landing was expected and then during the night of the 14 to the 15, we could hear far away the machine guns, and planes were flying over non-stop. Around 4 in the morning, we went down to the basement where a lot of people who were renters from the building and neighbors from around were already gathered. And then we waited... the sound of the engines and of the canons kept us awake.

Around 6 in the morning, we went back up and then came back down shortly after. It feels like people are constantly coming and going non-stop in the staircase. At 8 o'clock, we are told that the landing on the Mediterranean coast, the moment we were hoping so much for, has finally happened. The prospect of freedom rejoices in us, nevertheless we still dread the circumstances of this freedom.

What will happen? It is a mystery. The Boches, [a very derogatory term used by the French to describe the German soldiers] *forbid us to go outside, so we went upstairs and made lunch. At 1:30 we were told that we have to evacuate and be away from the harbor by 4 o'clock. In haste we gathered some clothes and food, and at 2pm we left with some friends.*

After walking for about one hour, we arrived in Saint Barthelemy where a name caught our attention: Salvation Army. Our parents asked for hospitality which was granted to us, and we setup in avenue Bardi. We were lucky to have a large garden and many bedrooms are at our disposal. We can do our own cooking, but it is a lot of labor. We have to walk to Saint Augustin, which I do twice a week with Madame Grandjean, her son, and his friend (11 miles round trip). The Germans imposed a strong curfew. We can be out from 7 to 9, 11 to 14, and 18 to 20. It is forbidden to circulate using a bicycle. We went to Saluzzo [their apartment in Nice] *very often to bring back as much food and clothing as possible. The days are fairly quiet. We can hear far away the canons and machine guns, some bombings of the harbor, [one bomb fell in front of the Palace of Monaco] but we did not have too much damage. All would be fine if a nasty Boche would not keep us awake every night. The nasty plane flies low near the roofs and drops bombs where he wants (apparently he is looking for lights).*

We sleep on the floor of the living room or in a chair, but it is tiring and we usually fall away. I read a little, I sew or I knit during the day, and I knit orders during my free time. Finally the battle is coming close as Cannes and Antibes are liberated. The Allies are getting close to Nice. Monday August 28th Mamine and I are going to Gairaut for vegetables. The restless night made us feel that something is happening, but now all is calm, we got a few vegetables after a wonderful walk. I've never come to this part of Nice, it is magnificent. Nice is in front of us under a wonderful sky, nature seems to be joyful, but nevertheless the Battle of Nice is starting. [They were in the hills above Nice looking down on the city.] *As we are walking back, we are told to be careful because the Patriots are coming to free us. Carefully, we keep walking and reach the Salvation Army.*

Three hundred meters from our place the battle is in full rage. Machine guns and gunshots are going off. Around 11, the men across the street will be able to join the Patriots. One hundred meters from our place, a roadblock is made. Around 1, the battle quiets down and we go out for a little while, but around 2pm the battle starts again. Gun fire is going off everywhere, a fight is engaged 150 meters from the Salvation Army and it's a victory for the FFI. Around 6pm a reprieve, but not for long because the Germans from the Gairaut battery start to bomb the city with explosive shells « those pigs ». A bomb dropped 150 meters from our place, and then the shooting stopped and we learned that the Polish occupying the battery surrendered after killing their colonel. It was a close call for Nice. [The Polish men who were forced to fight for the Germans killed the German Colonel, knowing the Allies were coming, then they surrendered rather than face the possibility of death.]

We are sleeping in the dining room on a mattress on the floor and we close all openings with bags filled with dirt. [A makeshift barricade]. *I sleep well even with the gunfire, the explosion in the harbor, and all that the Germans are bombing. Our parents are watching over us. Nevertheless in the morning everything is back to normal. Around 6am I get up and go outside to see what's going on. I met an FFI across the street and he tells me "they are gone". I ran back home to tell the good news to Mom. We washed up and went outside. Shortly thereafter everybody went out and around 9am the news is confirmed by loudspeaker, Nice is liberated!*

There is with a great joy that starts shyly at first, then progresses to a celebratory outburst. Houses are decorated, each one with a rosette made of ribbon, faces are relaxed, we are not afraid anymore. *Everybody talks to each other. The liberation is a miracle. France is back, but it is the next day Tuesday that the enthusiasm of the crowd reaches its paroxysm with the arrival of the first American troops. In town it is delirium. People are happy and forget their misery. Cafes closed for the last 3 weeks have redone their terraces. Military marches are sung by everyone. Finally the Boche is really gone. We are free again, and it seems that we are having a dream too magnificent to be a reality, but nevertheless at each street corner the truth is there. We are free from the Boche yoke. The same day Tuesday August 29, we went back to clean the house from top to bottom and the next day came back home.*

Surely the war is not over. The Allied armies continue their victory march but a big weight has been lifted from us. Traitors will be punished, abuses will be repressed, France will start again to live and Nice is a part of this beautiful country.

Today September 12, Nice is reorganizing. Bridges are being repaired, mines are removed from the harbor, food transportations are beginning to arrive, and roadblocks are removed. Little by little life is starting again. Almost all stores have reopened. Everyone is back to their routine but with joy and hope in their hearts."

Three days later after receiving this glorious news my mother writes again in her journal, unaware of the surprise hidden in one of those planes that woke them in the early morning hours of August 15th.

"Journal entry September 14, 1944, *"On 31, August we came down from the Salvation Army. The next morning Mama, Coco, and I cleaned the house and around 11:00 o'clock Colette went back to the Salvation Army, and we were going to join after her. When we went downstairs two American soldiers wanted to put their communication lines up and they asked Claud but he didn't have the key."* Claud was a teenage neighbor who along with his parents had gone to the Salvation Army with the Poulains.

They lived downstairs and his parents who had the key had stayed in the hills.

"*So I asked him if he could put the lines on our balcony. We offered him a drink and some cookies and he put the lines up, and I told him to come back. I wasn't thinking about him and when I came back from work on Friday Mama told me an American came to see me two times and he will be back at 7 o'clock. And just at seven my American came back. He does not speak French and he brought me some candy, cigarettes, chewing gum, and he wants to teach me to dance and his name is Johnny. He is from California and he is 20 years old. He said he will be back and he came back Sunday at 6 o'clock*".

My mother's journal entry from Sept. 14, 1944 when she writes about meeting Johnny. Notice on line 5, you can read the words "Johnny" and "California."

And that is how my parents Johnny and Monique met. With a vast ocean between their homelands it was Hitler's war that brought them to this moment. Was it by chance Claud didn't have the key and my mom and grandmother hadn't left with Colette? I believe it was fate as my mother had constantly prayed for and written of such a chance encounter. Even his age was just right, being three years older. Had her wishes finally come true?

Johnny and his Army buddy Batton pulled up in a jeep that pivotal morning. My mom would tell me later, *"He was drunk and smelled of wine."* It was already getting hot, and with the mixture of alcohol and the mid-morning sun, Johnny was shirtless. With his olive complexion he was so tanned that at first Monique thought he was Mexican. My charming father probably prompted my mother to offer their balcony, as for Johnny, it was love at first sight. James Batton shared his memory with Gregg, *"He walked back from the balcony with a pretty young lady. That was it for Johnny."* After all the fighting and stench of death this naive young French gal was medicine to his soul.

Having the streets filled with American soldiers gave the Poulains the sense of security they needed, and decided no more trips to the hills were necessary. When Colette returned, the young sisters bursting with excitement decided to mingle with the masses. G.I. Johnny was still fresh on Monique's mind as the pair took to the streets. Reveling along the way, they entered *Place Garibaldi*, a public square named after Giuseppe Garibaldi.

Euphoria was palpable as soldiers partied amongst the *Nicoise* continuing the day's long celebration. Strolling through the crowds the pair was giddy with laughter with a *que sera sera* outlook on the days ahead. A new life most certainly had begun. In the middle of the square is a tall ornate statue of Garibaldi that sits in a gushing fountain. As they approached, who does Monique see, but Johnny and his friend with two French dames flirting and drinking, unabashed to the world. Admittedly, my mother had felt a spark between her and this wild G.I. Their eyes locked and instantly he recognized the innocent beauty he had met earlier that morning. Seeing him in such a compromised position with an obvious floozy brought a rush of jealousy throughout Monique's unaccustomed fragile state. My mother gave him the dirtiest look she could summon, grabbed the sides of her dress and swished them back and forth with exaggerated force. Tossing her head back in defiance she stormed off in a huff with Coco doing her best to follow. My mom has never been one to hide her emotions, and the words "French temper" come to mind. She made certain the young soldier boys' actions were met with complete disapproval. I'm sure her feelings had been hurt as she wrote in her diary she had stopped thinking of him. So, when he came by the next day, not once, not twice, but a third time while bearing gifts, well, all was forgiven. Her entry continued.

"We were having dinner and we asked if he wanted to stay and he said yes. He brought us some cheese and milk chocolate bars. My mother let us go out until 9:30pm".

Monique had never had milk chocolate bars before, and knowing how much she loved her sweets, this was a very wise choice on Johnny's part, and when they went out it was always a threesome with Colette tagging along as chaperon.

"He told us he has two sisters and one brother and he had been fighting in North Africa, Casino, Anzio, and Naples and that he is a parachutist. He told us about all his battles and that he parachuted in Le Muy, France. And when we came back he gave

me a medal and he asked me for my address and we are good friends. He has to go back to Monte Carlo at 10:00 pm, but will have some free time Monday and Tuesday. So he came back at 7 o'clock until 10 pm. We went out and we tried to talk to each other, and I found him very, very sympathetic. I think I might fall in love."

Young Johnny, the soldier Monique was falling in love with. Picture taken in Nice, France.

The innocence of their youth in a budding wartime romance made me breathe a heavy sigh. Raised in an extremely strict Catholic household and having never had a boyfriend or even been kissed made this relationship for my mother even more special. Fortunately, my mom's family really enjoyed Johnny. There was nothing pretentious about my father, and when describing him, I tell people, *"He never knew a stranger."*

My mother continued, *"He is very honest, but you know we should never believe a soldier. And then no more of him until Saturday when I got back from the office, Johnny is the one who opened the door. I am happy because I was thinking about him these last few days, and I was really in a hurry to see him again. He eats with us lunch and dinner. He is supposed to go back at 10:00 pm".*

Food, especially meat, was still scarce and Simone wanted to make a good impression with Monique's suitor. For one of these meals Simone asked Colette if she would be willing to give up one of her pet rabbits. Even though it was a difficult choice, she agreed, and Louise, having grown up on the family farm, saw to the butchering. At dinner that night, while the family had a delicious meal, Colette barely nibbled on her vegetables and excused herself early from the dinner table. She quietly went to her room and cried, mourning the loss of her *petite lapin*. My mother was equally unable to eat any of the meat, but naturally had no intentions on leaving the table. When I heard this story and I've heard it several times, I thought what a great love Coco must have had for her sister to make such a sacrifice.

Continuing the journal entry, *"We went downstairs and he bought me a scarf and he taught me to dance again. And then he took me to the balcony and he told me after the war we would get married, and I would go with him to California. I could not believe a word of what he was saying."*

My mom had left out some key elements which she embellished upon in the cassette recording. My dad's marriage proposal that day was anything but romantic although it did make me laugh. *"Then he came back and after about the third or fourth time he wanted to kiss me. And naturally, being raised the way I was Catholic, I thought I'd go to hell if I kissed a soldier or anyone else. You don't kiss a boy unless you are going to get married. So, I told him. I'm sure he thought I was nuts. But he said, "Oh, okay then we'll get married". And he kissed me. And that's the way we were engaged. After that he always came with flowers. I don't know where he found them, it all happened so fast."*

My beautiful mother Monique taken at Erpe Studio. Johnny and Monique went together when they had their pictures taken.

And with that first kiss while her family kept busy in the apartment, my mother felt both fear and excitement. The passion between these two hot-blooded lovers was intoxicating. I'm sure my father felt a special honor to have been the man to consume the first kiss from her soft lips. But the fact remained, he was an American soldier, and as she had mentioned, soldiers couldn't be trusted. There was no guarantee she wasn't one in a string of women he had made the promise of marriage just to steal a kiss. With a war still in their future he would leave to continue the fight with the threat of bullets, grenades, and mortars. And the sad truth is, this man who held her tightly in his arms could very well end up a casualty before wars end. Monique would have to take her chances as falling in love, getting married, and having a family was all she ever dreamt of.

The last of her September 14, entry: *"The heavy chains that were put around us by the Germans have been broken and we can go back to living. I wanted something new, and I got it. With the liberation we are free from the war, and it came for me from an event that I would not think would have come. It's like a fairy tale. But I don't know what will happen from it. God only knows."*

Chapter 12

THE BATTLE OF THE BULGE

Reclaiming normality was important in the lives of the French who were finally free from German rule. Food, though still scarce, would gradually become more available. Bombed buildings lay in ruin and would take years to rebuild. The shackles may have been broken, but the physiological damage would take time to heal, and for some it never did. There was chaos in the streets as German sympathizers were apprehended and given swift mob justice. The father of my mother's friend Ester was Italian and had sided with Italy and Germany during the occupation. After the liberation he was found murdered. No one knew when the end of this brutal war would come, but at least for the majority of France a unanimous exhale could be heard.

The Gingerbread men still had a job to finish, and although champagne continued to flow, their unit along with others of the 1st ABTF had orders to secure the surrounding area. The Jerrys had fled to higher ground with the 509th PIB in hot pursuit. Flanking the Seventh Army they pushed north through the French Maritime Alps toward the Italian border. Thick brush and trees provided ample camouflage for the Germans, making for a risky situation. Mine sweepers cleared paths as the tenacious unit was steadfast in their mission to eliminate the enemy. For three months the men patrolled the dangerous mountains, engaging in close knit battles. And yet the war would not become a barrier for the love that had evolved between Johnny and Monique.

Downtime in the Maritime Alps, re-spooling wire to smaller wheels. Left to right - Jim McCann, Walter C. Pope, Reginald S. Marshall, and Johnny G. Aleck

It wasn't long before my mother received her first letter from the man with whom she was falling in love. On a simple 5x7 lined piece of paper, torn from a notebook and folded in half, my mother read his hand printed words.

Dear Monique   *Sept. 26, 1944*

Hello Angel, how is the girl of my dreams today? I am very fine and am very glad it isn't raining. It will be about 9 days before I will get to see you, dear, so please do not worry.

I wish I had a picture of you, Monique. I can picture you in my mind, but that is not enough. I want to see you all the time. How is your work coming along? I hope you're not working too hard, dear.

Monique, there is something about you that relaxes my mind very much. I can't explain that feeling, but I love it. Maybe you get that same feeling. The mountains here are beautiful, and the sound of the river flowing is really relaxing. All I really need is you here, Monique, to make me very happy.

Well, Monique, I will close for this time, so be a good girl and write as soon as possible.

All my love,

Johnny

In all the letters my dad wrote, he downplayed the danger he and his comrades faced each day. Johnny never wanted his new love to worry, and always mentioned that he was fine. I found this to be very sweet and protective. In reading my dad's letters I know I have gone against my mother's wishes. My mom had told me once that she had his love letters and that she didn't want anyone to ever read them. But in all honesty, the innocence of their love is refreshing. There was a war going on with uncertainties and miles between them. Letters were precious. And now, our family cherishes the three-inch binder filled with his words, along with our mother's journal. I think she'd forgive me if she knew.

Monday 23, October 1944:

"Happy people don't have any stories, and since I was happy I did not write for a long time. But today I want to write a little of what has happened to me since the last time I wrote. I love Johnny like a crazy woman. We are engaged and when we can, we will get married. I am so happy! I wanted to be in love, and I don't want anything to give me sad ideas. I trust Johnny and I can see he will be helpful in life. He wants to have four children and a ranch. We have the same desire that the war is finished. I will be very sad to leave Coco and my mother, but the wife must leave everything and follow her husband. That is the only shadow in my joy. But I will

be happy when we will see each other again. I don't have the same ideas as the Americans. I don't want to think that he is a wolf. I think he has good morals, and he is originally Greek and they are Latin people.

Right now he is on the front in Italy and I see him every ten days for one day. And in two days he'll be back, but the last time he was very tired and he had a cold, so I took care of him and told him to sleep, because if he kissed me I would get his cold. I was very happy with the little time we had together. And like they say those happy in love don't have stories to tell. I have a lot of work to do at the office and I don't even know where my head is? Since the last fifteen days I made 800 francs a month, which came at a good time as I have to prepare my clothes." In France, my aunt told me it is customary for the wife to provide linens and bedding and such upon marriage. "*I bought a new dress and I like it very much. This evening I wish that Johnny poor darling was with me.*"

Before the lovebirds met, Monique's life was full of boredom from their restrictive lives and she had fantasies of falling in love. Never had she imagined complications would arise from this new emotion. Now my mother was met with the hard reality that even in love life isn't perfect. Teenage boredom had been replaced with teenage worry as she wrote this entry.

November 1st, 1944:

"*Today is All Saints Day and naturally it's raining and it's also raining in my heart. I am very sad and have the blues. Johnny came to see me on Tuesday for two days. But since he left I think about him without stopping and I love him more and more. Now all the soldiers are moving to Belfort, and I have no news. We were talking about getting married in four months. I am going to say a little prayer for that intention. I have lots of work at the office, but I still can't think and I have a terrible headache. At the house everything is fine and Papa is good too."*

Belfort, France is a good 500 miles north of Nice near the Alsace region. With such a distance, he may as well have been back in the U.S. In my research I was unable to determine that the 509th did in fact go to Belfort. It may very well have been a rumor Johnny had heard, or the plans had changed. Fortunately, young Monique's world had not ceased to turn on its axis, as with another entry I learned the 509th PIB had a much deserved leave.

Ray Chapin kneeling far left. Johnny sitting on rock with hands on knees. This, and the following pictures were taken in Maritime Alps - Peïra-Cava. Location provided by Loïc 'Jack' Jankowiak.

Left to right - Chapin, Blass, and Aleck.

1 Left to right - Aleck, Blass, McCann, Chapin, and Marshall.

Johnny sitting in foreground holding his knee with both hands. Notice to the far right there are two spools of wire.

Finally, Johnny and fellow 509ers were relieved of their patrol duties and trucked to join forces with the 82nd and 101st Airborne Division camp in Villers-Cotterets just northeast of Paris. It would be the calm before the bitter blizzard in Belgium. For as the Allied forces regrouped, the Nazis were organizing for one final push. Would she ever see him again?

January 7th 1945:

"First of all in November all the Americans were on leave in the Alps, and Johnny spent fifteen days at Saint Jeannet and he came every other day to see me." Saint Jeannet is about thirty to forty five minutes north-west of Nice. *"We spent the days together either at the house or at the office. We went to the movies and our love is growing."* With Simone's insistence, Colette was still an ever-present chaperon when the pair went out. *"I was very happy and I didn't want to think about anything but the present. We were making beautiful dreams with lots of kisses. But alas, everything on earth that's beautiful can be sad, because we have to think about him leaving. And Thursday the 7th of Dec. he left for the war and since he left I am always thinking about him. I am very sad and am in a hurry for his return because I love him."*

And just like that, my mother, just two months shy of her 18th birthday had the most wrenching ache her young heart had ever felt. She thought of how her mother never really loved her father, and the chill that filled the air when both were in the same room. She had vowed her life would be different, but alas, why must it hurt so bad?

Operation Herbstnebel, or Operation Autumn Mist in English, was the name given to the German Offensive brewing in December of 1944. The Americans referred to the campaign as the Ardennes Counter Offensive. Once again the Ardennes region was to become a battlefield, as it had been for Sebastien, Emile, and Jean. Now it was Johnny's turn as German plans called for Panzer's to split the Allies in half, thus weakening any chance of a counter attack. Their intention was to push onward to Antwerp, Belgium and proceed to surround and destroy the Allied armies. Hitler's goal was to break down their enemies and negotiate peace in Germany's favor so he could concentrate the balance of their military strength to the Eastern Front.

The German forces went to great lengths to make the element of surprise a key role in overtaking the Americans and their allies. They moved tanks, artillery, heavy equipment, and soldiers during the night with minimal radio use. To the German's advantage, cloud cover kept important aerial recon virtually non-existent. Even though Ultra intelligence project members (the highly regarded British military surveillance and code breakers) knew a German offensive was in the works, the allies were still caught off guard. Some say along with the lack of aerial viewing, the Allies were filled with over-confidence. The concentrated efforts in planning their own offensive attacks have been said to be another reason our troops were idling. But as my mother once wrote, *"Perfection is not of this world,"* and mistakes, even though costly, are made every day. It could be the Germans simply out-maneuvered the Allies and some just didn't want to admit it.

Whatever the reason, history shows that the results were devastating for both sides as it was the deadliest and largest battle fought throughout WWII. During the conflict the manpower grew to over one million American, British, and German soldiers scattered across an 80-mile front. On Dec. 16, 1944 at 5:30am the temperature was an icy 14° Fahrenheit as Hitler's 6th Panzer division was one of four German outfits to launch their offensive in the Ardennes Forest of Belgium. On a lone stretch of frozen land our men sustained a barrage of fire for ninety deafening minutes from some 1,600 pieces of artillery. At the initial attack the Allied defenses were greatly outnumbered as past battles had left heavy American casualties and exhausted troops. Replacements helped fill the ranks, but many of these newcomers had never seen combat. General Eisenhower and his staff had deduced the Ardennes region was an unlikely route for Hitler to launch a full scale attack, thus there were roughly only 80,000 U.S. troops protecting the Belgium-Germany border. Although a glance back through history would have shown this region to be a favorite gateway for German forces in the past. Eighty thousand men sounds like a high number until compared to the Nazi head-count which had assembled to 250,000 strong. The Krauts outnumbered the ill-equipped Allies in all areas such as manpower, tanks, artillery pieces, and tracked equipment. The sheer unbalance of troops would lead one to believe the Germans would have trampled our G.I.'s. Not so, for the tenacity of the American spirit was something to be admired for generations to come.

Heavy overcast weather and fog grounded the Allies superior air support, allowing the Germans to make their advances. Fortunately for the good guys, waist-deep snow slowed the Nazis forward progress of tanks and machinery, causing a nature-made bottleneck. The winter of '44 had been one of the worst on record. This and the favorable defenders' terrain threw a wrench in the German timetable. For the Panzer soldiers that did get through, fierce resistance on the northern shoulder of the offensive around Elsenborn Ridge and the town of Hofen and in the south around Bastogne blocked German access to key roads they counted on for success. Even though they were greatly outnumbered, the Americans held their ground. After about ten days of fighting, the Jerrys finally overtook the small villages, but not the ridge, resulting in heavy casualties on both sides. The 99th Infantry Division, which was outnumbered 5 to 1 had amazingly inflicted German losses with a ratio of 18 to 1. Leaving these brave men battle weary, it was obvious the greatly outnumbered Allied forces were in desperate need of reinforcements as the Nazis rears seemed endless. Their advances had nearly split the Allied armies in half, which Hitler had planned, and in the process formed a bulge inward as was evident on wartime news maps. Thus the press dubbed this bloodiest of battles, The Battle of the Bulge.

Meanwhile, my dad, along with other members of the 509th PIB, was enjoying their much deserved downtime, sleeping on feather beds while savoring hot meals every night. Charming the local French *femmes* had become part of wartime curriculum. With the 1st ABTF now disbanded it was widely thought that the worst of the war was behind them, and still others had heard rumors they may be shipped to the South Pacific. But Johnny had his own French beauty on his mind and was enjoying his R&R, leaving the string of battles far from his mind.

As a huge fan of big band leader Glenn Miller, he and some buddies found themselves in Paris on the evening of December 21st. Tragically, the night would take an historic turn as the acclaimed United States Army Air Force Band was two hours late starting the Christmas concert minus their famous band leader. Not seeing his musical hero must have been a great disappointment for young Johnny. After all, when would a small town boy get another chance to see one of the most popular names in music of that era?

Johnny on left with unknown soldier, wearing the new M43 uniforms that replaced the M42's worn in Southern France. Information provided by Matt Anderson. Picture was taken while on leave before the Battle of the Bulge.

My dad had always believed Glenn Miller died that night while flying over the English Channel, but in truth his single engine plane had gone down a week earlier on December 15th. It wasn't until after December 24th when Miller's wife living in America was notified that he was listed as Missing in Action, that the news was made public. Even without his hero the band played on, and as the last horns blew, the satisfied men returned for what they believed would be another comfy night's sleep. A soldier's life is never that simple, and as they entered their toasty rooms, orders were given, *"Get into the trucks, we're moving out."* An old veteran by the name of Jack Darden of the 509th PIB recounted to Gregg, *"We were pulled off leave and shoved into cattle trucks driven by colored soldiers."*

My mother's entry of January 7th continued: *"I think I am going crazy because I have only received two letters for the past ten days then no news at all. I know very well all my friends are in the same boat, but I am worried because those dirty Nazis have two big offensives, the last I hope. Anyway I have to wait and pray. Two big holidays the one I like the best Noel and the other, the first of the year have passed. Johnny sent me an evening robe and two perfumes. At the house it's beautiful sometimes and sometimes not so good. Papa sometimes is charming and other times you can't go near him. I really want my relationship with Johnny to be sweet and warm and full of happiness and love. I hope that 1945 will be the year of peace and of my marriage."*

Riding all night in the early morning hours of December 22nd the paratroopers may as well have been sides of beef in an ice box as they huddled in the back of the open bumpy trucks: destination hell. Some were fortunate to crowd under tarps, but this did little to break the windchill which yielded sub-zero temperatures. Arriving at 6:45 a.m. it was obvious when they reached the war zone at Manhay, Belgium. *"We drove up to the front and got fired on immediately."* Word had spread about the massacre at Malmedy just twenty miles up the road.

On December 17th the out-gunned Americans of the 285th Field Artillery Observation Battalion were engaged in a lopsided firefight shortly after pulling through the town of Malmedy. The survivors, realizing their plight, surrendered to the Krauts to be taken as POW's. Numbers vary but it is said some 150 American soldiers were looted, marched out to an open snow-covered field and machine gunned down in cold blood. Those who survived, when thinking it was clear, made a mad dash running to the woods. Miraculously, some of the soldiers lived to spread the word. *"A couple of men escaped and told what happened."* My dad would recall later, *"They were outright slaughtered. That made everybody mad, Americans, British, everybody. It was a huge mistake by the Germans."*

Now the soldiers found themselves on the front line under a full scale attack. A, B, and C Companies of the 509th PIB, along with parts of HQ Company were assigned to various Task Forces of the 3rd Armored. The next day on December 23rd, A Company proceeded to drive the enemy from high ground south west of Soy, and held their position against constant pressure. C Company was loaded back onto trucks and moved out immediately onto Route 15, also referred to as "the most important road in Belgium." This was the truck line running north from Bastogne to Liege. With orders in hand, the Gingerbread men, including Aleck, were headed straight into the the German 2nd SS Panzer Division toward the strategic crossroads of Baraque de Fraiture. What followed was a massive firefight. As he had at Anzio and Southern France, my dad was fighting on the front, which is exactly where he wanted to be. *"I had one dread all the time I fought. I dreaded getting pulled off the front line. You want to know why? Because the most frightening thing was going into a new battle area not knowing what was there. I dreaded that more than anything else."* It wasn't long before the Geronimo unit ran head on into the German's sights and were fired upon before they could even reach the crossroads. After two days of intense fighting both sides suffered considerable fatalities. As a result, the 509th PIB was given orders to pull back.

Pulling back isn't the same as surrendering as they continued to cripple their foe. Tanks engaged in tit-for-tat warfare, filling the air with one thunderous boom after another. The brave soldiers gave it their all, keeping the German grays at bay. Still, the enemy Tiger Tanks continued to roar down the corridor. Hours into the conflict lady luck smiled on the 509th PIB. The clouds lifted and Major Brewster, recognizing the seriousness of the situation called for air support. The P-47's were already doing fly-overs and it was determined that the ground troops were in dire need of their birds-eye view. The air-strike was radioed in and the pilots didn't disappoint, bombing the exposed German tanks. I know it was a very welcome sight for the freezing Gingerbread men below.

One would think the Allies would have taken advantage of the success of the hit. Instead, General Eisenhower had turned over command of the First and Ninth American Armies to British Field Marshal Montgomery. Montgomery made the decision for the troops in the 509th PIB and others in that sector to retreat. The entire 82nd was withdrawn since Montgomery didn't like the way the 82nd front bulged out ahead of the battle-line. As one can imagine, his decision was met with much American criticism, but an order was an order.

Meanwhile, what remained of the Panzer Division had halted its progress, hiding their tanks under the canopy of the Ardennes forest due to the aerial bombardment. It was Christmas Eve as they waited in the frigid cold till darkness fell to move out. The Allied retreat left a hole through which the 2nd SS Panzer Division had easy access; an early Christmas present from Montgomery. To make matters worse, a captured US Sherman tank led the way for the Panzers, causing confusion amongst the Americans. While the 7th and 3rd Armored Divisions were in route through Manhay, the hijacked American Sherman tank reached a US roadblock and quickly destroyed four other American tanks. This chaos played out at another roadblock down the line creating a heightened withdrawal for the bewildered Americans.

From there, the situation seemed grave for the Allied soldiers. With the men out of position they became easy targets for the aggressive German offensive. Again, one would believe this would have been the time for the Germans to take full advantage of the momentum they had gained. But instead of continuing north toward Liege and Antwerp, they veered west toward Manhay, and other neighboring towns. The Geronimos who had incurred scores of losses in just three days rode atop the remaining tanks racing toward the northeast. More casualties ensued until the 509th PIB were able to reach a safer destination.

By the 27th December most of the 509th had gathered at Erezee and was under the control of Battalion Headquarters but still attached to the 3rd Armored Division command as a mobile reserve unit. They were ordered to dig in and hold their positions with the enemy close at hand. The men, including my dad, crammed into two small houses and barns, sleeping shoulder to shoulder on the floor to avoid well below freezing temperatures that night. When you're exhausted and finally have a chance to lay down, the conditions are irrelevant. By the following early morning hours around 1:30am the sounds of enemy attack rang loud in the distance. The men, ready to rock-n-roll, held their positions, awaiting orders as the Gingerbread Men were about to enter yet another battle.

General Rose of the 3rd Armored Division had given strict orders to Major Tomasik not to engage in any combat without his prior approval. So, when the night sky lit up about a mile away, the Major was in a quandary. After having learned the attack was on their 87th Mortar Men at the Belgium town of Sadzot, he spent the next 30 minutes trying to reach the General without success. It was obvious that come daybreak his own troops would be next in line and he was well aware of the importance of protecting the Erezee road at all costs. Without permission from Rose, and putting his own butt on the line, Tomasik ordered his platoon leaders to gather the paratroopers and prepare to move out. In the pre-dawn hours, Johnny, along with the other soldiers, marched in the tenaciously bitter cold night.

Reaching their destination they found there was approximately two hundred yards of open snow-covered field that lay between them and a dozen or so buildings that made up the tiny town of Sadzot. With TD's (or tank destroyers) for added cover, the brave Gingerbread Men made their push over the exposed fields. What followed was a fierce battle between the 25th SS holed up in village houses, and the good guys. Tank destroyers shot heavy fire power into the structures as seasoned troopers scrambled across the snow-covered field. Those who were fortunate enough to escape death and reach the small town of twelve buildings, began to systematically clear house after house. Loss of life continued to fall on both sides although the Americans fared better. When the Germans scattered to the surrounding wooded area and upon hearing familiar voices of American soldiers, surviving Mortar Men crept slowly from their hiding places. These battered men, who by all accounts should have been dead, were forever grateful to their comrades, and by 9:30 a.m. the town was almost secure.

The gingerbread men continued to push the Krauts back to the woods. The fierce battle raged on as at one point the G.I.'s shot blindly into the dense forest with a wish and prayer. Heavy shelling from the well-hidden German 25th SS Panzer Division forced our men to fall back about 150 yards. But the troopers formed a strong defensive line and held their ground despite the freezing temperatures. Eventually the enemy fell back as well, possibly due to being out of ammo, and by noon, the 509th slowly withdrew to reorganize. They hadn't eaten anything for a full day. Many had frostbite as my dad would say in regards to entering their next battle at St. Vith, *"I was already frost-bitten by then. We only had Barbasol shaving cream with its alcohol to rub on our frost bitten skin."*

My dad mentioned a package from home he had received, *"I remember when I was at Sadzot, I got a food basket from my mother at home. It contained a fruit cake and two pairs of grey underwear with trap doors in the back. I really took quite a razzing about them. I ended up wrapping them up in a package with a piece of that fruit cake and giving them to an old farmer."* Obviously this was after the fighting had ended.

Johnny wrote another letter to the woman of his dreams, dated December 28th, written on stationary called V-mail. It's a one page letter on one side that when folded properly is used as its own envelope on the other. In the upper left hand corner of the letter is a red circle with the words, "censor stamp" typed underneath. In the circle is a stamp that reads "Passed By Army Examiner," then a signature in the middle. This would explain why my father was often vague in his correspondence. He wasn't able to give out any specific information about what he was doing, although it wouldn't have served any positive purpose. My mom didn't need to know the dangerous reality his Army life entailed. With mail delivery very slow, it is evident Monique had not yet received this letter before writing her January 7th journal entry.

Dear Monique   *Dec. 28th*

I received your six letters the other day and was glad to hear from you. I had a lovely Xmas. With your watch to tell what time it was and a drink of Scotch to set me on fire, I was very content.

I am somewhere in Belgium and having a good time so don't worry about me Dear. Say hello to the family and don't forget to send that picture to me.

All my love,

Johnny

After the battles he had just fought in, I had to smile. Dad had been having anything but a good time. With the addition of replacements after Southern France the battalion of some 827 strong had been reduced to 62% of its combat strength. But their efforts did not go unnoticed as the 509th PIB was awarded its 3rd Presidential citation on March 20, 1945.

Print the complete address in plain letters in the panel below, and your return address in the space provided on the right. Use typewriter, dark ink, or dark pencil. Faint or small writing is not suitable for photographing.

TO: Monique Poulain
Palais Saluzzo Porte A
Rue Barla
Nice

[CENSOR'S STAMP]   SEE INSTRUCTION NO. 2

FROM T/5 Johny aleck
39406966 HQ Co
509 Para Inf Bn
a.P.O. 464 % P.M
US Army
(Sender's complete address above)

PASSED BY
ARMY EXAMINER

Dear Monique,   Dec. 28th

I recieved your 6 letters the other day and was glad to hear from you.
I had a lovely x mas. With your watch to tell what time it was and a drink of Scotch to set me on fire I was very content.
I am some where in Belgium and having a good time so don't worry about me Dear.
Say Hello to the family and don't forget to send that picture to me.
all my Love
Johnny

HAVE YOU FILLED IN COMPLETE ADDRESS AT TOP?   REPLY BY V---MAIL   HAVE YOU FILLED IN COMPLETE ADDRESS AT TOP?

The Vmail letter sent from Johnny to Monique. December 28, 1944.

During the period 22 - 30 December 1944, the 509th Parachute Infantry Battalion was given the mission of assisting in the slowing down of the enemy thrust toward Liege, Belgium. By its aggressiveness, the Battalion destroyed leading elements of the enemy south of Manhay and permitted other units to reorganize along the Grandmenil-Manhay axis. Opposing the finest enemy troops, the 509th Parachute Infantry Battalion contributed materially to the destruction of elements of the 25th SS Panzer Grenadier Regiment and kept the enemy from cutting the Grandmenil-Erezee road. The aggressiveness and extraordinary heroism displayed by the 509th Parachute Infantry Battalion were in keeping with the highest traditions of the service and contributed materially to the blunting of the enemy spearhead thrust toward Liege.

By command of Major General RIDGEWAY.

Chapter 13

BATTLES END - LOVE LETTERS BEGIN

After Sadzot, the remainder of the battalion was given time to patch up, rest, and regroup. In an excerpt from Johnny's letter dated January 6, 1945 he does his best to put his sweetheart's mind at ease.

"This will be a short letter so please don't be surprised or disappointed. This morning I washed myself for the first time in four days and I feel like a new man. I sure needed a shave. For dinner we had turkey, coffee, beans, rice pudding, and gravy. Now that I have told you all this I hope you realize I am happy so please don't worry. I would be more happy with you here but that is impossible now."

My dad's C-rations sounded more appetizing than I'm sure they were, but food is food. Knowing my mother, her letters must have been wrought with worry for my dad to impress upon her that he was doing well.

It wasn't long before orders to retake St. Vith were issued to the Geronimos. It would be the final crusade for the 509th PIB. As they entered the battle zone, mortar shells continued to pound, and the relentless death grip of the biting cold was ever-present. Death from over-exposure wasn't to be taken lightly and had taken the lives of countless soldiers on both sides. Gloves seemed useless with frostbit already nipping at Johnny's fingers as he tied lines off onto dead soldiers. *"I wouldn't tie off onto our guys only the Germans."* One of the troopers in their communication unit had begged to be transferred to the S2 scout unit so he could see more action. The others tried to talk him out of it, but to no avail. About a week later Dad and James strung lines over his stiff broken body. While moving from outpost to outpost the pair came across bodies of dead G.I.'s stacked like frozen cord-wood. All in a day's work while wintering in the Ardennes Forest in '44.

Again, when Johnny was up when he should have been dug in, my dad had another close brush with death. Gregg heard this tale from Mr. Batton: *"While stringing communication lines during the Bulge, Johnny was in front carrying the phone and I was 25 or 30 feet behind him when we came under artillery fire. We both dove into a ditch spread-eagled and a shell came down and landed between your dad's legs, then flipped him over so that he was looking at the sky. The shell was a dud, didn't even break the skin."* They had developed nerves of steel, or just the realization that if their number was up there was nothing they could do about it.

For a good week the Geronimo unit saw its numbers dwindling but continued to persevere. The German artillery shells ripped through tall pines, shattering trees, sending shrapnel whistling through the forest. Finding a safe haven was no easy task as the Nazis found a band of US troopers who had regrouped on lower ground. Another account from Gregg: *"Scouts from dad's unit had found fresh boot prints in the snow that led up to a small hill. It was obvious two German scouts had been out the night before and spotted their location. The American scouts reported back, and the order was given for the men to surround the area and wait. When the Germans arrived they thought they were going to surprise and wipe out the Americans, but instead the Germans were ambushed. Dad said, "It was like shooting fish in a barrel." They took no prisoners that day."*

Johnny had become a hardened soldier. That sentiment is best described in the book *"Bloody Clash at Sadzot"* by William B. Breuer. When a young soldier was asked what unit he belonged to his reply was straight forward, *"We're not from any unit. We are the famous 509 Parachute Infantry Battalion—the Kraut killers!"* Yes indeed, this was a very proud brotherhood who had earned the respect of officers and fellow soldiers alike. They were feared by the enemy; those unstoppable devils in baggy pants!

After intense fighting at St. Vith, on the 28th of January, what was left of the mighty Geronimos was pulled off the front line and relieved by members of the 345th Infantry 87th Division. A note from Lt. Morton Katz of the Battalion read, *"After this last action, seven officers and forty-eight men came down the hill on 28 January 1945. All others were either dead or hospitalized."* I have read this line many times, and each time my eyes tear up knowing my dad was one of the fifty-five who had survived and walked down the hill that day. My brother Gregg had the opportunity to correspond with Lt. Morton Katz. Of our father he said, *"Your dad was a fine soldier and you should be proud of him."*

After the 509ers had rested near Paris prior to the Battle of the Bulge, they had a headcount of 827 Gingerbread Men. Two months later, only a handful was left standing. Aleck had miraculously survived the major battles he fought in with nary a scratch, while so many others had perished.

But a different axe was to fall as the 509th PIB was officially disbanded March 1st 1945. The reassignment had already been in the works prior to the Bulge. The original order, dated December 1,1944 in regards to the disbursement of the Battalion stated in part, *"...will be disbanded at the earliest practicable date,"* and that *"Personnel rendered surplus by this action will be absorbed within the replacement system."* Apparently, my dad and the others were considered "surplus" by the U.S. Army.

On the fiftieth anniversary of the Battle of the Bulge, Johnny made the front page of our local paper with his picture and an article from his personal perspective. Regarding the disbanding of the 509th he commented, *"It made me sick! I fought with that outfit for almost four years. I felt like dying when it happened."* And again in a letter to his love back in Nice, dated April 27, 1945, the only reference he made to Belgium and his paratrooper brothers, *"I'm in good health but still wish I was in the 509 with all my hard-fighting men. We had it very hard in Belgium, but that is all over with now, and just another page in my life."*

Casualties and losses for the battle that lasted 41 days vary, but show it was enormous. For the Americans, approximately 19,000 killed, 47,500 wounded, and 23,000 captured or missing for a total of 89,500, with approximately 800 tanks destroyed. The British fared much better since the American troops greatly outnumbered them in combat. The count for the British was 200 killed, 969 wounded, and 239 missing for a total of 1,408 soldiers. For the Germans, between 67,200 and 100,000 were killed, missing, captured or wounded. Some 600 German tanks and assault guns were destroyed along with hundreds of aircraft. The innocent Belgian civilians who were simply in the wrong place at the wrong time were not immune to the slaughter as 3,000 lost their lives. Most were outright murdered in cold blood by the frustrated SS troops. In the end, the official date of the Battle of the Bulge that lasted just shy of six weeks was December 16, 1944 to January 25, 1945.

The paratroopers of the elite 509th PIB had made their mark in history even though few today have ever heard of them. They were the first U.S. Airborne unit deployed overseas and arrived at Glasgow, Scotland on 10 June 1942. The Gingerbread men executed the lowest altitude mass parachute jump in history, exiting the aircraft at 143 feet in England during June 1942 rehearsals. They were initially awarded the "right" to wear red berets by British MG Sir Frederick A.M. Browning, Commander, 1st Airborne Division, who made the 509th honorary "Red Devils," which was a very high honor. The Geronimos performed America's first combat parachute insertion on 8 November 1942, following the longest combat invasion in history of 1600 miles from England to North Africa. The men conducted five combat jumps during World War II: three into North Africa, one into Italy, and one in France. The troopers led an amphibious invasion with Darby's Rangers at Anzio, Italy on 22 January 1944, which Johnny participated in and subsequently participated in that successful Allied campaign that lasted 70 days. Also, they were the first Airborne unit awarded the Presidential Unit Citation, 29 February 1944, a second Citation on 14 March 1944, and yet a third Presidential Citation on 20 March 1945. Paul B. Huff, a member of the 509th, was the first American paratrooper to receive the Congressional Medal of Honor on 29 February 1944 at Anzio, Italy.

The list of campaigns the 509ers fought in during WWII were, Algeria—French Morocco (with arrowhead), Tunisia (with arrowhead), Naples—Foggia (with arrowhead), Anzio (with arrowhead), Rome—Arno, Southern France (with arrowhead), Rhineland, Ardennes—Alsace, (aka the Battle of the Bulge). In addition, six 509ers received the Distinguished Service Cross while numerous Silver Stars, Soldiers Medals, Legion of Merit, Bronze Stars and the Croix De Guerre with Silver Star were awarded for extraordinary heroism to this outstanding and fearless band of paratroopers. As if that wasn't enough, they were awarded the right to wear the Insignia of the 3rd Zouaves Regiment, and the Gingerbread Men were Cited in the Order of the Day of the Belgian Army for action in the Ardennes and for St. Vith. The 509th PIB that my father was so proud to have served with is still the most decorated American parachute battalion with 1,718 Purple Hearts awarded. And so, when my father said he felt like dying when their Battalion was dissolved, I believe he really did. For that reason I felt it necessary to list the aforementioned accomplishments to honor my dad and his brothers of the 509th Parachute Infantry Battalion; the Gingerbread Men of WWII.

While young Johnny had just fought through one of the worst battles in WWII history, my teenage mother had completely given her heart to her beau.

January 31, 1945: *"Not very much changed this month. I got some news from Johnny two letters per week, and that's my whole life. I think of him more and I have beautiful dreams. I hope he comes back quickly mon Chéri. I write to him every day, and I hope that the war will finish soon. The Russians are starting a very strong offensive against Germany and it is formidable, and they are advancing rapidly. It is very cold. I am freezing from the cold. It is even snowing which is very rare. Papa is half drunk and in a very bad mood. What a life at home. I don't want to work anymore. Oh my God bring me back my darling Johnny, I adore him!"*

Again, in an entry on February 17th my mother expresses the affection she has for Johnny and that she hadn't heard from him for three weeks – a lifetime for a teenager in love. But then she writes she received a letter and is in even more of a hurry to become Madame Aleck. In a letter dated February 1st my father again assures her that he was fine and that *"the war news is going good and I hope this war will end soon."* He mentions that he received 9 letters from her including her picture which he loves. He then adds, *"I'm sorry I haven't written sooner but the Army had things for me to do."* In another paragraph, *"From the way you write I don't think you like those Jerrys, do you? Well more than half the world* doesn't like the Jerrys so that's the way it will be until they learn to be like people should be." And of course he ends the letter, "All my love, Johnny."

My mother's journal entry March 23, 1945: "I believe in you, Chéri, I believe in love, but I am very blue and think I'm going crazy. I don't have any news of Johnny for 5 weeks. The last letter was from February and I am very worried and I learned that his regiment was not a regiment anymore because lots of soldiers died. But I'm sure he will come back to me, I put all my hope in God. God is so good! I can understand now how I love him and want only one thing, to see him again. Please God bring him back to me I beg of you!"

Three days before my mother wrote her plea to God, she had sent a request to the Red Cross asking for information about her fiancé. Five weeks was much too long for her to stand by and do nothing. On March 31, my mother received a reply from Headquarters, European Theater of Operations, United States Army. The letter included her home address and was typed in both English and French.

Dear Miss Poulain,

Your letter of 20 March 1945, in which you request information concerning T/5 Johnny G. Aleck, 39406966, has been received at this headquarters. Records of this headquarters do not indicate that T/5 Aleck has been reported as a casualty in the European Theater of Operations.

Yours very truly,
Leonard R. Litman
Captain, AGD,
Asst. Adjutant General

HEADQUARTERS
EUROPEAN THEATER OF OPERATIONS
UNITED STATES ARMY

RR/hs

APO 887
31 Mar 45

AG-704.02

Miss Monique Poulain,
Palais Saluzzo, Door A,
Rue Barla, NIZZA(Alp. Mar.)

Dear Miss Poulain,

Your letter of 20 March 1945, in which you request information concerning T/5 Johnny G. Aleck, 39406966, has been received at this headquarters.

Records of this headquarters do not indicate that T/5 Aleck has been reported as a casualty in the European Theater of Operations.

Yours very truly,

LEONARD R. LITMAN,
Captain, AGD,
Asst. Adjutant General.

Chere Mademoiselle Poulain,

Votre lettre du 20 Mars 1945, concernant le Caporal Johnny G. Aleck, a bien ete recue a ce Quartier General.

Le nom de ce soldat ne figure point dans les dossiers des victimes du Theatre Europeen des Operations.

Recevez, chere Mademoiselle Poulain, mes salutations distinguees.

LEONARD R. LITMAN,
Capitaine,
Assistant l'Adjutant General.

The letter Monique received from HQ.

It was a difficult romance to be sure. My father finally did write, and along with the letter from the Army, calmed my mother's nerves. He wrote of how torn he was having met her. *"Being a soldier I never know what or where the Army has plans for me. As long as I am away you will always have doubts as to the love I have for you."* He then added his awareness of God, *"Today is Good Friday and I once more find myself very much devoted to God. No matter how tough a paratrooper thinks he is, he is never too tough to realize God is always with him. Easter must be lovely in Nice. I sure wish I could be there with you. We would go walking together over the shore road without a worry in the world."*

My mother has always been an incessant worrier. I thought this was the result of trauma that would come later in her life. In reading the letters from my dad it was obvious that fretting was second nature. In a note dated April 7, 1944, I can feel my dad's frustration as again he mentions, *"Monique I know that you worry over me a lot and that only makes it harder for me. I sometimes wish I had never met you because to be in love with a soldier isn't very good. I want you very much dear, but if the Army will ever let me marry you is very hard for me to know. If I leave France and we aren't married it will hurt you very much. So you see why I sometimes wish I did not meet you."* Then in the last paragraph he adds, *"Well angel I'll close for this time. Don't forget the picture for me. I prefer it in a spring dress like you wore the day we liberated Nice, remember? All my love, Johnny"*

My young father it would seem was just as pre-occupied with my mother as she was with him, yet torn. Up to this point he had always written Dear Monique, but with this next letter I saw an awakening of Johnny's heart, or maybe he just finally vocalized his deeper emotions.

April 15, 1945: *"My Darling Monique, Well, Chérie it is about 11:30 at night now and I must write to you once more before I go to bed. My life without you is beginning to really drive me crazy. At the dinner table my friends often see me sit there with a fork in my mouth day dreaming about you. I often ask myself, "Johnny you are in love and you want to be in love. Then why are you so far away from your darling wife Monique?" Chérie I can't answer that last question but I'm in love with you and God himself only knows how much I really need you. My mind now is very heavy with all the thoughts of you and you alone. Darling I am becoming stupid with my love for you. Angel if you only knew how strong my love for you is. I wake in the morning with you and die every night with you on my mind. If I could only hold you in my trembling arms and tell you all the things that are on my mind. Chérie I love you. Monique we will spend the rest of our lives together and I hope I make you the happiest girl in America. I must my darling angel, I must, I must."*

Two more handwritten pages express his love for her and he adds toward the end, *"Chérie, a man is as good as his wife makes him, and believe me you are making me the man I have always wanted to be."* He signs with, *"All my life, my love, and passion to you Madame Aleck. Your only Johnny, Always, Chéri."*

Young Monique must have read his words until her eyes were heavy with sleep, then read them some more; especially when he referred to her as Madame Aleck, even though they had yet to exchange their vows. I loved reading that they called each other *Chérie* (female) or *Chéri* (male), which is a French term of endearment our family heard our parents call one another for as long as we could remember. Even their friends would jokingly call my mother or father Chéri in their best French accent. I had no idea our parents had used this pet name even before they were married.

After the disbandment of the 509th the remaining troops became replacements for the 82nd Airborne Division where my dad found himself with more idle time as the war was winding down. Planning a life and making arrangements to marry the French beauty who had stolen his heart allowed no time for war.

My father's letter on April 27 mentions, *"The man who is giving you this letter is a very good friend of mine. I tried very hard to come and see you but my friend Bill got the pass instead of me. Have a little faith dear and someday we will be together forever."* My mother's journal entry of May 6 tells us his friend had made it. *"I got news from Johnny, at the end of the month we'll get married and I will be Madame Aleck. Thursday three of his buddies brought me a letter from Johnny and they asked me for some papers for our marriage. Johnny is going to come for a leave for eight days. The war is almost finished and we are waiting for the church bells to ring when the war is done. Oh, my God let me get married this month with Johnny."*

My dad's April 7th letter continued, *"Yes Monique we are all very sorry that President Roosevelt died. We Americans thought very much of him and he was my choice as well as my father's choice. I finally got a 10 hour pass to Paris the other day and really enjoyed it. I drank a little but not much so don't start thinking I'm beginning to drink, because I'm not. Paris is very lovely in the spring. I also had a chance to fly over Paris on a clear day. Your picture is very lovely dear. It makes me very lonely being so far from you. I can still remember your lovely lips and white teeth that make any smile like a flower. Monique I don't know if we will marry before I leave France but I hope so. I need you very much and I know it with all my heart. Please don't worry about me getting wounded because I haven't, believe me please. Well I'll close for now, dear, say Hello to the family and keep your chin up. All my love Johnny"*

Then a jubilant journal entry from my mother, dated May 11, 1945: *"The war is over in Europe and we had Armistice Day, but for me the war will be finished when the Japanese ask for peace. But anyway I am very happy because Johnny is going to come and it's finished very soon. Those dirty Krauts got the punishment they deserved. The three of us,"* [my mother, Simone and Coco,] *"got together and we partied for three days!"*

What a party that must have been, with bottled emotions finally able to burst forth like the champagne that flowed.

The Nazis ground game had been stopped dead while consistent air-strikes over Germany finally forced their unconditional surrender on May 7. In Europe May 8, 1945 is the celebrated V.E. Day or Victory in Europe Day. Ah, but there was still trouble in paradise as my mother's see-saw emotions were seeing green.

Journal entry May 23, 1945: *"My God I cannot stand it anymore. I haven't heard from Johnny and I don't understand why. Why doesn't he write to me? He is on vacation in France. Did he find another girl? I cannot believe this, but my God I suffer. I cannot stand it please take care of me. At the house I try not to show it, but the first minute I am alone I feel like I am at the end. Why do I suffer so much? I was just asking you to have some happiness on earth. I see some women who are no good and they want to flirt and they are lucky in love. And I don't have any chance, and that revolts me. Anyway, I hope to have some happiness. Maybe Johnny will come soon. Maybe he did not forget me and I will forget everything in his arms. It's raining!"* Was there any part of my mother's heart left untouched? I think not.

Journal entry May 31, 1945: *"Oh my God I am so happy and I savor my happiness. After all the hard luck that I had it has been exactly eight days since I received a letter from Johnny saying he was leaving for Japan and we could not get married. So I was going crazy and Mama decided we were going to see him in Chartre before he left. On Saturday we left and had a tiresome trip with very bad weather. But we got there and Monday we went to the camp and we asked to see him. Everything went very good they brought him to see us and I want to get married next week. I love him so much. I don't think anyone could love him more. I left my job at the office and I am getting ready for the big event that will decide my whole life."* This was the second to last writing in my mother's journal, with the last entry seven months later.

I never found a letter from my dad telling her he was leaving for Japan, so it is quite possible in her frustration it was torn to bits. Then I had to ask myself, had my dad really heard that they might be going to Japan? After going to Paris, did Johnny have a change of heart? Had he gotten cold feet and decided the easy way out was to tell a little white lie? In May of that year he had turned 21 with a full life ahead. Whatever the truth, it was Simone who finally came to her daughter's rescue.

Years later my mother's recording added more details. *"When we got to the train it was standing room only, and the ride from Nice to Chartre took almost two days to get there. We were packed like animals, and many of the people had their chickens with them and other farm animals. It was so crowded! It's a long ride and we had to stop in Paris to change trains. When we got there I didn't know if he was there, I mean I had no idea if he was there or not! We just left and that was that. We got there and asked where they* (the American soldiers) *were. We got to the gate and they didn't let us in. We had to stand with the guards while they looked for him. And then here he comes, I'll never forget that! And he was just twisting his little butt, he always twisted his butt."*

John interrupted, *"Cocky, huh,"* to which my mom laughed, *"Cocky as hell! They said we had so many hours, so we went for a walk in the country with my mother. We went to see the Chartre Cathedral, and then we went to eat somewhere."* My mother had told me how accommodating dad was as he scrambled around looking for chairs and a table for the three of them. *"And then we took the train back that night and that was in May."* I'm so glad my brother had the recordings.

I'm sure seeing Monique with her mother so far from the French Rivera was a very unexpected surprise for my father. Now standing face to face, any doubt he may have harbored melted away as they held each other in a long, tender, embrace. It is possible after months apart and his preoccupation surviving the Bulge, her memory had begun to fade along with his promise of marriage. It's a possibility, given Johnny's age and all he had just gone through that he was second-guessing whether or not he was even ready to be a married man. But now, with his spark rekindled, letters once more found their way to my mother's hands. In all I found five written from my father before their wedding. On June 4th he writes that he will be re-assigned to Frankfurt, Germany and wishes he would have known they were going to stay as long as they did in France because he would have had her come to Sissonne where he had been stationed. I doubt Simone would have allowed her oldest daughter to live so far from home un-chaperoned.

An excerpt from another letter also dated June 4, 1945, my dad mentions going to a movie. *"I saw a movie tonight called "Saratoga Trunk." It was about a French lady who returns to America, and believe me, it sort of made me fear French beauty. I hope you have a chance to see it."* While in Germany he mentions *"I will be a Sergeant next Saturday not that it makes any difference to me. I'm still just a private deep down inside."* In Frankfurt, the soldiers live in civilian houses and my dad says that his section has the best one. Johnny waters the roses every night and mows the lawn weekly as he tells my mother, *"All I need is you by my side."* On the lighter side he states, *"It's raining today and I'm devoting the day to ironing and housekeeping. I think I'll make you a good wife, don't you think, Ha Ha!"*

Sgt. Johnny Aleck - Frankfurt, Germany - June 1945.

Finally in a note dated June 17, 1945, my mother read the most important letter of all. *"Dear Monique, I'm sorry I didn't write to you in the last two days, but I have been very busy. This morning I saw the commanding officer and he said I could get married any time after the 25th of June, and I think I will be in Nice about that date. We should be able to get married as soon as I get there now that we both have our papers ready. I haven't received a letter from you in five days now and do I feel in the blues-yes-yes.*

I saw the city of Frankfurt yesterday and the air-corps really did a good job of bombing. There are very few houses left standing. You know, Chérie, I can picture you in my mind now. Reading each other's letters is like a hope of freedom that really starts our hearts to beating. I love you Chérie very much, much more than you can imagine. I need a girl like you to make a better man out of myself. I'm sorry that I can't be as pure as you will be when we get married, but what is done is done. I'll close for now dear so be good.

All my Love to you forever,

Your Johnny"

Johnny's *Chérie*, pictured in his mind~

Chapter 14

MONSIEUR ET MADAME ALECK

All of the heartache and disappointment Monique had been experiencing miraculously disappeared as my parents' wedding day approached. It had been just ten months since the young lovers met on that hot August morning. With the uncertainty of war, those ten months had felt like decades, but now anxiety had at last shifted to exhilaration as preparations for the big event were at hand. With less than two weeks to prepare, thankfully, Simone lovingly and hastily stitched both her daughters' dresses for this blissful occasion. Colette naturally would stand at her sister's side as maid of honor.

Keeping it simple yet fashionable, the bride-to-be's white dress came to just below her knees. Sleeves rested at the elbow and were accented with a soft ruffle at each shoulder. Her delicately embroidered v-neck surrounded a modest necklace while my mother's thick flowing hair was held loosely in a netted veil. The style was *tres chic* and emphasized the fullness of her wavy mane with white flowers tucked on either side. In her hands she held an arrangement of the same fragrant flowers with an added splash of greenery. Keeping with the summer theme, open-toed wedged shoes, and a pair of white gloves dressed up the attire. Monique's natural beauty required very little makeup as all she wore was a little face powder and red lipstick for that all-important first kiss as husband and wife.

My father looked as dashing as a movie star in his paratrooper dress uniform with the trademark pant legs billowed at the top of his boots. It was a uniform of distinction, worn only by those brave enough to jump behind enemy lines. Johnny's waist length jacket fit perfectly on his firm body, affixed with the stripes and medals he had earned. He too wore a pair of white gloves along with a *boutonniere*, and his brown boots were so polished they gleamed in the afternoon sun. As was the style of the times he displayed a pencil thin Errol Flynn mustache and thick, wavy, jet black hair that was parted to one side. What a handsome couple they were.

My dad had two of his army buddies attend, with one of them, Jim McCann standing as best man. They too were very hunky in their Army dress uniforms. Johnny escorted his bride-to-be as the family followed to their first stop. Arriving at Nice's Town Hall they had an intimate civil service, as a marriage in France isn't considered legal if they marry only in a church. Besides my parents and dad's Army brothers, Colette, Jean, Simone, and a family friend were present. There wasn't time or money for an elaborate wedding, and only those who mattered most were present. Unfortunately, my mother's grandmother Louise was visiting relatives in Upper Normandy and was unable to attend.

After the civil ceremony my parents received a booklet known as the *livret de famille,* or family book. A copy of their marriage is recorded in this official booklet, and had they continued to live in France, their children's births would have been recorded in it as well. I still have the original *livret de famille* and their yellowed, tattered marriage certificate that my mother held as precious keepsakes from their special day. Town Hall wasn't the most romantic place to wed, but it made no difference to my mother as at last on June 30, 1945 they were officially Monsieur et Madame Aleck!

Introducing Monsieur et Madame Aleck, just outside of city hall in Nice, France. June 30, 1945.

From there the small group made their way to John the Baptist Parish Church for the Catholic mass and wedding. The church was beautiful as the afternoon sun shone through stained glass windows. The entire ceremony was in French, but Johnny needed no help when it was his turn to say "I do" or *Je fais, en Francais*. When it was time to place the ring on his beautiful bride's finger, the young Sergeant fumbled a little, as he had tucked it in the wrong pocket. A small mishap he would mention months later in a letter as he reminisced about their wedding day. The newlyweds exchanged simple gold bands, signifying to the world they were now one.

The same beautiful blue skies my mother had written about several months before made for a delightful reception held in an outdoor restaurant setting in Mont Boron. The view was exceptional as was the exquisite French cuisine. Our family is very fortunate to still have the wedding party photo taken from their special day. Everyone is standing with arms interlocked, smiling at the camera. Everyone that is, except for my grandfather Jean.

Instead of being in the picture my grandfather snapped the photo, leaving him noticeably absent. His friend, who I was told was a city official, stood smiling between my aunt and grandmother. My mother to this day does not know why her father didn't hand the camera to his pal so Jean could rightfully take his place. But in a way, the picture is symbolic of her father's emotional absence.

After the glasses were raised, wine bottles emptied, and all that had been said was being said again, the reception finally wound down for the evening. Kisses and hugs were met with the wiping of a tear, and soon all embarked on their journeys home. Even though the war was over in Europe tourism was still a distant memory as many of the local hotels were now occupied by the Allied military. The Hotel Negresco well known as the hotel for the Rich and Famous, was one of these beautiful hotels being run by the U.S. Army. The place was crawling with U.S. soldiers taking much deserved rest and relaxation. With its ornate architecture the Negresco resembled a palace and my mother it's princess. Again John's recording years later would serve as a page into the past as my mother recounted the day she married her Greek.

The newlyweds' wedding party photo taken in Mont Boron. From left to right: Unidentified soldier, Monique, Johnny, best man Jim McCann, Colette, unidentified family friend, and Simone.

*"I remember when we got married, after we had the civilian, then the church wedding, and after we had our dinner at Mont Boron, we walked back down and **we walked!** I mean we walked I'd say about six miles – it's a long, long, way! I was so embarrassed when we got there. They knew, the Sergeant and his guys, that we had been married, and they were giving us such a hard time,"* she said, laughing. *"After we got to our room I didn't want to come out. I would sneak out of the room. We had a*

suite and there was an armoire that was white with green trim, and the walls were pale blue. The sitting room had big windows. And they used to bring us our lunch or whatever we wanted anytime we wanted to eat. It had a big bathroom, I mean, it was gorgeous! And it was just the two of us."

My parents' wedding photo. June 30, 1945.

During their conversation my brother had to ask, *"Knowing you had no experience with men before, were you embarrassed?"* To which my mother replied, *"I was, but I was curious."* My brother, his wife, and my mother are heard on the tape howling in laughter with that last remark. Then my mom added, *"It worked out fine."*

When my young parents did venture out, Johnny was thrilled to have live entertainment that played to dinner guests. Even though he had given several dancing lessons to Monique, my mother never developed the confidence to dance with him publicly. In a sympathetic gesture he guided his new bride behind a large column where she'd feel more comfortable while out of sight from the others. My mother recalled how romantic it was to be held in his strong arms and gaze into those dark brown eyes as if they were the last living souls on earth. Glenn Miller's "Moonlight Serenade" held a special place in both their hearts that night and forever more.

With their hotel situated on the famous *Promenade des Anglais* the newlyweds took many a stroll as Monique clutched the arm of her man. She was living the fairy tale she had wished for. The views along the Mediterranean still held remnants of the war with concrete bunkers, but the young couple was oblivious as they spoke the universal language of love planning a lifetime together. One week would prove far too short as reality woke the couple from their blissful dream. With their honeymoon over duty called for Sgt. Aleck. He returned his young bride to her parents who were now his parents too. The family said their goodbyes with hugs and kisses. As my mother took her turn, her heart was both overflowing with love and anguished with thoughts of their separation. It could be months before she and her Chéri would fall asleep together again, waking with smiles and soft kisses. She sobbed and sobbed in the arms of her husband as he did his best to comfort her. With their last goodbyes, Johnny drove off in a jeep much like the one he was in the day they'd met.

Sgt. Aleck's new job in Frankfurt was as one of the honor guards for General Dwight D. Eisenhower. We have a picture of our father wearing his dress uniform including a garrison cap, white silk scarf tucked under his jacket, and a pair of white gloves in hand. He's in front of a wooden sign with three parachute drawings and the numbers 5 then 0 then 8 in each of the open chutes. With the 509th disbanded he had been reassigned to the 508th PIR. "Don't Fence Me Inn" is written below. It was a far cry from the adrenaline rush on the front lines.

Now back in Germany, it wasn't long before letters started to flow, sharing their love, fears, and the frustration of Army life. Even though they were now married, the miles between them became prison walls. At last they had shared a bed and consummated their marriage. Many of the letters are very private about the intimacy they shared. It was clear they ached to be in each other's arms as now their passion had ignited.

July 10, 1945 - Germany: *"Hello Monique, Another day will soon be over with and life isn't what I want it to be. Monique many things run through my mind all day and they all have something to do with you. As I told you before we only have our love so far and the hard part of making our home is yet to come. There are so many things I want to do and being in this Army my hands are tied. I am sometimes afraid of our future, but I know with your prayer and lovely smile everything will be okay.*

I love you and to say I miss you isn't strong enough but I think you know what I'm trying to tell you. I love you Chérie! Today I sent home the papers for you to go to America so now all we have to do is wait and pray." He continues: *"I just finished taking one of the coldest showers in my life and I do mean it was cold. I sure miss you washing my back. My life and love to you forever, your Johnny."*

Sgt. Johnny G. Aleck - Frankfurt, Germany - July, 1945

For the next three months my dad wrote letter after letter, sometimes two and three a day to his new wife. Likewise, my mother took pen to paper as letter writing became their life. My father's Army duties had done a full 180 from wartime battles. He bounced between the honor guard and a desk job manning the radio, *"Tonight I am responsible for all communications to and from battalion #9 so I think I will have time to write again."* You can feel the boredom as he shares his mundane life. *"I received my PX rations today and I got some good razor blades. A man's day is no good if he doesn't have a good shave in the morning."* The enthusiasm of Army life has all but left him. *"Some of the boys had to make a jump for some inspecting General, but I didn't, thank God!"* And again, *"This Army is sure a dull life for me. I think I shined my boots 20 times today just to keep myself occupied. I just came back from a walk but that didn't help me much. I miss you Chérie very much and I wonder if I'll go crazy at times."*

In keeping with his love of music, Johnny writes July 22, 1945: *"Last night I saw Glenn Miller dance band and they were really good. It was the last time the band will play overseas. Now they are going to America and from there no one knows. Gee but that postman is very bad to me, I have received only one letter from you so far and I feel lost."*

The letter continues, *"Chérie on August 22 at 09:00 at night you go out on the balcony and for half an hour we will be together because I will also be with you even though you are many miles away. I feel very near you if I know that we will be thinking about each other at the same time. I will talk to you and you to me. Okay. I'm crazy aren't I, but love makes me that way."*

In reading my father's words I was touched at such a romantic notion at the young age of just twenty-one remembering the balcony where they had their first kiss. *"There is a very lovely song over the radio now called "Dream" and it is very good. Maybe you have heard it?"* The Johnny Mercer hit song fit my father's mood to a T, as it has a melancholy melody with the opening line *"Dream when you're feeling blue."*

With well over a hundred letters to sift through, it was difficult to decide what to include. The romance between my parents was magnetic. They anguished from being apart from one another with their sole communication dependent on the mailman. It wasn't until July 24th my dad finally started receiving multiple letters from his wife.

"Hello beautiful, guess what? I received 3 letters from you today and gee do I feel much better. They were written on the 9th, 11th, and the 13th of July. It took them 15 days to get here." One of those letters had some very good news as he expressed, *"I'm glad to hear that you are not pregnant believe me. It is a relief, a very big relief."* In another letter Johnny paints an innocent, yet I'm sure, sexy picture for my mother, *"I just finished swimming and feel fine. I am getting to be very tan like a Spanish boy. I like to sleep in the sun with only my shorts on. Angel, are you as lonely for me as I am for you? The day that we will meet again will be like a new life for both of us. I am afraid that I will melt in your arms. Every time I think of you I tremble like a helpless baby. I always think about the 3 days we spent before we were married. You were so tired and yet so sweet. You had the red dress on, do you remember?"*

Pictures were exchanged as these photos kept their images alive. My dad spoke of how he would kiss her picture and wrote other personal words meant only for my mother to read. Monique in turn expressed conditions of her home life, and since she wasn't writing in her journal anymore, shared the intimate bothersome details with her husband. My father responded with great empathy. *"I am sorry that Mother is obliged to make love with Papa because it is hard to do without love. You understand? Give your mother a big kiss and tell her I pray for her."* My father understood the emptiness of Simone's heart as in another letter he wrote. *"I prayed for us and for your mother Chérie. Your mother is very lonely for real love. I know I can see it in her eyes. I often think about your darling mother."*

Johnny was also taking care of business. July 27: *"Your passport will be ready by the time you receive this letter and we will be one step closer to California."* He talked about going swimming with his friends when the weather warmed, and wrote often of shaving and how wonderful it was when he had hot water. *"I was very good with my mustache. I was thinking about you while I was fixing it. You really like my mustache don't you Chérie. Sometimes I think about shaving it off, but if you want it I will keep it for your kisses, okay."*

His letters reminisce often about their honeymoon in suite 132, expressing passion, and intimacy etched deeply in his soul. He did his best to be patient while waiting to be discharged from his military obligation, passing away the time with daydreams of his wife. The Army would only release him when he had earned enough points, but there was no way of knowing when that day would come. In the meantime, my dad spent many days alone manning the communication radio while listening to music on the transistor radio. Many songs take him back to thoughts of his new bride while they danced.

Then on August 9th, he writes, *"This morning the radio said that the Russians have declared war with Japan. Monique, do you realize what that means? It means the war will end sooner and we will be able to be together sooner. When I heard the news my heart started to beat and all of my dreams started to work in my mind. Chérie, when will our dear God let us be together? When you are in America some people will always talk too much about America always going over to France and freeing her from the Germans. Please, remember I love you and I know it will be a little hard for you, but if you love me like I know you do all will turn out okay. You see what I am trying to tell you?"* Already my dad was being protective of his young vulnerable bride.

With distance between them, fear crept in along with underlying concerns of losing one another. August 10th, *"Your two letters of Aug. 1st and 2nd really left me thinking very much about you darling wife. Angel I sometimes think that you are afraid of losing me. Please, write and tell me if you are afraid of this, because of your father and other French men you will always have that fear in a man. I understand you Chérie because I sometimes think the same way about losing you."*

"I want to give you a good kitchen, clothes, life, and most of all a happy life with my love for you. I want to be very tired at the end of the day just to know all my labor is for my lovely little Angel, Madame Aleck. I pray to God that I will be a good husband. All I want from you Monique is your heavenly smile, laughing eyes, tenderness, and warm love to make me know that I am really alive and slaving for you my darling wife. I love you Angel with all my tears, suffering, passion, and love that God has given me for you my darling wife." Your Greek, Johnny.

In another letter from the same day my dad writes that, *"it has been raining for two days now and today the wind is blowing very hard. It is a cold rain and wind and I had enough of that cold in Belgium. The boys really got drunk last night and I could hear them yelling up until 03:00 this morning."* There were entries in other letters as to the rowdiness of his fellow comrades. In one he mentions he had gotten into a fight with one of the men and wrote, *"I put him to sleep."* I'm guessing by this he meant he knocked him out. What a tough group of soldiers this was.

On the last page he writes, *"Chérie last night I was thinking how we would act when we saw each other again. I could see you running into my arms with your hair flying in the air and your chubby little body looking so cute. We will kiss each other for a long time and maybe cry a little too. I am really looking forward to being together."*

With so many letters much of what my father wrote would repeat. But there would always be something I didn't expect. In a letter dated August 13th he writes, *"I miss my mother very much. It is very hard for me to explain how much, but I think you understand me. Monique, my sister Bessie wrote a very nice letter to you. I am very proud of Bessie because she has helped me in many ways. You know how nice it is to have a big sister to keep you from doing bad things? You two will be very good friends, I'm sure. Everyone seems to like her."*

In a previous letter my dad wrote about a fellow soldier who had been with a German girl and had gotten "sick" between the legs – his reference to an STD. Again on the subject he wrote, *"Do you remember those two boys that came up to us in Chartre and talked a little while with us as we were sitting down? Well they are both sick between the legs. Yes Monique, their passion is too much for them so they must go out and sin. Some people never learn do they? The more of my friends that I see get sick like that the more I am happy that I have you my angel to guide me along like I want to be."*

There was an occasion when one of my dad's buddies, Wilkins and some of his other buds were on leave and paid a visit to my mother. She was told they were coming and was very excited to see fellow soldiers that could tell her news of her husband. August 13, 1945: *"Chérie last night Wilkins returned and was I glad. I made him sit down and tell me everything. When he first came to see you, you were wearing that red dress that you always have on the first thing every morning. You know the one that I can always see your lovely legs with. After that you changed into your dress that you sent me in your last picture. The one that is brown and then light brown."*

Monique in the red dress my father speaks of. On the back of the picture my mother wrote, "To my Love, your Monique for always." She underlined 'Monique' once and 'for always' twice.

"Monique, Wilkins said that you were so beautiful and all the boys could hardly control themselves. He said you were so excited you could hardly speak. I can picture you so easy. They took many pictures of you and I'm sure they will all be lovely. I hope you don't mind my friends coming to see you. They all wanted to see you because I always speak about you and they see your pictures. Monique, Wilkins told me about your facial expressions when you were excited. You must have been very lovely, Chérie."

"I couldn't sleep all night long. I was trembling to the thoughts of you. I kissed you a thousand times, and turned over in bed two thousand times more." My father writes of the intimacy they shared that out of respect I will not include in this writing. The letter continues with the memories my father had of their romance in Nice. *"I can see you watching me shave in the morning, playing with my hair at night, holding my arm as we go walking. Always smiling for me, and oh so many little sweet tender things about you that are in my blood like salt in the ocean. My Angel, please always love me. I am sometimes afraid I will lose you. I would die. Please always love me."*

"Wilkins said that I was the luckiest man alive. He said you were very beautiful and had natural beauty. Monique if you were in America you would never look at me. I have seen girls like you before and they would always put their nose up in the air at me. That is why I am sometimes afraid of losing you. I was the first man that ever really looked at you and you never had much of a chance to see other men like me."

And the love continues: *"Monique, remember the first time I kissed your lips? I will always remember that night. Your lips were so sweet, tender and soft that I was in heaven all that night. I couldn't sleep all night. Your lips are my food of love. I must have you Angel. Monique why do you love me so much? I can't realize that the most beautiful girl in all of France married me. Please write and tell me. Oh if this war would only end soon so we can be together. Wilkins always says, "How were you ever so lucky as to meet such a lovely girl like Monique?"* My mother must have been beaming with all the wonderful compliments and attention. This was all new to her and I'm sure she relished every moment. *"My Angel I seem to walk with you all day long. You are always talking to me and saying many lovely things. Monique why are our souls as one so much? Love is so powerful that it sometimes makes me a little afraid. I always listen to the radio for the news. I pray that the war will soon end so we can be together much sooner."*

August 14, 1945: *"Well by tonight we should know for sure if the war is over with or not. I pray that it is Chérie. It must be."* The accumulation of the damage done by Hitler's Panzers along with the death of so many of his friends had taken it's toll on my father. He finally shows his disdain of the German people as his letter continues, *"Monique these German people are so bad that I don't even like to look at them. I can smell them as I could smell a German soldier."* Dad had told me the Germans always wore something along the lines of talcum powder and you could actually smell the strong scent. *"They had everything here that they ever needed and then they started destroying the world. I really hate these stupid people. Every time they ask me for some food I always tell them to go ask Hitler, and that puts a stop to our talking together for good. The city of Frankfurt is destroyed forever now and it will never be any good. They will have very little to eat this winter and I hope they will get no help from no other countries. These people are fools and God has seen all their crimes. I have no pity at all for them."*

Then finally in a letter written exactly one year from the date Johnny jumped behind enemy lines in France, good news arrived. August 15, 1945: *"Chérie the war is all finished with, do you understand? Monique, Monique, Monique, I am so happy I can hardly sit still. Oh, my darling wife our lives are coming closer and closer every minute every day. Wilkins and I and Bill listened to the radio up until 01:10 in the morning to relive the news of the wars end. It is raining very hard here today, but it is still a lovely day. Monique I don't know how long it will be before I am out of the Army but everything will turn out for the best."*

My father writes that he thinks he'll have to make another parachute jump in September but hopes he doesn't have to, because now that he is married he realizes how dangerous it is. Fortunately he didn't have to. He also believes he will be out of the Army within half a year but isn't sure. The unknowing and separation from his wife has his nerves on edge. Then Johnny receives a letter that puts his mind at ease.

August 20, 1945: *"I received a letter from my father today and he made me feel very good. He did some very important things for us and I'm sure we both love him more for all he is doing. He said he is making plenty of money and needs me very much to go to work with him. He is trying to buy another business and hopes to succeed. Monique I'm sure you will love my father. He has always worked very hard for the family and we really love him. He is very funny and a little shorter than me. I am always laughing with him. I am in a very good mood today Chérie. I guess father's letter made me very happy. In fact I'm sure his letter made me happy. Also Madame Aleck loves me very much and that to me is the most important thing in the world."*

About the middle of August Johnny grew tired of pulling guard duty, and writes that he sometimes wished he was still in the war because he was so bored. But then follows up with how crazy that is. In another letter he writes, *"Gee sweet, I'm on guard again tonight. For five hours I must drive a jeep and patrol the town to see that there is no trouble."* On August 29 he writes: *"I saw Mickey Rooney in person today and he is really just another soldier at heart. He is very funny and a corporal."*

How wonderful it was for me to read that my father remembered the anniversary of the first day my parents met. August 30: *"One year ago today my eyes first saw Madame Aleck and she was very chubby and lovely like she is now. I can remember that day as if it were yesterday. I can remember the first time I kissed your lovely lips and how I almost melted in your arms. You thought I would never see you again, but after you saw me with that other girl I said to myself, 'Johnny you are crazy. Monique is the girl for you to marry. Don't lose her because there is only one Monique.'"*

Chapter 15

HAPPY PEOPLE DON'T HAVE ANY STORIES

Since their nuptials it had been two and half of the longest and most trying months for Mr. and Mrs. Aleck. Their distance encompassed all the emotions of a long distance relationship with a thread of patience keeping them sane. At long last Johnny writes in a letter on Sept. 4th that he had been given a three-day pass and was arranging for a flight to Nice. He informed the love of his life that he now had 86 points in his service with the Army and would be able to go home soon. After war's end with millions of troops waiting to go home, the Army implemented Operation Magic Carpet. Points were given with straight forward rules. Those who fought the longest and hardest should be honorably discharged to return home before all others. My father definitely qualified. Now they were one step closer to beginning their new lives together as he adds, *"I hope I can have most of our home built by the time you come home."* Ambitious aspirations for such a young man.

Finally in mid-September my dad was able to reunite with my mother once more at the Hotel Negresco. My mom saved the letter they had received from Headquarters United States Riviera Recreational Area. APO 772, U.S. Army. It is dated 18 September 1945 to T/4 and Mrs. Aleck, Room 137, Hotel Negresco NICE. My dad had been a T/5 prior to the disbandment of the 509th PIB, but when reassigned to the 508, as is common he dropped a notch.

Dear Sgt. and Mrs. Aleck: It is a great pleasure to welcome you to the Riviera, and it is my sincere wish that your stay here will be a most enjoyable one. Please feel free to call on our staff for anything that will make your stay more pleasant-- all of our services and facilities are at your disposal. Special arrangements have been made so that if you desire to have your meals served in your rooms, you have only to call Room Service and they will gladly oblige. Again I extend my greetings and hope that you will be able to visit us again in the near future. Sincerely, Riley F. Ennis, Brigadier General U.S.A. Commanding.

HEADQUARTERS
UNITED STATES RIVIERA RECREATIONAL AREA
APO 772, U.S. ARMY

18 September 1945

T/4 and Mrs. ALECK
Room 137, Hotel Negresco
NICE -

Dear Sgt. and Mrs. ALECK :

It is a great pleasure to welcome you to the Riviera, and it is my sincere wish that your stay here will be a most enjoyable one. Please feel free to call on our staff for anything that will make your stay more pleasant -- all of our services and facilities are at your disposal. Special arrangements have been made so that if you desire to have your meals served in your rooms, you have only to call Room Service and they will gladly oblige.

Again I extend my greetings and hope that you will be able to visit us again in the near future.

Sincerely,

RILEY F. ENNIS
Brigadier General, U.S.A.
Commanding.

Letter from the Hotel Negresco dated September 18, 1945.

In many ways it's good that Monique had no idea this would be the last romance my parents would relish for some time. There's a reason we're shielded from future tribulation. It allows us to appreciate the here and now. My parents met with intensity and fervor as their rapture for one another was unstoppable. Being in each other's arms was all the pair had been praying for, and not a moment was taken for granted. My father had written in earlier letters to excuse him if he became like an animal when they finally had the chance to be together again. I doubt my mother took issue with her wild hot-blooded Greek and welcomed his amorous advances. Instead of three days they were blessed with two weeks of total immersion. But, once again their time together would be just a tease of what could be as young Johnny had to return to the mundane Army life he began to despise.

Sgt. and Mrs. Aleck out on the town. Monique is wearing the red dress my father loved so much. Picture taken by Colette. Nice, France - September 1945

After a turbulent four-hour flight back to Frankfurt, more letters from Sgt. Aleck would find their way to his wife's hands. *"Cherie, this is very good news for both of us. I am leaving for America October the 13, 1945 and should be home by November, easy. Write and tell me if you are going to have a baby. I know it is hard for you to say "I don't want a baby" after I gave you that speech, but if you are to have a baby, you just are, okay? I thought I would be excited about going home, but I really am not. All the glory of war has died away now and I will just be one of millions I guess. From now on send all my letters to America for me, okay? Thanks."*

Instead of leaving on the 13th my dad and the other men heading home left for Paris on the 9th. First though, the soldiers had to have their feet inspected due to the extreme frigid weather in Belgium. Then they held a big parade for the officers. My dad made reference to his feet many times throughout his letters, saying they were getting better, but still ached if he was on them for too long. On Oct. 12th Johnny sent a letter from France in which he wrote something that I found puzzling as I will never know the answer. *"The letters I left with you, you can burn them or do what you wish, okay."* Since they are not letters he had written, I can only assume he had saved my mother's letters to him and did not wish to keep them. Maybe because there were so many it would be a burden for him to pack for his journey home. But again I can only assume as I never found any written by my mother to my father while they were in Europe.

What I did find were a few letters from my mother once he did arrive back in California, and a letter dated 15 Oct. 1945 from Johnny's new mother-in-law Simone. It is a two page letter that is written in her best English. She is very sweet in wishing him all the best and talks of how happy his family must be to have him home again. A mother would think that way. Mame speaks of how much her daughter suffers from their separation, and asks him to write to them as they love reading his words. It is signed, "Your mother of France." My grandmother always loved my father as if he was the son she never had.

The last letter my father wrote to his bride before leaving for the states was on 17 Oct. where he tells her the next day he and other soldiers are leaving for Marseilles. Now that the war was over, a mass exodus was put into motion to reunite those who had served with loved ones back home. While all this was taking place Monique was exhausting her efforts toward getting the last bit of paperwork in order and arranging for her own passage to America. At first she was given the false hope that she would be there by Christmas, and then on Oct. 18, 1945 she writes to my father in her best English:

"Since Monday I'm very much in the blues. I've gone to Navigation Company there is not boat the next month because the U.S. have taken the ships for the American soldiers discharged and I would be in America before January. I'm gone another company I don't think it's possible before the end of this year except if I have my immigration papers, but the American Consulate to Marseilles does not give the papers. You see Chéri, I'm going crazy!"

What a predicament my young mother found herself in. All of her letters were filled with the blues and frustration. She even writes of being physically ill and going to the doctor to find out why she is "puking" to which the doctor answers, *"It is because you miss your husband."*

At last Johnny's ship docks in New York harbor and he jots down a quick letter on November 10th letting her know he is safe. He had the chance to telephone his father, and the next day had a 14-hour flight to California. Awaiting the young war hero was a jubilant welcome home. A write-up in the local paper mentioned Johnny's honorable service. Even though the facts weren't altogether correct it sounded good just the same, with the last paragraph alerting all the single ladies his new French bride would be joining him soon.

My father's letter dated November 13th, *"Dad is really proud of me and he has taken me all over town to meet new people and I really had the time of my life. All the people want to see you very much and I know they will all love you, Angel. Our home we will live in until we can build our own home is all remodeled and it really is very nice. We will have the bedroom for ourselves and it is really nice."* This was the gesture he had spoken of when he mentioned that Gus had done something really nice for them. Thanks to his parents the old house on C Street where my father grew up, was now going to be their new starter home.

November 16, 1945, *"I think I will go to work for my father next week because I am going crazy with nothing to do. The new place we were to have bought didn't happen so we will wait. I really prefer to work for Father more because I learn more. Dad is very smart and has many, many friends as you will see."* Now that Johnny was over 21, finally he would be able to tend bar at the Liberty Club, instead of just doing the stocking and cleaning.

Hanging up his stripes, Sgt. Aleck was easing into civilian life as he tells his bride about buying new clothes, *"Well baby, I bought 3 suits of clothes yesterday, one dark brown, one gray, and one sport suit. Also two shirts and some other things. I spent $160.00 but then to get clothes one must pay plenty."* He continues, *"Mother and I are always talking about you, and mother just loves your pictures. She said you look like you want to be kissed all day long and then tells me to kiss you always."* He also writes of seeing his old girlfriends but not to worry. Monique mentioned his old flame Barbara in a few of her letters to him letting her husband know of her jealousy. Trust had not been fully developed at this early stage in their marriage and with her man thousands of miles away

Monique's only comfort was going to church daily. Hopefully with so many temptations looming, God would protect their marriage.

Letters with these words didn't help. *"Monique, really I do love you and I want you to always know this and not worry about your Johnny going out with other girls. If I were to flirt with other girls I couldn't look you straight in the face. I love you Angel and I always will."* Just the mere fact that my father even mentioned the words, "flirt with other girls," would not sit well with Monique. It was an invitation for trouble. But her letters continued to be consumed with her complete adoration of her husband, still mentioning the 22nd as their time together.

Many of my mother's friends had married American soldiers and were in the same limbo she found herself in regarding getting the necessary papers together to be with their husbands. At least she found comfort in knowing she wasn't alone and had even asked her husband to write to the appropriate military department for help. The process would be slow with the mail taking at least two to three weeks to reach one another. Letters my mother lived for. My father was sending money to her to help in any way that he could. Working for his father at $8.00 a day also helped keep him busy, as he writes of driving to Chico with him to buy cigarettes for the Liberty Club and that they bought plenty. With the war now over many of the returning service men from Camp Beale in Yuba City packed Oroville's bars.

Once again my naive father had my mother seeing green with this entry on November 23rd: *"Yes, Monique before you ask me, I have seen Barbara, and all the other girls too, and they are still lonely as ever but don't worry and please don't cry, okay now promise me. Thanks Angel."* What was he thinking?

November 26th, he again tells his wife how much he loves her and that he is saving for their future. He talks about how excited he is for them to have their first baby when she is finally in America, and includes personal words of love for Madame Aleck. But oh how quickly that sentiment can change. There had been an underlying message in his letters, that until I came upon the most difficult of all, I had not noticed. It is true my father was young at just 21 and full of testosterone. He was an alpha male to be sure, a Taurus full of confidence, with GQ good looks and a passion for life. Being a local war hero, if it wasn't for the ring around his finger Johnny would have been a busy man indeed.

I call this picture of my father, Mr. Handsome.

Upon reading the words of his next letter I was shocked, angry, and cried, knowing the terrible pain that would have seared through the heart of my poor unsuspecting mother. Only my older brother later would disclose that he had known the truth, but none of the seedy details.

November 29, 1945: *"Dear Monique, Monique this letter is hard for me to write to you but I think it is necessary. You remember in your letter you said, "Our habits, our customs, our ideals, our way of life and many other things are different." Well, all this has been on my mind now for a long time since I have been back. Everything seems to be different and very hard for me. I always want my freedom and want to go places with other girls. This is very hard for me Monique and I am sometimes afraid that I will never make you happy. Many girls here still want me and one in particular. No it isn't Barbara. Monique how can I explain it to you. You have always wondered if I really love you and it is the same way with me. If you didn't come to Chartre I never would have married you I don't think. While I was out of Nice in the mountains I always came to you mainly because I wanted to be a good boy or maybe I loved you. I really don't know even now. The devil is in my mind Monique and I really don't know what to say. I don't want to hurt you and again if you come to America and find that I don't love you and make life bad for you it will hurt you more. I must be crazy for writing this letter but I want you to understand me. I know how much you love me but I'm afraid for you. I am the bad man for writing this to you but I want you to know how I feel. I can't tell you about any other girl because I can't even tell my own father. Well Monique, please answer only to me and me only. Not by telegram. What should I do, or should I say, what should we do? I can't understand myself and again I can understand myself. So I want your words on our future. Love Johnny"*

My heart was shredded after reading this letter of betrayal. Words cannot describe my feelings while I succumbed to both tears and rage. I paced about the room cursing my father for the pain he caused my mother. In less than three weeks Johnny the war hero had fallen back to his old comfortable ways. As handsome as he was my dad didn't have to chase after skirts, they chased him. But now things were different. Now there was a Mrs. Aleck. I do believe that had my mother been able to make the journey with him my father would have remained faithful. Instead, he fell weak to fleshly desires. Full of doubt while riddled in guilt, Johnny became as moldable as a lump of clay. He was the perfect target for the vixen that preyed upon his vulnerability.

Half way around the world my mother read the toxic letter. All she dreamt and lived for was shattered. She became short of breath, never suspecting her Johnny was the wolf she swore he wasn't. Not even the Nazi SS was capable of destroying her delicate heart and yet it lay open now, barely beating. Young Monique was devastated. Colette told me how much the entire family suffered and sobbed together in the wake of these dismal words. For they too loved the carefree American soldier boy, and to see Monique agonize even further was more than they could bear. How could this have happened when they were so much in love?

A follow-up letter was sent, dated Dec. 4th 1945, "*My Darling Lovely Monique, Angel, I don't really know how to start this letter because the last letter I am sure made you cry.*" He says he has many things to explain about his life before he met her and asks for her forgiveness for the "Bad" letter he wrote the other day. He tells her how much he loves her and to forget about the letter. But as it turned out he continued his ruinous behavior, as this was the last letter from my father that I was able to find.

My mother recapped the events in her final journal entry January 19, 1946: *"Here for some long months I didn't write to you my little journal and so many events have happened. I became Madame Aleck the 30 June 1945. Since then I belong to my husband but alas happy people don't have any stories so I didn't write to you for so long. But tonight, my little journal, tonight I cannot stand it I am so unhappy. After 5 months of happiness of marriage I was receiving everyday a love letter from my Johnny, my husband declared he does not love me anymore and wants a divorce. It's so terrible I don't even want to think about it but it is the true reality. But my God it's so hard, I suffer so much. I am going crazy, but I don't want to sign it because in spite of that I still love him. But let me tell you how that happened."*

"Johnny went back to California after living 12 days with me. I was sad to know he was so far away but the news from him helped me to support our separation. Alas the 13th of December a dirty bitch told me about it. I cannot call her anything else. She has the nerve to write to me to ask me to divorce Johnny because they are in love and voila. This was an American wedding. Oh my God why always suffering why it's always the same people? I sure pay a big price for my happiness that has left. And the worse of it I cannot rejoin him in California because the papers have changed because he is asking for a divorce and no ships are available. So that girl cannot profit! What a dirty bitch. I don't work anymore so now I am the housekeeper. My mama and coco are still working in Monte Carlo, and my grandmother is at Nanterre in the east of France." Then in English my mother writes, *"I prefer to not speak about my father....understand?"*

"My God help me to support this crisis. Give me back the love of my husband. Have pity on me I have suffered so much. Pray that

I go soon. Excuse the writing I just had a screaming fit. Whoever reads this... Salute!"

The only medicine for my mother's soul was the same who had poisoned it. How I felt for her young brittle heart.

Decades later in the recording from John, my mother described her feelings in another way, *"I could have killed him I was so darn mad at him. The American girls didn't like the French women, and naturally the nurse kept telling him, "She's never going to be happy here. You should never have married her. She made your dad believe it was a mistake and it never was going to work out. He believed her and she cleaned him out. Then she went to another and cleaned him out."* I was amazed to read that it was the other woman who had the nerve to ask my mother to divorce my father.

It wasn't long before Gus and Angelica figured out what was going on and completely disapproved of their oldest son's behavior. Gus may have had his share of infidelity, but he never divorced his wife and was always an exceptional provider. That's not to say my grandmother was not hurt by his actions, but she was also aware theirs was an arranged marriage with no promises. But Johnny's behavior was of a cowardice nature in Gus's eyes, and as Simone had stepped in to save Monique by taking her to Chartre, Gus would intervene regardless of his son's immaturity and make things right.

On Liberty Club stationary, a handwritten letter signed by my mother's new in-laws told the extent of the situation. I'm glad my mother had the foresight not to listen to her husband and did in fact write to Gus of her predicament. The words that follow are verbatim. February 13, 1946: *"My Dear Monique, Your letter of February 7th received. Johnny went to Reno, Nevada to stay there 6 week to apply for his divorce and after 6 week have to advertise in the Reno newspapers another 4 week* and if I don't get answer from you the divorce case will be postponed for another 2 months. Yesterday I took Nick, Bessie, Laura and went up to that town and your case to a lawyer to put a stop to divorce case until you arrive in America. We drove 200 miles good highway but lot of snow. Last week I sent Bessie to San Francisco and showed the French Consul and he wrote letter to Superior Judge at Reno, and he received his letter. The lawyer put a stop on the divorce case, but he want your consent to fight the case. Johnny don't have chance to win the case. You send a cable to this Lawyer the same as I cable you."

The letter my mother received from her new in-laws dated February 13, 1946. One day before Valentine's Day.

My grandfather then wrote out the lawyer's address and instructed my mother to write this in the cable: *"Please deffert my divorce case for me until I arrive in America. Monique Johnny Aleck."* On the back the letter continues, *"Send me all Johnny's love letters to me by air mail. I want them to send them to Lawyer for evidence. Do this as soon as possible. Day before yesterday I sent you 100 dollars for expenses. You don't have any idea how much we care for you. We all want to see you come to America so we can feel very happy. You do this at once. Love from Pop and Mama"*

The rest of the letter on the reverse side.

Honestly, had my grandfather not stepped in to lead the charge, who's to say what would have become of this inexcusable situation? I'm sure my father got an earful from all the members of his family for the stunt he pulled and felt like a wanted man. Obviously my mother never sent the love letters since I have them now, but in the end they were not needed. Colette shed a little more light on the infamous woman by the name of Darla, who took complete advantage of my dad's lack of self-control. The very control he had condemned other soldiers for in earlier letters to my mother. I'm not letting my father's actions off the hook by any means, for as they say, it takes two, but it would be both my father and mother who would suffer in the end.

"When Johnny ran out of money she ran away too. See how much she loved him, but she got all that he had. Bessie was in charge of his money for him, his Army checks used to go into an account in Johnny's name, but Bessie was in charge. He had a few thousand dollars which was a lot back then. And she took all his money. He didn't have a dime left. He even bought her a brand new car and put it in her name." I found out later that when Darla, who was a nurse, realized my dad was penniless, she rode off in her new car to try her luck with a local doctor.

It was obvious the odds were not in my dad's favor. With the humiliation it was time to face some hard realities about the mistakes he had made. Clearly, Madame Aleck was his one true love. After the divorce was dropped my mother's travel papers were finally able to go through. Relief was felt thousands of miles away with news Monique would finally rejoin her Chéri. Gus, who was always both prosperous and generous, held family at the highest and lived by the motto, *"The more the merrier."* He helped many of his family members, be it cousins, brother, or daughter-in-law an ocean away. Colette informed me Grandpa Gus also helped by sending some money towards her journey *home*.

My mother recalls it was March of 1946 when her father took her by rail to Marseilles to board her ship. First she said her tearful good-byes to her loving mother and sister and hoped they would visit soon in America. It was another bittersweet occasion, and even though she longed to be with her Johnny her heart was fresh with remnants of the axe that had almost split their marriage. Once in Marseilles, Jean and Monique went to a local hotel a friend had recommended as the ship was to sail the following day. To their surprise the hotel had become a brothel and there was a bit of confusion when it was found that this was a father with his daughter – not their usual clientele. All made light of it and the situation provided for a good laugh for my mother's over-burdened nerves. They, of course, were able to get separate rooms.

The following morning on March 8, 1946 the pair found their way to the docks where my mother's Liberty ship was awaiting her arrival. The port was bustling with military personnel as father and daughter held a tearful embrace. An embrace that would be their last as they would never set eyes on one another again.

Bon Voyage, and may God be with you in your new life *ma chérie*!

My mother's Liberty Ship that brought her to America in early 1946.

Chapter 16

COURAGE AND CONFIDENCE

It must have been a surreal moment as Monique's ship embarked to a foreign land. What a strong woman my mother was to make such a journey with promises scribbled in the sand. The war was over, but would a new one arise on the home-front? Would the ebb and flow of Johnny's love cause further disappointment or would he come to his senses? Imagine how scary it must have been for this naive young woman. Monique wouldn't be arriving with love pounding in her heart, knowing the man in her life was eagerly awaiting her arrival. Instead, she would be filled with anger, fear, and uncertainty. For all she knew, her husband might resent her for coming all that way, for putting him on the spot in front of his family. She had no way of knowing if this voyage would bring a fresh new start to their marriage or see its abrupt end. But for my mother, it was a chance she was compelled to take. Monique's complete adoration of Johnny could not be extinguished. If he wanted a divorce he would have to tell her face to face.

Thankfully there were two other French women on this ship full of men, who were watched over closely for their safety. The trio shared a larger cabin, housing two bunk beds with full length drawers under each bottom bunk. Soon after departing from Marseilles the Liberty Ship was met with turbulent weather. During the storm one of the over-sized drawers came unlatched, rolling in and out as the boat tipped to and fro. My mother's shipmate feeling sick, tried in vain to make her way to the bathroom, but teetering off balance, fell and was swallowed into one of the drawers like Jonah and the whale. With arms and legs flailing, for the life of her she was unable to crawl back out. The poor dear, already overcome with sea sickness, gave up, tossing her cookies on the spot.

At first my mother thought it was comical, until the vomiting began. Even though the relentless unsteadiness didn't affect her gag reflexes, smelling the foul odor was starting to take hold. So, with the ship still rocking, Monique steadied herself with handrails and made her way to the dining hall. Aside from a few sailors, she was the only one with the stomach to still eat. The bowls were held in place by rubber rings secured to the tables. Naturally, Monique ordered ice cream and gleefully chased mouthfuls of her favorite food group with delight.

After crossing the Mediterranean there first stop was Oran, North Africa. While there, a fight broke out on board involving some sailors and Nigerians, leaving a Nigerian national dead. The ship was quarantined for ten days during the investigation, and since no one could leave, time was spent swapping stories, reading, crocheting, and eating more ice cream. Monique had much to chat about as the three young women passed the time. Now that she had an audience my mom was able to let off steam about her husband's recent affair. The other gals became Monique's sisters-in-arms, hurling off-colored insults at the home-wrecker nurse like grenades from the trenches. For Monique, it was time well spent. My mother said for the most part, her trip was a lot of fun and I thought, except for the ice cream, what a drastic change from her life back home.

Monique with her shipmates in route to America

Passing the time reading and crocheting.

Monique with other passengers. Notice her cheeks are sunburnt.

I doubt my mother knew the magnitude of the heartache she left behind in Nice. Her attention lay squarely on thoughts of her Johnny, be they good, bad or indifferent, and the excitement of this new adventure. Just two days after her departure on March 10, 1946, Simone, Louise, and Colette wrote letters and shared their deepest emotions to the one they missed so much. I found the thin folded pale blue air mail papers amongst my dad's letters and the *Liberation de Nice* and had them translated, again by Anne-Marie. Until reading their words, I had no idea how deeply my mother was missed and deeply loved by her French family. With the thoughts they shared that day to their Momo, my commentary is not needed. They bare their souls with vulnerability indisputable.

My Darling Monique,   *March 10, 1946*

You are already away from us for the last two days and today is Sunday. How many memories this brings back, but for your happiness I need to have courage. Hence my thoughts are not away from you. Most of all I pray, because I know my darling how much you will need courage and strength to get your Johnny back, who being so far away has failed you.

Because of your suffering you are already a woman and I know that you will understand your duty. You will forgive and you will be happy together because I have no doubt for one instance my darling, that your little man will come back to you. All will be a bad memory that will make you both appreciate each other. The happiness will come back to you. So my treasure, have courage and confidence and everything will be okay.

I will relive with you the last few days. Wednesday evening you were hoping to leave on Saturday or Sunday, maybe even on Monday. But then on Thursday morning when I was passing in front of the church I made a wish. Every day I passed in front of the church and in the evening I learned you will be embarking on Friday. I can't express how happy I was with just my pen. So all day Friday I spent it with you, and every day since, I hope your husband is next to you. I hope your travel finds you healthy because when you read this letter you will be in your new country. Guard yourself from the blues. Be open to the joy of your new family that is waiting and already love you very much knowing you only through pictures.

I know that you will know how to return that love back to them. And you can tell them that I am very grateful for all they have done for you. Love them my darling. You need to have people next to you who love you. Now that you are far away from us it is to them I entrust my treasure. God will bless their household and therefore the calm will come back to your heart.

This week on Wednesday and Friday I took communion for your happiness, and this coming Sunday I will go to Laghet and do a pilgrimage, because I know my daughter has great confidence in this. Don't be discouraged and pray with order and not with revolt. You will see that God will bless you and everything will go well with your Johnny. Read this little letter to him and tell him I always have a lot of affection for him and I will give him a good whooping when I come to see you.

[Continued one week later]

It's the second Sunday since you have left the house for your new life and a lot of others will pass before I can see you again. This letter is all I have in my heart during this harsh separation. With this letter you don't know how many conversations we have on this subject. If you knew how much pain is in your little sister. She finally understands this departure was necessary. Like myself she lives with the thought of our travel to the USA. Your ears must be burning because we talk a lot about you.

We received your papers for your boarding from the Army the day that you left as well as the papers from Lougares the lawyer.

Today Jack came and took your sister to see an operatic called The Happy Widow. He wanted to help cheer her up. I'm at the house with Papa and Mytzou. I straightened up everything as usual for him so he wouldn't be mad. I hope my letters will bring lots of love to you. It is with impatience I am waiting for news for you, but I know it will take some time before I can receive letters regularly. As promised every week you will have news from France.

Be careful with yourself my darling. More than anything else I believe very soon you will be full of happiness. Thank you my darling for all the joy that you give to me. I am reassured that in your departure you are well organized and your thoughts are in place and that is the best for you to be happy. You will see very soon.

For my work there is nothing new. I am very busy and the same for Colette. Your father was successful in his winnings. We needed it very much, but he did not win as much as we were hoping. Never the less we appreciate it. I hope you know my hopes and dreams for you. I know that in Marseille he spoiled you and hopefully you will have enough to get to Oroville. I just regret we could not have given you more. Colette also helped and everything we have done is to help you to get to Oroville.

My darling I want to end for today. I know I have more to write because I have neglected it for a week. Courage and confidence and prayer to St. Joseph and the Virgin Mary and everything will be better for your happiness. Give our affection to your Johnny and when you are back with him a big kiss to him from Dear Mother Poulain. Your papa and Coco join me in sending tender and sweet kisses always.

Mamine

France.   10 Mars 1946.

Ma Monique Chérie -

Te voilà déjà éloignée de nous depuis
deux jours, et c'est dimanche, que de souvenirs
ce jour me ramène, mais pour ton bonheur je
veux être courageuse - ma pensée ne te quitte
pas et surtout mes prières car je sais ma
Chérie combien il te faut de courage et de
forces pour reconquérir ton cher Johnny qui
loin de toi si faible, mais par tes souffrances
tu es déjà une femme, et je sais que tu
comprendras ton devoir, pardonner, et que
mes deux heureux très heureux ensemble, car
je ne doute pas un instant ma chérie, que ton
petit mari te reviendra, que ce sera un souvenir
mauvais qui vous fera mieux goûter votre
bonheur retrouvé - donc mon trésor courage
et confiance et tout ira O.K - (tu vois si je
connais les expressions USA) -

Je vais revivre avec toi ces derniers jours.
mercredi soir, tu espérais partir que samedi ou
dimanche, peut-être même le lundi; le jeudi
matin en passant devant l'Église du Pat
je fais un vœu (remarque chaque jour j'y
faisais une courte invocation) le soir j'apprenais
que tu embarquais vendredi; te dire ma joie
malgré ma peine - aussi toute la journée de
vendredi je l'ai passé avec toi, et depuis
chaque jour c'est souvent que je suis à
tes côtés -

The first page of the letter from Mame to her daughter. March 10, 1946.

Colette and Simone heading to work. Simone looks tired. 1940's France.

My grandmother's bus pass from Nice to Monte Carlo. Notice the date March, 1948. I believe this was the expiration date.

My Darling Momo, my little treasure Monique,   March 10, 1946

When you read this letter my Momo you will be in Oroville, but for the moment you are alone on the boat and believe me I think of you and I live with you. Your departure caused me great pain and words cannot express it, but you are courageous. Life is such that the wife must follow the husband, and this is why you left. You must have a lot of courage I know it very well because of the condition in which you are leaving, but your father-in-law is very, very nice to you. You will be strong and you will heal from Johnny's actions.

At this moment Johnny is lost on a path. Take him by the hand and take him back on the road, and when he comes back to you he will understand he has a soul, and you will be his light. His life will become clearer when the sunlight begins. You will still be close to him. You will still walk the path of happiness. It is a very pretty road and it should not be dirty.

Believe that a love so strong cannot die. There is a God and he blessed your union and will protect your love. Mom and I pray for you. God will not allow the heart of a mother to suffer.

I would like to know how life is in Oroville? The layout of the land, the attractions, and the girls and boys. You must be very busy with this change in your life. You are going to become a real American, but for me you will always be my darling Momo, my little French, just mine. So please send a detailed letter with pictures from Oroville if possible.

Today I went out with Jack. Can you realize your sister is getting out? hmm. I went to the city Casino to see a nice comedy called National. I like comedy a lot and prefer it even to the movies. When we got out from the comedy we went out with Jack's friend and she said frankly, "I did not have fun at all." We went with some young girls and we danced. They laughed for no reason. You know, the double entendre words. There were six of us, but you know I did not like the company. There were three young girls wearing lots of make-up. You understand the type. There was a type of Zasou who was talking about music, and mentioned Chopin, Mozart and other types of music. But since I was missing you Momo I was not listening and more than once I was thinking about you.

When I came home I went to your picture and I kissed it very hard. My little bedroom is very sad without you. Every piece of furniture tells me with one word and a sweet song is sometimes very sad. A little bit of my heart is sailing on the Atlantic at this time and it will go further and everywhere you will be.

I think of you so often that sometimes I say your name my Momo, but no one answers. Never the less I'm sure that our thoughts are crossing each other. And you know I will come to see you with mom at the end of summer. I promise. Our plan is well in place. Mr. and Mrs. Aleck who will be radiant with happiness will pick us up at the train station. Time will pass quickly and think about when we will see each other again.

The weather is great, but it has been raining since you left from Marseilles. You took the sun with you and maybe when you arrive in Oroville it will be sunny. The sun in America is the same as the one in France, because it left France to wait for you there. Therefore Momo darling take care of yourself. Stay the pretty woman that Johnny will like always, and eat well.

Don't have the blues. Think about all of our beautiful plans. Good night little sister and I hope to dream of you. I kiss you very hard. Big, big kisses from your little sister who loves you always.

Your

Colette

Mytzou [their dog] hopes to see you. In the meantime she kisses you and don't forget to kiss your new parents in Oroville from me.

My Dear Grandchild,   *March 10.1946*

I put some lines to this letter that your parents and darling Colette are putting together for you. When you reach the US you will receive these lines. My adored treasure you will be in the arms of your very dear Johnny and amongst your new family that you will love before you even know them.

My dear little Monique, kiss well your dear Johnny from your grandmother Louise. Johnny that I love much because I'm still convinced it will make you happy to be his wife. God will protect your home. This is my dearest wish that I have for your life. I know how much you love each other so I can guess your happiness when you will be back together after this cruel separation.

My darling Monique my thoughts never left you in your travels, so I think you must be happy to finally be back with the one you love so much as well as your new family which will replace the one that you left here. I'm hoping to see you again when I have great grandchildren. Please give to your new parents and brother and sisters my dearest affection.

For you my very dear grandchild from your grandmother that loves you I send the most tender and loving kisses.

Mamine Louise

Almost three weeks pass and still no word from Monique. The waiting is always the worst. It was a time for faith and great patience.

Dear Momo Cherie, Ma Niquette,   *March 31, 1946*

Today I think about you all the time. You must have certainly arrived in America by now and where are you? Maybe you are on the train to San Francisco. But anyway when you read this letter you will be in Oroville and we will finally receive some news.

I would like to know that you have arrived to your destination because I worry about you. Don't forget to keep us posted on information about Johnny and most of all tell us the exact truth!

I miss you a lot, Momo. My life is always the same. I go for walks. In one word it is life and now I am alone. Last night I took your picture and I kissed it and of course after that I cried. What do you expect Momo? Tears are running, they are a part of my heart that overflows.

I love you a lot, Momo and I want to know that you are happy, because you see when you love somebody you need to know that they are happy as when we loved them. I'm confident in God and I pray that your destiny is in his hands and he will not be insensitive to all my prayers. Courage and confidence, my Momo. Mom talks a lot to me about you and we really are serious about coming to see you at the end of the year. That is why we are working.

This afternoon I went to Mt Boron. So many memories came back to me. Especially a certain evening when Johnny was looking at you for a very long time. And our little walk with Mamine. I hope to hear from you soon.

I'm finishing this letter by sending you big, big, big, kisses from your sister who adores you.

Colette

PS. Dad is the same but I'm telling you now he is worse.

Mytzou kisses you a lot. Don't forget my suede shoes if you can. It is not polite to ask. Excuse me. Coco

Colette gave this picture to her Momo before she set sail for America. The back reads, "To my little Momo, the kindest little sister. Your Colette forever. 28-2-46"

Chapter 17

LIVING IN AMERICA

In April of 1946, a month after saying goodbye to her father, Monique stood on the deck of the Liberty ship where she could finally see the shores of America. After crossing the Atlantic, instead of docking in New York, the ship set anchor in New Orleans, Louisiana. There, Monique purchased some postcards which she mailed to her loved ones in France. Others she kept as mementos I found mixed with my father's letters. From there she headed for San Francisco, and upon her arrival was eagerly greeted by Gus, Angelica, Bessie and oh yes, the reason for her journey to California, her husband Johnny.

While Monique had gotten chubbier eating cartons of ice cream, my dad had lost weight and his face was broken out in pimples. A good sign he was stressed as to how his wife would react with the fresh wounds he had caused. Clad in his gray suit and stylish fedora it was the first time my mother had seen him in civilian clothes. She confessed to me that her husband didn't look the same as she had remembered and she preferred her soldier in uniform. Hugs were exchanged all around as Gus and Angelica were finally able to gaze upon their new daughter-in-law. It had taken a great deal of effort on my grandparent's part to clean up Johnny's mess, and I can only imagine their elation, finally laying eyes on his bride. Soon the family found themselves dining at an authentic Greek restaurant hand-picked by Grandpa. My mother wasn't accustomed to the cuisine and barely nibbled. She would mention to me later the food was awful, but everyone else loved it.

After most of their bellies were full it was time to check into a local hotel, also owned by Greeks. It was another disappointment and far from the Negresco, as my mother explained in the recording. *"So we stayed on skid row in San Francisco. And we had the suite, mind you, the bridal suite on skid row. I said to myself I'm not staying here, I can't stay here. I was so upset. I cried and I cried and I cried and I didn't want Johnny to touch me. I hated him and all that stuff that was bottled up inside me, I let him have it! I didn't care."*

John asked our mother to describe the room. *"Broken window, paint was peeling, an ugly bedspread. I mean, it was awful just awful. The next day they took us to I-magine."* To which John pointed out, *"From a dump of a hotel to a top of the line dress shop,"* as my mother continued, *"You should have seen the outfits they picked out for me. One outfit was nice but the rest were like my grandmother's clothes. Luckily, I got pregnant anyhow and I was so sick."*

Leaving San Francisco the family piled into Gus's Cadillac for the four-hour journey home. As they drove up to the house on Linden Avenue, Monique set eyes on the temporary home where she and her husband would rebuild the trust that had been severed. It was a far cry from the three-bedroom apartment with marble tiled balcony in Nice that her mother kept impeccably clean. Gus and Angelica had moved back down to the Oro Vista after the passing of great-grandpa Stefanis. Living above one's business made perfect sense and was akin to how it was in the Old Country. Aunt Joy moved out with her boyfriend Alford whom she would later marry in August of '47. That left the two-bedroom, one-bath house to her brothers and sister who didn't mind living in what Monique considered undesirable filthy conditions. With the VA loan for the C Street house still being processed, Johnny thought it perfectly natural for he and his new bride to live with his siblings. Considering that just three months prior he had wanted a divorce and was now living paycheck to paycheck, in reality, this was the only option available.

Her description of the living nightmare: *"When I think back, here I was 19 and naive, and what I had to put up with. I was away from everything. When I came here I couldn't believe it. I lived there with the whole family. Bessie and her boyfriend, Nick and his wife, and John and I, okay. All sick. Nick had syphilis, Bessie was just getting over gonorrhea and she had surgery so she couldn't have any kids. So that was the atmosphere. And I was pregnant and sick, sick as a dog! Even if I hadn't been pregnant I would have been sick because I was so homesick. And I hated it so much, it was awful. Your Dad was working night shifts half the time."*

With her religious upbringing Monique must have thought she'd just stepped into Sodom and Gomorrah. To make matters worse, since there were only two beds and three adult couples, they all took turns sharing the same quarters. Monique was constantly washing bed sheets. Thankfully, there was a constant flow of letters keeping her tethered to loved ones back home. April 14, 1946 from Colette:

My little Darling Momo, and Dear Johnny,

I cannot tell you my happiness when we received your telegram telling us you are back together. My darling Momo, God blessed your union and now he will protect you. You suffered a lot, but I am certain Johnny asked himself more than once where do I go from here. No light was shining on his soul and an obstacle was stopping Divine help. Now your love is strong. All my prayers reached Johnny's soul and you are certainly the light of his life.

Johnny, your daddy must be very happy because he loves you a lot and wants your happiness. Today, Momo darling, it is your first Sunday in Oroville. My thoughts do not leave you. I would love to visit and know you must be happy next to Mr. Johnny Aleck. I would like to receive a letter from you with some details of your life over there and your arrival etc. Most of all if you can send me a picture of both of you because I don't have any, and pictures of Oroville and your new parents. That will make us very happy.

Oroville must be charming country for two lovebirds like you. Is it nice weather? Certainly a little bit of sun from France shines in the California sky. Today the weather is magnificent. Mt. Boron seems sleeping with this beautiful spring sun. A lot of memories were revived within myself. Mom and I speak about you, and you know, Johnny, Mama loves you very much.

Today Mama and I went to see a movie called Strange Destiny. It was very good. After we came back home and had dinner we were talking about you. If you knew, Momo, how much I love you and I wish for you happiness. When you left you took a piece of my heart and now it belongs to you. It will always stay with you.

I'm sure that you think of me. Very often I look at your picture and every time I kiss it when I say good night. I think also of Johnny and I love him very much because he will make you happy.

Good night Johnny, take care of your little wife. If you only knew how much she loves you. Momo, I'm saying good night and I kiss you very much.

Colette

You know, Momo, Dad is even worse than before and he is hurting Mom and me very much. And he doesn't even have a steady job.

Again, I want to say I am very grateful for your telegram.

I don't think my grandfather was physically hurting my grandmother or aunt, but I can't be sure. Instead I think Colette was talking about emotional and verbal abuse, which in many ways is just as bad. My tight-lipped Mame would never have shared information about any abuse, but if he had physically hurt them I think Colette would have told me when we did the recordings. I only know after his incarceration he had become a consummate alcoholic. My aunt referred to him as a mean drunk.

Monique became pregnant in June and migraines were soon to follow. The only food she could keep down was oranges and chopped lettuce with French dressing so she was given intravenous vitamins from the doctor. As for her nerves, he recommended a pet so they got a little dog and named her Mytzou the same as their pooch in Nice. The doctor's wife was also with child and soon Monique had her first friend in the states. Having someone to talk to who sympathized with her situation was better than any pill could provide. In addition, the doctor's sister was a college student and soon my mother was giving her French lessons, and with that, it wasn't long before the migraines subsided.

As the months passed, instead of continuing to gain weight, her constant challenge with keeping food down caused her to lose weight and she slid all the way down to 120 lbs. People began to wonder what happened to the baby, thinking she had come to America already pregnant and now was slimming down. Young Johnny's military training didn't cover how to care for your sick pregnant wife. Since his in-laws goal was to be in America by year's end, a letter to the powers that be might help to expedite their arrival.

He wrote a one pager dated September 5, 1946 to the Commissioner of Immigration in Philadelphia asking for assistance in bringing Simone and Colette Poulain to

America. The letter was read by the Immigration department and returned with further instruction. My mother kept my father's handwritten keepsake which was stamped as received Sept. 9 1946.

During that same week Mame sat down and wrote another letter. It is dated September 10, 1946, six months after my mother sailed to America. Letters and telegrams were their only form of communication, but then I found a very nice surprise within my grandmother's words.

My Darling Children,

I still feel like I am dreaming and am thrilled from your phone call the other evening. What a pleasure to have been able to listen to your voices. I'm still turned upside down! Thank you my loves for this great happiness. Colette received the telegram during the day, and made an appointment at 8pm, but we had to wait until 10:40pm. What time was it where you live? Probably 4 o'clock in the afternoon. We left the post office at 11:20pm. Colette and I couldn't stand still we were so excited! Thank you again for giving us such wonderful pleasure.

My grandmother and Colette received a telegram instructing them to be at the post office at a certain time in order to receive a phone call from Johnny and Monique. After pacing in anticipation, and waiting a very long two hours and forty minutes the phone finally rang. The family was able to enjoy thirty minutes together with each receiver huddled over at both ends. No one wanted to miss a word, a nuance, nor joyful laughter. Unfortunately, while they were still talking the line suddenly became disconnected. The operator was unsuccessful in making a second call, but all went home happy having at last been able to hear the familiar voices of those they missed so much.

Her letter continued, *"My Momo, I think that you forgot your French because on the phone you were not talking very much in our language. I could also feel that you were so excited! Anyway everything is well, and I see that you found a house. You've gained weight and Johnny is in love, and you cannot wait for us to come!"*

Simone's words lead me to believe my parents moved out of the Linden house that they shared with Bess and Nick while still waiting for the Veterans paperwork to go through to purchase the C Street house. This would not surprise me, given my mother's total dissatisfaction with the living arrangement with her in-laws while being pregnant.

It is really nice to hear Johnny speaking in French. I just wish we could have talked longer. Send him a big kiss from me and tell him how happy I am. Yesterday I received a letter from the third. [It took a week for the air mail to be delivered.] *I see you are doing well in your state, and that the baby is starting to show. I am sharing in your joy. I keep praying to God to keep you and your household safe. Johnny has a lot of work so take good care of your loving husband. A big thank you to Johnny for his nice letter to Colette. She was so happy that she cried. She reads your letters over and over. It fills her with Joy. Colette is beyond the moon, mom is okay, and for myself, I am very tired, but my morale is excellent.*

And please tell me what kind of perfume you want and anything else you want me to bring in a detailed letter. We hope to be in America by October if all goes well.

Your father's health is compromised again since he is losing his strength. The doctor has come by twice, but they cannot do surgery because it is too risky and he could die. He needs to be on a very serious diet, but last night he was not in as much pain.

At the end of the letter my grandmother adds her salutations and sends her love to Gus and Angelica then adds that she is still making the baby clothes.

Finally after nine long months the VA papers went through and Mr. and Mrs. Aleck purchased the house on C Street in November of 1946. What a blessing it was to finally have some privacy. My mother was pleased to have a new electric refrigerator, gas stove, ringer washing machine and a handy clothes line in the back yard.

With his bride now six months pregnant, my parents continued to receive dozens of letters from Nice. This one written by Simone on December 22, 1946 reveals a shift as my grandmother comes to terms with the inevitable. It is the last letter I found from Mame or Colette.

My Darling Loves,

If God permits, in one month we will not be in Nice, but on our way to our big trip! You can imagine the happiness that is within me! Days are passing very quickly now. Every day we are getting closer and closer to the time.

This week Colette and I emptied our armoire so we can choose what to take with us and throw out anything that we don't have an interest in. We are going through our things and discarding those items that hold bad memories for us. You can imagine how many memories there are both good and bad, but this is the past. Now we are going toward the future. We hope according to Johnny's words that the future will be better than the past. My thoughts are always with you and I think of the joy you must have spending your first Christmas together.

With left over yarn I'm going to finish a pair of mittens without the thumbs for its first few weeks. This way the baby will have two pair, one with and one without thumbs. Right now we already have packed two suitcases, but I will have to buy another one which will make it a total of four.

I made a trousseau and filled half of one of my suitcases with baby clothes. I hope I will be able to bring your doll and I packed the Nativity scene as well. I am also asking permission to bring the dishes, but I haven't had an answer yet from Paris. I have to have my list notarized from the American consulate in order to bring the dishes and other things with me. I will be so happy if I can bring them so I can give them to you as a present for your new home.

Are you settled in your new home? You have not talked about it so maybe there has been a delay. Colette and I want to know if you have a garden, because you know everything that has to do with nature interests her. Here it is cold, but it is the season. You must still be feeling winter. Make sure Johnny takes good care of himself. I remember the big cold that you gave to him. "REMEMBER"!!

My grandmother talks about Colette having health issues that I assume were due to an improper diet from the food shortages. She was concerned as to whether or not the she would be fit to travel to which the doctor replied, *"Go, just go, it will be a good change of climate, life, thoughts, plus good food."*

We have so many projects that we are working on. This morning I worked on my Assimil that I had started a long time ago to learn English. I'm counting on you to translate this to Johnny. I remember last year and I was thinking about you and it's our turn now. Maybe it's the last time here as well.

I have to admit to you that my heart is so happy at the thought of seeing you. I feel in myself a lightness. This departure will bring for me a very different life than the one I have lived up to this day. It will be calm, serene, and peaceful.

Most of all, darling, listen to the advice of your doctor. Don't do too much and tell me honestly the results of your consultation with him. I know that your Johnny must be very attentively checking on you. Tell him that I pray a lot for you and for your happiness together. I am sending a lot of kisses toward him. Colette is sending her best kisses and she will send a letter in the next mail and she is thinking only about our trip and her arrival to be next to you. Mom and Jean are sending you kisses.

Friendship and hello to Pop and Mom Aleck. I hope that you have finished your purchase of the house and that you are creating beautiful memories. It must be wonderful for you to have Christmas the way you describe it in your last letter, especially with a happy family.

I send my tender kisses to you and I am forever your,

Minette

The baby was born in March of 1947 and shortly afterward Simone and Colette managed to make their way to America. Their reunion was a moment of elation with numerous kisses and tears, hugs and smiles.

Colette's depression vanished now that she was with her Momo again. The French ladies torturous separation was but a distant memory. With the hardships imposed by the war and constant outbursts from Jean's abusive drinking, the threesome had become an emotional tripod supporting one another. Now reunited, they were whole again.

The young couples' first-born was a healthy baby boy given his father's name Johnny Gus Aleck Jr. Nick-names are important in this family and the newborn was christened JoJo pronounced Jsho-Jsho with a long "o." Mame wasted no time unpacking the one-of-a-kind crocheted *petit* outfits she had lovingly fashioned for months.

Gus gave my dad a few days off from his work at the Liberty Club and Johnny treated his in-laws to a beautiful trip to Lake Tahoe. We still have some old photos taken of the family standing on a dock taking turns holding little Jojo. My father's pride is obvious as he tenderly holds his son while my mother is filled with the blissfulness of motherhood. Colette and Mame now saw and experienced for themselves the life they could only envision through letters. If Monique harbored any traces of resentment toward her once unfaithful husband, none were visible.

Monique, Jojo, and Johnny - Lake Tahoe - 1947

A happy family: Simone, Monique, Jojo, and Johnny. Lake Tahoe - 1947

Sisters united with John Jr. Lake Tahoe - 1947

Two twin beds had been set up in the extra bedroom since it had been decided the French ladies would stay for a while. Johnny had talked with his parents about work for the pair and when they were ready, Gus and Angelica had jobs waiting. Simone and Colette took turns behind the counter of another business, the Oroville Liquor Store, Gus opened a year prior to their arrival in '46. It was conveniently located right next door to the Liberty Club and my father was given the responsibility of being the manager while still tending bar at the Club. Colette worked the day shift from eight to four, Mame worked swing from four to midnight, with Gus wrapping up the evening from midnight till 2am. My French grandmother even helped Angelica in the Oro Vista, changing sheets and helping with the laundry. It wasn't the most glorious job, but even while paying a little rent on C Street, Mame was able to put money aside.

Oroville Liquor Store matchbook cover. Color: royal blue with yellow lettering

Bustling downtown Oroville. The Liquor Store sign can be seen on the right just past the 'DRUGS' sign. It says Oroville on top and then has a neon arrow that bends downward and toward the building which says Liquor. The buildings across the street on the left were torn down in the mid-1960's. Montgomery Street circa 1940's

It wasn't uncommon in those times for the Oroville socialites to gather for teas and invite special guests for a meet and greet. In such a small town everyone had heard of and even spied the beautiful French lady who now resided amongst them. It wasn't long before Monique was invited to one of these teas by Mrs. Griggs, wife of Dr. Griggs. How noteworthy it was for others to finally meet this French native. My mother told me it was interesting as the host "showed her off" to the others. Monique had her own charm and quick wit, and I'm sure, along with her intriguing accent and grace made for an exceptional guest.

Now that they had tested life in America, Johnny's in-laws made a trip back to France in '48 to gather a few more belongings. Being a devout Catholic, Simone never divorced her husband, but there was no punishment of excommunication from the church for leaving the father of

313

her children. With the end of the war, Nice had begun to rise from the rubble. An easier task than rebuilding the Poulain's marriage.

When translating my mother's journal, Colette confided that when they first came to the states she was not impressed with America or Oroville. There's a reason why it's called culture shock. As much as she yearned to be near her sister and best friend she was torn and ached to be back in the familiar surroundings of her homeland of Nice. Fortunately, she knew her health and heart could not withstand a long-term separation from both her mother and Momo. Not that Simone would have allowed such an absurd notion. Colette's place would be at her mother's side, and over time, she grew to accept and even enjoy life in America.

Front side of Simone's immigration card.

This is to certify that
Simone Wacker Poulain
was admitted to the United States on **June 11, 1948**
at **New York**
as a **Nonquota** immigrant for **Perm Res**
under Sec. **4-B** of the Immigration Act of 1924 and
has been registered under the Alien Registration Act, 1940.
Visa Application No. I **641152**

DATE OF BIRTH	SEX	HAIR	EYES	HEIGHT
July 6, 1906	F	Br.	Br.	5-4

Commissioner of Immigration and Naturalization.

GPO   16—48499-2

Back side of Simone's immigration card.

Colette holding her baby niece Michele Colette. Summer 1948.

Their stay in France was brief. After Mame gathered her favorite treasures and dishes, she arranged to have them properly packed and shipped back to the U.S. With goodbyes exchanged, the two arrived back in New York on June 11, 1948. Thankfully, they made it just in time for the birth of my parents' second child, my sister Michele Colette born June 25, 1948, affectionately nick-named Menu, (pronounced Mee-New.)

Having said *au revoir* to their former lives and *bonjour* to anew, Simone and Colette settled into a duplex on Montgomery Street between Pine Ave and First Ave. Resuming their employment routine at the liquor store, Simone found the pair had time to take on a few house-cleaning jobs. Ever the workhorse, she knew the importance of saving for a rainy day. The same Mrs. Griggs hired the French ladies to keep their home, which overlooked the Feather River, tidy. Mame even showed some of the beautiful glassware that she had shipped from France to the misses who admired the uniqueness of their design. Knowing its origins were from France the small town socialite jumped at the opportunity to purchase this uncommon Parisian glassware.

Living in America had its adjustment period to be sure as Colette shared a funny anecdote. In France during the '40's, the toilets were very different than in America. They had a good sized hole and I'm assuming did not have P-traps where items could get stuck. It wasn't uncommon to use the toilet as a garbage dump for small unwanted items such as food scraps, bones, and such. The sewage pipes led to the outside of the building, taking the waste to God knows where. Hopefully not the magnificent Mediterranean Sea, but my gut tells me during the forties it could very well have.

At any rate, without a thought, my aunt, put some bones down the potty as she was accustomed, and upon flushing, naturally it became plugged. Water flooded the bathroom floor and poor Colette was baffled as to what she had done wrong. The two were in panic mode throwing down towels to sop up the water, and frantically called for help. Any problems the women incurred were addressed by Johnny or Gus, as surely they would be able to remedy the situation. With my dad busy, Gus made a house call asking what Colette had flushed down the toilet. Disclosing it was bones and thinking nothing of it, Gus had to scratch his head and wonder why anyone would even think to do such a thing. The French ladies explained it was a perfectly normal practice back home. Well, Gus got his tools out and rectified the situation, but before he left, Grandpa, with a wag of the finger exclaimed, *"No bones, no more bones. Just your business, but no bones."*

Keeping with the family theme, Gus had also hired Jim Banos, husband to his niece Helen, who also hailed from Greece. Helen was Angelica's niece – her sister Anastasia's daughter. Anastasia if you will recall was the sister who had the measles and was unable to come to America to marry Gus. She had stayed in Greece, married a man by the name of Spyros Zaxos and the couple had four children including Helen. Helens' three brothers all remained in their homeland. Gus helped pay Helen's way and get settled in Oroville. With Grandpa's commitment to family, if you needed employment, he had a job waiting or he'd create one. So, while my dad tended bar from 6am to 4pm Jim Banos took over the 4pm to midnight shift. There was always money being made at the Liberty Club, especially with the back room poker games. It wasn't long before Aunt Bessie and husband Don opened a barber/hair salon next door to the club calling it Don's Barber Shop. With that, downtown Montgomery Street became a family affair with first, the Oroville Liquor store, the Liberty Club in the middle, and finally Don's Barber Shop to the right, complete with the Oro Vista rooming house perched above.

With my mother carrying their third child the Aleck couple put the little house on C Street on the market and searched for a larger three-bedroom which they found on Manzanita Ave. In the 1960's Manzanita was renamed Oro Dam Blvd. It wasn't long before Monique gave birth to another gorgeous baby girl given the name Christiane Simone on January 9, 1952. Her round face and chocolate brown eyes had unmistakable French characteristics much like her mother.

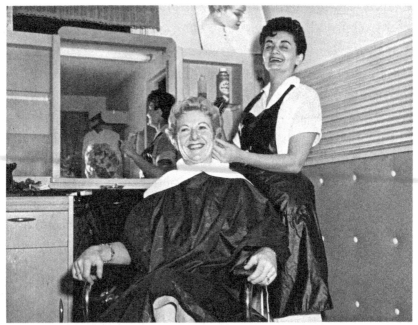

Aunt Bess enjoying another day at the salon. Early 1950's

Almost a year after Christiane was born Colette shared that after they had moved to America, she and her mother had taken a final trip back to France. It would be the last visit with Jean Andre and their native land forever. A failed marriage from the start, it was sad to see my French family had suffered as a result. At least he still had their dog Mytzou.

Mame soaking up some sun on deck. 1950's

Colette enjoying the fresh air on one of their trips across the Atlantic. 1950's.

Now having a larger house, Johnny decided it was time to pursue his biting ambition and take a stab at the world of songwriting. My mom recalled having the living room floor covered with albums while my dad played his favorite melodies for his Chérie. They'd sit on the carpet as he could hardly contain his excitement, pointing out trumpet, clarinet, and deep sexy sax solos. My mother reminisced how they laughed and danced, having many a date night right there in the comfort of their home.

Johnny scraped together a few extra bucks and finally purchased a used upright piano. My dad's energy was tireless fulfilling his hunger for music while working full time and helping with the little ones. With fellow collaborator Urthel G. Weston they'd stay up till the wee hours of the morning composing many originals. One was a song called *"Vegetable Ball"* I remember our dad singing when I was a kid. It made me laugh since it was about vegetables that actually went to a ball. The other, *"I'll Toss a Kiss to the Moon."* was copyrighted April 22, 1953. It includes twenty-seven pages, meticulously written for a full fifteen-piece band. Maybe someday I'll be able to hear what my father and his partner put so much time and passion into creating.

In the same box with the sheet music I found a few 1950's music publications for amateur songwriters. I know my dad sent out several of their songs in hopes of getting published and landing that big one! Unfortunately, he received an equal amount of rejection notices. John Jr. said Dad had told him he swears a record company stole one of their songs and changed it up just enough to pass it off as their own. Hard to say if that was true or not, but I do know my father loved music, and throughout his life he was usually whistling or humming some tune. He'd stand at the kitchen sink while washing dishes or tossing a Greek salad, half singing musical notes, sounding something like, "la da de dum...la da de dum... la de dum." I still catch myself humming that same soothing melody, and one day realized I had absorbed it from my father.

My mother never liked the house on Manzanita. The rooms were too small, but also Monique had a sixth sense as it would become apparent this house possessed a dark side, if one believes in such things. With Christiane still a toddler, the family moved once more, buying a house that Gus had built on Linden Avenue on one of the three lots he had purchased back in the 30's. Along with the house, which Gus sold at the discounted family-rate, he included the over-sized lot in the middle that sat at the corner of Linden and Grand View avenues.

In one of the letters my father had written to his bride, he said that he had wanted to build their dream house before she made it to America. We all know that didn't happen, but now the time was right. With the corner lot now theirs, they hired an architect and builder and were heavily involved in the creation of their soon to be 3-bedroom 2-bath, ranch style home. The custom living room had a full wall of bricks with a large fireplace, vaulted ceiling, and exposed beams. The back wall held three over-sized ceiling to floor solid glass windows overlooking their back yard that would later be filled with flowers, crape myrtles, and brick hard-scapes my dad would build. Each bedroom had a closet with double sliding doors and all the other doors within the house were pocket doors, which was unusual in the '50's. And finally, one of the children's bedrooms had a built-in book shelf and desk for school studies.

At the same time, my great-grandmother Louise, as mentioned in her letter, made plans to visit her America family. I can't be sure but she may have had half a mind to make the move herself. Fortunately, in Nice, she did have the love of Jean's family who were very kind. Still it might be nice to be near great-grandchildren and a change of scenery could do her tired old eyes some good.

With that in mind, three years after Simone and Colette's final excursion to France, Louise decided to test the shores of America for herself. Not able to speak a word of English, Grand Mame' MeMille made the bold decision to leave her comfort zone. I was able to locate the ship's manifest from the Cristoforo Colombo, where Louise departed from Cannes, France on May 20th, 1955 and docked in New York on May 28. Under her typed name, 2707 Oro Vista, Oroville, CA was listed as her final destination, which was Gus and Angelica's rooming house address at the time. But I know she stayed with her daughter and Colette. It must have been quite the adventure for this woman who was pushing seventy at the time.

I'm not certain if she had any preconceived ideas of what she'd find in America, or in Oroville for that matter. Sadly, the adventure was short lived. Even though she thoroughly enjoyed seeing family and great-grandchildren, my great-grandmother liked nothing of the town, the people, or the customs. Oroville was no match for the century-old buildings, open markets filled with fresh vegetables and flowers, and of course, the mesmerizing sea. At the northern end of the Sacramento valley, Oroville had its own small town charm, but it wasn't home.

What bothered my great-grandmother the most was seeing her only daughter cleaning houses and changing bedsheets for the well-to-do. Simone's former employment as manager of the finest women's dress shop in southern France carried with it an air of prestige and pride, and Louise was a very proud woman. She considered a job cleaning bathrooms to be beneath Simone's credentials and dignity. Simply put, it was humiliating to have a daughter become what she considered a maid, much like the maids who worked for the Poulains back in Dijon and Vichy. Clearly, this would not do, but Louise could do nothing to fix it. She stayed for two weeks and complained the entire time. It is sad to think they had such an unpleasant visit since it would be their last.

Grand Mame'-MeMille in her later years.

Still, the early 50's was a magical time for the Aleck family with loved ones dropping by to enjoy the children. In the warmer weather, outings to Chico's Bidwell Park became a weekend ritual as the in-laws and little ones piled into the bed of my dad's truck. My mother said it was one of the happiest times of their young lives with windows rolled down and the tickle of Christiane's hair against her bare shoulders. Motherhood came as natural as flowers in springtime, and she felt blessed having her Mama and Coco be a part of the memories being made. My mother's gray skies with its parade of black butterflies had transformed into Ozzie and Harriet perfection.

The perfect family. The adults with children, John Jr., Christiane being held by her mother, and my sister Michele - Christmas 1953 at the Manzanita house.

Prayers had been answered with Johnny and Monique's lives filled with child-rearing, a job my father loved, and planning and preparations for their new home. As Mame's letter had once said, Johnny wanted the same as Gus, as he too was living the American dream. To help pick up the slack, it wasn't uncommon for the three children to spend time with Mame and Colette down on Montgomery Street giving my parents a much needed break.

Tragically, unbeknownst to all, the unthinkable was creeping into their lives. The day was near that no one would forget. A day everyone would have liked to have back, but there are no "do-overs" in life. And somehow we continue the best we can.

Chapter 18

CHRISTIANE

On the way home from one of their weekend excursions to Bidwell Park, out of the blue, Christiane asked, *"Mom, what's it like to die?"* Cri-Cri, (pronounced with a long e,) as they affectionately called her, was just three-and-a-half years old. The family had piled into the family car that day, with John, now eight, sitting in the backseat.

My brother later said about that time: *"It just sent a chill through me, and I told mom within a day or two, 'Mom, I have this feeling that Christiane is going to die.' When I say I had a premonition or a feeling, I mean, how could a kid remember that? How could a kid at that age remember unless it really made an impact? It emotionally just hit me."*

Monique didn't want to alarm her son and told him not to worry. What she hid from him and her family is that she too had a premonition in the form of a dream that Christiane was going to die. It was the first week of August 1955 and Monique, already blessed with three healthy children, was due in December to give birth to her fourth.

I had always known about the eerie feeling my mother was overcome with, but never the full details. All my life I was curious about the little girl whose 8x10 black and white baby picture sat framed on my parents' dresser. I never had the heart to pry, knowing how painful it was to relive. With my mother now in her eighties, I thought possibly enough time had passed for her to finally share the full details. Fortunately, this particular day, she was able to bear her soul.

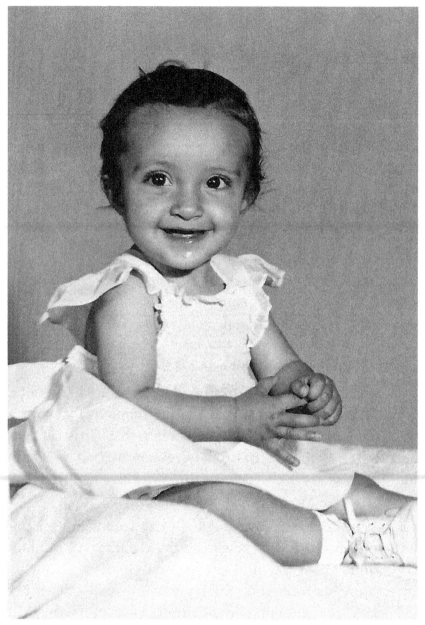

Christiane's baby picture that sat on our parents' bedroom dresser for decades.

"In my dream, my grandfather Emile, my mother's father was holding Christiane in his arms. They were standing on a beautiful wide marble staircase that gently sloped upward toward heaven.

On either side of the stairs were banisters and candles lit at each step. I asked him what he was doing with Christiane and he said, 'We need her now.' Knowing that my grandfather was dead, I became frantic, saying, 'No, you can't take her.' When I reached out to try to grab his arm to get Cri-Cri free, he turned his back to me and started walking slowly up the staircase. I continued to beg for him to bring her back but he kept walking and then I woke up. I was so scared that I couldn't go back to sleep. The next day we all went to Chico to play in the creek. I never let Christiane out of my site, thinking she might drown. But she didn't, and I thought, okay, maybe she's safe."

A few days after the dream my parents dropped their kids off with Mame and Colette so they could meet with the builder and go over house plans. Upon returning to pick up the children, Mom said they heard sirens but thought nothing of it. As they got closer to the duplex the ambulance had stopped very near to Colette and Simone's house. Blood rushed from Monique's face. How does one describe what she knew had come true? Police were already at the scene and a small crowd had gathered around the little girl who'd just been hit by a car. Johnny quickly stopped the car as his wife flew to her side. The little girl was their beautiful angel, Cri-Cri.

I cannot even begin to imagine the shock, anguish and utter disbelief my parents encountered when they saw her laying there. Mom said when they pulled up Christiane was still conscious and kept saying she was sorry. Sorry, I suppose, for crossing the street. Poor sweet young thing. There was no way anyone could have averted this. It was fate and there is no avoiding what has already been decided on a higher level. Perhaps the premonitions were a way for the Universe to try to ease the pain in that moment. If that was the case, it had no effect. There are no words, no touch, absolutely nothing on earth that can console the parents in the wake of losing their child.

My brother John shared his account of that horrific day. *"Christiane wanted to visit this little girl that somebody said looked like her, and I said, 'You can't go over there, you can't cross the street.' And I pulled her back one time because she was wanting to go across the street. We were in the back yard and she had gone to the front and I saw her standing there by the trees. The trees were between the sidewalk and the street. And I said, 'Come on, you can't be doing that.' I remember saying that and I got her to go back with me and we were playing some more and the next thing I know she was missing.*

She had snuck off and I went around front where I looked and I saw her in the street. I saw all these people around and I went across there and said, that's my sister, you know, that's Christiane. And I said, Christiane, you know, I felt horrible. She was crying and people were holding me. I don't remember Michele being there and I barely remember Mame and Colette. I remember being put in the ambulance and taking off.

I also remember being at the house later and Mom was in bed just crying and stuff and I remember Dad coming in and leaning against the door, crying and saying Christiane is dead. We all broke down. Actually, I didn't cry, I didn't cry at all. I just felt real sad and then the next morning I remember going outside and just walking around where the garden is now. Mr. Lucasie our neighbor came over, he knew what had happened. I don't know what he said, but I just started crying in his arms. He just held me and I sobbed and sobbed and sobbed. And that's what I remember of it. I remember the suffering mostly by mom and dad over her death. It was wailing – it was pretty goddamn emotional."

"Shortly after, we all took a trip to the Redwoods with Mame and Colette. Just to get away from what was going on. There are pictures in the old album of our trip. I don't recall the funeral – not

sure that I went. That's all the memories I have of Christiane. I do remember mom changing her diapers on the bed when she was younger. And I remember praying that God would bring her back again.

At the Redwoods after the funeral. Simone, Jojo, and Colette. 1955

Mom was never the same after that. Every time August rolled around or January, Christiane's birthday, there was some mourning going on. There were tears and it was a very somber day. There was not a lot of action. It was a day of staying in bed or dad sometimes would take us for a ride. And this went on for several years. She started having more children to help with the sorrow. She was pregnant with Gregg, but wanted another little girl."

Little Christiane's death took its toll on the family, and the town as well. Oroville was very small back then and everyone knew each other or knew of each other. To lose a sweet innocent little girl in such a nightmarish way sent shock waves through the entire community. There was a huge turnout of mourners at the Catholic mass and graveside service. I had been told for years that my mother didn't go. That the doctor had wanted her to stay in bed because they were afraid she would have a miscarriage. But she told me she did in fact go to her baby girl's funeral, as hard as it was, she had to be there.

It is difficult to read the newspaper account of that day but I think it's important to know the truth. With the date of her death etched in my mind, I found it on microfiche at the local library. We had been told Christiane was hit by a drunk driver, but I found from the article the young man was completely sober. I don't know why my mother told us he was drunk. Maybe it was a coping mechanism, making it easier to believe it wasn't entirely their little girl's fault. We'll never know for certain, but at this point it really doesn't matter.

On Tuesday August 9, 1955 the Oroville Mercury newspaper's headline read, *"Oroville Tot is Fatally Injured When Hit by Car."* The article from the paper follows: *Christiane Aleck three and one half years old daughter of Mr. and Mrs. Johnny Aleck, 1559 Linden Ave, Oroville died at a local hospital at 2 a.m. today as a result of injuries suffered last night when she was struck by an automobile driven by Charlie Floyd Stafford Jr. 23, Route 5 Box 2158 Oroville. The accident occurred on Montgomery Street near Leah Court.*

Rosary will be recited at 3pm tonight in St. Thomas Catholic Church. Exact cause of death is not known pending a pathologist report.

CAR RUNS OVER GIRL

Police said Stafford going west on Montgomery struck the child with the left side of his car throwing her to the pavement. His car ran over the girl and dragged her over three feet before he could stop the car, police said.

No citation was issued to Stafford pending police investigation. The accident was the first pedestrian fatality in Oroville since 1953. It ruins Oroville's perfect record of no traffic fatalities for all of 1954 and to date in 1955.

Christiane was staying with her Grandmother, Mrs Simone Poulain 1343 Montgomery St. while her parents were downtown. She started to cross Montgomery Street to see an unidentified child on the other side of the street. She was crossing from south to north and was just north of the center line where she was struck.

She suffered a broken right leg, fractured pelvis, arm abrasions and a laceration on the side of her face. She was in surgery for two and half hours.

Requiem Mass will be held at 9 a.m. tomorrow in St. Thomas Catholic Church. Hamilton and Riley is in charge of funeral arrangements.

Christiane who was born in Oroville on Dec. 9 1951 [she was actually born January 9, 1952. The paper got it wrong] *is survived by her parents, a brother Johnny Jr. 8, sister Michele 7, paternal grandparents Mr. and Mrs. Gus Aleck of Oroville. Maternal grandmother Mrs. Simone Poulain, Oroville. Great grandmother Mrs. Louise Wacker, Oroville* [she was living in France] *and the following uncles and aunts. Mr. and Mrs. Nick Aleck both of Oroville,* [Nick and his wife were living in Florida] *Mrs. Al Harvey, Palermo,* [my aunt Joy.]

Investigation of the accident is still under way.

I was able to find another story in the following day's newspaper.

Funeral Rites Held For Christiane Aleck

Rosary was recited last night in St. Thomas Catholic church for Christiane Aleck three and one half year old daughter of Mr. and Mrs. Johnny Aleck 1559 Linden Ave. who died in a local hospital as a result of injuries suffered when she darted into the street and was hit by a car Monday night.

Requiem Mass was held in St. Thomas Catholic church this morning. Burial was in Oroville Catholic Cemetery. Father Joseph Farraher officiated at the services.

Pallbearers were Joseph Ghianda, Ed Johnston, C.E. Grafe, and George W. Custer. A coroner's inquest into the child's death will be held 7pm August 16.

Chief of Police A. F. Kessler said today that he "probably" would issue no citation to Charlie Floyd Stafford Jr. age 23, Route 5 Box 2158 Oroville, driver of the car that struck the Aleck girl. Stafford told police he was traveling around 20 miles per hour at the time of the accident. Witnesses corroborated his statement officers said. A police spokesman said Stafford stopped his car in 34 feet, and that he couldn't have been traveling much faster than his stated speed.

Chief Kessler and the officer investigating the case conferred this morning on a possible citation. According to Kessler, two eyewitnesses following the Stafford car discounted the possibility of negligence on Stafford's part.

I found it a bit calloused and inappropriate to mention that the death of my sister had ruined the cities record of pedestrian fatalities. I doubt the writer gave it any thought. I also thought how this must have impacted the young driver,

Mr. Stafford. I did some research after finding his name and address in hopes of finding him but was unsuccessful. I'm not even sure he is still alive, but there is no doubt in my mind the events of that day weighed heavy in his heart throughout his life.

It would seem the old house on Manzanita was cursed after all as my mother had insisted. Christiane was the first child to die, followed by two other young girls whose families had lived in that house one after another. The second was another three year old little girl and the last young victim got sick at age three and died from Leukemia three years later at age six. Three little girls who had all lived under the same roof. What are the odds? That house and a couple of others were torn down years later and a Walgreens now sits there. I'm not a big fan of progress, but in this case I'll make an exception.

John Jr., Christiane, and Michele - Christmas 1953 at Manzanita house.

Michele, Monique, Christiane, John Jr., and Mytzou. 1953 - Manzanita house.

I've visited her grave often. Christiane's headstone is very large and thick for such a small child, standing at least four feet tall to the stone cross that sits on top. The inscription reads simply ALECK on top, then under that CHRISTIANE SIMONE. The next line, Jan. 9, 1952 and finally, Aug. 9, 1955. Since my parents were in the process of building their new home and my father didn't have a lot of extra money, knowing my grandfather, Gus probably paid the entire funeral costs. I have learned enough about Gus that he and his wife would have wanted to help in whatever way they could during such a great loss. This was, after all, their grandchild too. My parents were in such deep grief I doubt they were fully functioning, and planning Cri-Cri's funeral was beyond their abilities in such a state. Not wanting Christiane to be buried amongst strangers, four years later my parents purchased two more plots one on either side of Cri-Cri. Johnny and Monique's eternal resting place would lie with their little girl whose life ended far too soon.

My parents received letters of condolences and dozens of flower arrangements that filled their home. My mother was never able to part with the old-fashioned flower-cards bearing the sender's names, along with the type of flowers that filled each vase. I found the cards and letters years later on the top shelf of my parents' closet. From those cards I was able to visualize sprays of pink and white gladiolas, and arrangements of both pink and white carnations accented with daisies were abundant. Even pink and red roses along with asters in lavender and pink added fragrance and color to their living room. And from the Aleck family, a wreath of white carnations with clusters of pink baby roses had stood graveside.

Within the same box that held the sympathy cards was a small white book filled with signatures from the townsfolk who had the courage to attend a child's funeral that day. I thumbed through the pages and recognized many names of people who have since passed, while others were the parents of children whom I would later have as classmates. The four pallbearers mentioned in the newspaper article also wrote their names as the men who carried her tiny casket that day. How could such a small box bear the sadness of an entire community? I wondered to myself how my parents not only managed to survive such an overwhelming heartache, but also raise four more children.

I found another item in my sister's sacred box. A small pair of poll parrot black patent leather shoes that my mother used to slip on Cri-Cri's little feet. As I held them in my hands I felt tears roll down my cheeks. From the few pictures I've seen of Christiane during her short life here on earth, I remember thinking, what a gorgeous woman she would have grown to be. The sister I never knew was a beautiful child with wild brown hair, an angelic round face, big inquisitive golden brown eyes, and infectious smile. I wonder how different our lives would have been, how enriched, had she not been taken at such a tender young age?

Besides the flower-cards, signature book, and tiny black shoes, there were still the condolence cards and letters. One was from the Butte county Sheriff's office, signed by Sheriff Larry Gillick. Another was in an envelope affixed with a three-cent stamp. The envelope itself was from the Shriners Hospital for Crippled Children in San Francisco. The card inside revealed that Mr. and Mrs. Pittman, our neighbors up the street on Grand View, had made a contribution in Christiane's memory to the hospital.

There were a small handful of notes such as, *"Dear Mrs. Aleck and Johnny, I know words mean very little at this time but I wish to extend to you both my very deepest sympathy. Sincerely, Alice"*

One in particular just didn't seem right. I understand how they would have misspelled my mother's name, but it was the content that was unsettling. *"Dear Monic and Johnny, We are very sorry to hear about Chri-Chri, but it's just one of those things. Both of you must be brave. It was meant to be this way. Our very sincere regret."* It could have been that the person who wrote, *"It's just one of those things"* struggled with their word choices, always coming up short. I don't know that my parents ever actually read any of the cards. I had to ask, having just lost their little girl, would they find comfort in the words from others, or would it deepen the sorrow to their already shattered hearts?

In the stack of cards I found a yellowed one page letter dated August 10, 1955. *"Dear Johnny and Monique: Pat and I didn't have an opportunity to see you two, and we want to express our feelings to you at this time of your great sorrow.*

Only a parent can realize the love one has for their children and we know the sorrow you have at the loss of Christiane. One thought we have is that she doesn't need our prayers, but you and Monique are in our prayers to bear up under this cross. Our ways are not always God's ways and we are sure He had a good reason, although at the moment it's hard to bear. But you have your faith and we are sure if God needed another angel in heaven you won't deny Him in your heart.

We know the sorrow and heartbreak you are experiencing and while what we say cannot lessen your grief, it may soften it just a little to know that we feel sorry for you and Monique and that you have our prayers and sympathy. Sincerely ...."

The Feather River Inn was a bar on Montgomery Street a couple of blocks down the street from the Liberty Club. I came upon a card that had been passed around and signed by well over two dozen patrons that day. I'm sure many of them had Johnny as their bartender when they frequented his club.

There was another handwritten note that showed it was written at 10:30am on the morning of August 9th. *"Monnick and Johnny, I just now talked to Juanita and heard about your tragedy. I'm just sick! You have all our sympathy. God just sends things that we can bear. In his pattern there is a reason for everything. All of our sympathy to you all..."*

There was even a typed letter on Bank of America stationary dated August 10, 1955. *"Dear Johnny and Monique" Words are futile at a time like this. There is nothing that we can say regarding the loss of your daughter that can possibly assuage your grief. We want you to know that we sympathize deeply in your bereavement, and if there is any way in which we can be of help to you, do not hesitate to call on us. Sincerely, H. J. Cochran, Manager."* It's signed, Herman.

There were many more but I will end with a Western Union telegram sent on August 10th at 11:02 a.m. *"Dearest Monique and Johnny, our thoughts love and prayers are with you. Words are futile. You know how we feel if you want or need anything call Long Beach".* The phone number and address are listed. *"Wish I could be with you but impossible. Love, Nora and Ray".*

Nora and Ray Guthrie were very close friends of my parents who had lived in Oroville at one time and moved to southern California. Nora would face her own battles succumbing to cancer in 1966. Even though I was a youngster at the time, I recall my father holding his wife in his arms as she wept upon learning of Nora's passing.

News of Christiane's premature death made its way across the Atlantic to Louise and Jean. My aunt told me Jean had sent a letter addressed to Monique, Colette, and Simone giving his sympathies for their loss and the loss of his granddaughter. Colette said my mother didn't want the letter and that she still had it, but had no idea where it was. I am hopeful that one day it will turn up.

Sadly, my grandfather Jean Andre Poulain died just two years later on May 28 1957. Consuming alcohol daily had ravaged his body. It was a slow, lonely suicide. Colette said he had been renting a room from a friend and died in bed. Louise, who was still living in Nice, identified her son-in-law as he and Simone had never officially divorced. I contacted the city hall in Nice to get any information I could about his death or where he might be buried. In the mail I received a copy of his death certificate, but cause of death wasn't listed. Likewise, there was no evidence of where he had been laid to rest or if he was cremated. Since he was penniless, Colette thought her Papa was probably buried in a cemetery reserved for paupers.

Grandpa Jean Andre Poulain gambled with their future and lost. Lost his family, his grandchildren, and worse, himself. He died alone at the young age of just fifty-seven.

Jean [wearing glasses] with unidentified family members from his side of the family. On the back of the photo is written, "Jean 1947 en barque"' On boat.

As the days drudged on it became apparent my mother couldn't bear to have reminders of her little angel in their home. Still with child, it was important to do everything possible to avoid needless stress. Even the sight of Cri-Cri's clothes became unbearable, so my parents at just 28 and 31 kept a few of her outfits, packing them into a small red suitcase. The rest, my heartbroken father carried across the street to his parents' house and piled them onto a chair in one of the bedrooms. They'd know what to do with them. The suitcase was stored for years on the top shelf of the carport closet. I recall the day my mom decided it was time to revisit her daughter's tangible memories. I was just a young child myself as I sat next to her on the cold concrete floor under our carport while she set the suitcase in front of us. Upon opening it a slight musty scent filled the air. Mom reached down and gently smoothed her hand over Christiane's clothing. She held up a crocheted jumpsuit, then a lacy white dress that had yellowed through the years. It wasn't long before tears rolled down her cheeks as she quickly closed the hard case and walked swiftly back into the house.

I'm glad I was too young to grasp the agonizing yet loving emotions that filled her heart and mind in that moment. I sat quietly by myself feeling helpless and very sad. Without asking, I knew the clothes had belonged to my older sister. Once again, the many questions I wanted to ask about my sister and her untimely death would have to wait. Instead, I reopened the suitcase and stared at what could have been, as I felt the wetness of my own tears rolling down my cheeks. I don't believe my mom ever opened her case again. I think my father put it back on the shelf when he came home from work.

Decades later I would learn Christiane's suitcase had somehow wound up in my younger sister's storage unit, then in her garage. She called me to ask what she should do with it. Almost six decades later, touching her clothing turned the cloth to dust. Her cute little outfits were disintegrating before my sister's eyes, and the case had molded over the years. I told her it was time to let the past go, and toss the old case, knowing we would always hold the memory of the sister we never knew.

After my mother lost her little Cri-Cri her faith in God was tested. Her devoted Catholic upbringing was no match for the devastation she endured from losing her precious baby girl. Why had the same God she prayed to her entire life, the God she wrote to in her journal during the uncertainty of her marriage with Johnny, the God who had always been there for her, suddenly wrapped a crown of thorns around her heart? Monique's ingrained faith changed forever that day. To put it bluntly, her trust in God could no longer be trusted.

My dad holding Cri-Cri in front of the Manzanita house.

My mother, Michele, and Christiane.

I'll close this sad chapter with the words I read from one of the many sympathy cards I still keep in the small box. The quote was written by James Whitcomb Riley and reads as follows:

"I cannot say, and I will not say that she is dead-she is just away!

With a cheery smile and a wave of the hand, she has wandered into an unknown land.

And left us dreaming how very fair, It's needs must be, since she lingers there.

So think of her faring on, as dear In the love of There, as the love of Here;

Think of her still as the same, I say, She is not dead-she is just away."

Rest in peace my dear sweet sister, rest in peace.

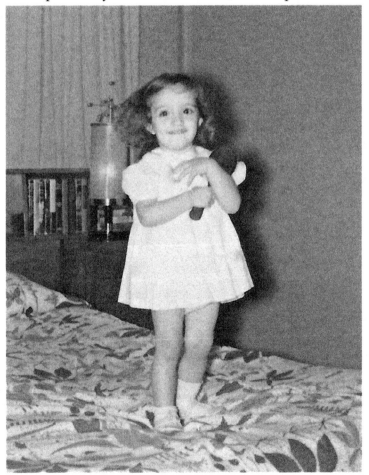

Christiane Simone Aleck

Chapter 19

GRANDMA'S GIRLS & UNUSUAL UNCLES

The expression "life goes on" sounds so callous after such a tragic loss. The cold reality is that life does in fact go on, and by year's end their new house on the corner was finally complete. The ritual of packing, wrapping, and unpacking had begun. Hopefully, the expended energy of the move helped as a distraction during their grieving. In December, just four months after losing one child, my brother Gregg was born. But as John had said, the mourning was ever-present as January 9th of the following month would have been Cri-Cri's 4th birthday.

Except for the heavy loss of Christiane, the 50's still held many fond memories for the family. My grandparents' famous parties at the house were still a large part of the Oroville Greek culture. Gus was looked upon by the community as somewhat of a Godfather, being one of the more successful immigrants, and was respected by all. Living conveniently across the street, my parents and siblings never missed these festive gatherings. Our mother, being a fabulous cook had learned how to prepare her husband's favorite meals, and would bring a casserole filled with the aroma of authentic Greek cuisine. As John put it, *"Hers were even better because they weren't as greasy.* She was complimented many times, which is high praise for a non-Greek to receive.

There was one older gentleman of about 70 at these parties who made an impression on young Johnny Jr. With dinner plates cleared, he took advantage of the long runway-like table to show off his stuff. While the music played, he climbed atop the dining room surface and placed a half-filled juice glass of wine on his bald head. John and the others were amazed as he demonstrated his dexterity, leaning and twisting then stooping way down and slapping the table without a drop being spilled. The onlookers went wild with clapping and *opa's* galore.

Gus on left enjoying friends at one of their many dinner parties.

Alcohol seemed to be a common denominator with this energetic family. Now living next to Gus and Angelica, young Jojo and Menu used to run across the street to help with their grandparents wine making adventure. With the fall harvest, grapes were tossed into the large vat that sat in their old one-car wooden garage. I had flashes of "I Love Lucy" when John told of how he and Michele were lifted into the rustic container and to their utter delight had the good fortune to be the stompers of the grapes. With purple-stained feet and out of control giggling they marched in circles, mashing, mashing, mashing.

At the Liberty Club, dad and Nick and some of the other men would hoist a full metal keg of beer onto their shoulders. Balancing the heavy load, they'd race two at a time down the worn floor with beer sloshing to see who was fastest. Even grandpa showed he was still no slouch as he'd pack a keg on his shoulder and carry it from the beer truck parked a good hundred feet away to the swinging club doors. It was all for show, giving the locals a good tale to embellish upon later. Life for these Greeks was a competition, but a fun one at that. Amusing others came easy for the Aleck family, adding to the welcoming atmosphere that always kept the club alive.

During the 50's the Oro Vista was still in its heyday. My mother said during WWII soldiers came to visit from Camp Beale which was about an hour's drive away. It was about this time my grandparents introduced the oldest profession to the Oro Vista by hiring prostitutes for their tenants, and hourly customers, as a very lucrative side bar. I wouldn't be surprised if they had actually started earlier. John Jr. confirmed there definitely were "working girls" up there who kept the boarders happy, and Grandma's coffers full. Being about twelve or so, he remembers going upstairs to visit with his grandparents. As he got to the top of the landing, a door to his left was ajar. He heard some rustling and as he peered through, saw an attractive *naked* lady getting dressed. Her ample breasts immediately got his attention arousing and shocking the active imagination of this inquisitive lad. In the same room was a man sitting on the bed putting on his pants. Instinct told him neither looked like they belonged there. But with her suggestive figure staring him in the face, Jojo wasn't saying a word. Being just a kid, he assumed the only tenants upstairs were men. It didn't make sense in this young boy's mind for a lady, especially *this* lady, to live with all those stinky old guys. He later learned from our dad that Grandma had acted as *room provider*, aka Madame for the *ladies*, who besides paying rent, gave her a nice piece of the pie.

349

The steps that led from Montgomery Street to the rooming house above were steep and many. They became part of Angelica's arsenal as my brother John shared another story from the early 60's. *"I used to clean the Oro Vista as a young teenager. I was on the landing, mopping, when I heard a commotion at the top of the stairs. Went up and saw a middle-aged woman in a skimpy nightie. She was shouting, I can't remember what, but pointing to a guy who was coming down the hall, tucking his shirt in. Grandma was in a rage, grabbed a broom and hit him with the stick in the head. He tried to squeeze by her, going toward the stairway. She kept popping him and he lost his balance and rolled down the stairs hard. Grandma caught up with him on the landing and continued her whacking. He just covered up and stumbled out of the hotel. I can't remember exactly what it was about but I sensed it had to do with hooking. I had already been told by Mom and Dad that was how Grandma and Grandpa made extra money. It was just no big deal. During my cleaning days I saw a couple ladies giving Grandma money. I wasn't shocked since I already knew it was business as usual. Grandma had a temper and was strong, really strong. She could flip mattresses like they were bed sheets."* At four foot, eleven, Grandma took care of business like a Marine.

While writing this book I was fortunate to meet a woman by the name of Barbara Evans, now in her seventies. Barbara had been a hair stylist employed at Aunt Bess and Uncle Don's salon during the 1950's. She was a pretty, petite, naive young lady of just eighteen, straight out of beauty college when Aunt Bess took her under her wing. *"They had prostitutes living upstairs – they were my first customers. Now that was interesting."* I did my best to have her share some of their stories, but she insisted, *"Some stories are best left secret."* I couldn't have disagreed more, but finally got one account as she told me one day a "John" from upstairs hit one of the prostitutes over the head with a beer bottle. They didn't take her to the hospital since, as she put it, *"hooking was illegal,"* so Barbara was the one that had to pick the broken glass out her bloodied head. With Dr. Kusel in the building next door, I hope Grandma had him discretely on file for such matters. Barbara remarked that she didn't like the sight of blood, but *"Those gals tipped real well! Got a dollar every time, instead of the usual nickel or dime."* With haircuts .75 and a wash and set $1.25, a buck tip was well worth feeling a little faint.

The gals upstairs loved their perfume, with Chanel No.5 one of the more popular dabbed behind the ears and unmentionables. It didn't hurt that in 1954, when asked what she wore to bed, Marilyn Monroe replied, *"Five drops of Chanel No. 5."* Barbara recalled, *"They may as well have taken a bath in it since the scent was so strong."* To make matters worse, seems the young hairdresser was allergic to the cocktail of fragrances, causing her to sneeze on a regular basis when in their midst.

Aunt Bess had a varied and very loyal clientele. It was a unique setup with five cumbersome red barber chairs in the front section for Don, and Bessie and the gals' work station toward the rear. Aside from Grandma's prostitutes, Barbara recalled that the salon had a reputation of coming up with fashionable new hairdos, attracting rich women from all over the county. Back in the 50's Don's Barber Shop and Bess's Salon was the jewel on Montgomery Street.

Grandma Aleck felt very comfortable in her daughter's business as Barbara recalled. *"Mama Aleck was a large-busted lady who didn't trust banks. Anyway, she would tuck rolls of $100 bills under each breast. Being young, I was so shocked to see her pull out her money to pay for something. We had a back room at the salon where she did this and then go on her way to do her shopping. She was hard to understand since she spoke the Greek* *language most of the time."* Then Barbara added, *"I remember all of the fun girls when I first started working on Montgomery Street, the best of my working years."*

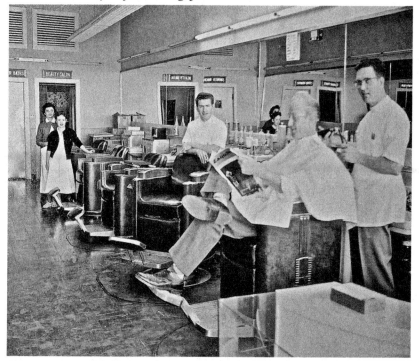

Don's Barber Shop 1950's. Aunt Bess in back behind Barbara Evans. Uncle Don cutting hair of unidentified customer. Picture provided by Barbara Evans

Aunt Joy had another tale of the rooming house above. *"That's how dad's business partner Andy met June. She used to "work" upstairs and he would go see her. Guess they really liked each other because they ended up getting married. When we were still in high school, dad rented out our house again and me and Bess shared one of the back rooms at the Oro Vista. When some of the guys started making advances at us, Dad kicked out the school teachers that were renting our house and had us move back home."*

A few years later Joy found herself living at the Oro Vista again. I imagine it became a revolving door for some of the Aleck clan. Barbara recalled an event that would be hard to forget. *"When I first started working, Mama Aleck had kicked Joy out and threw her clothes out of the upstairs window so Joy wasn't around the family very much. Although Bess did keep in contact with her. Don't remember why she was kicked out. You didn't want to get Mama Aleck mad."* What a sight that must have been. Women's clothing scattered in front of the Liberty Club below with a trail of Greek cursing from above!

Then there was Uncle Nick. My uncle was described by John Jr. as the bad boy type; feisty, strong, and full of the devil. He was a handsome dude and liked to show off, doing one-handed push-ups, and according to John, did this disappearing cigarette trick. He would bite off the filter and spit it out, then put the rest of the cigarette in his mouth. Nick would show the cigarette then pull it back in several times with a "now you see it now you don't" look in his eyes. This little act would end with him actually chewing then swallowing the gnawed, wet tobacco and paper. He must have enjoyed the reaction from his audience because I can't think of any other reason one would do such a crazy stunt.

Uncle Nick wasn't around much and had a string of marriages throughout his life. John thought he had wed six or seven times, but my count confirmed five. Laura was his first wife who he met while still in the Navy in Washington State. In one of the many letters my dad wrote to my mother, he said that Nick and Laura were going to have a baby and name him Johnny if it was a boy. Unfortunately, in another letter I learned that Laura had miscarried. Esther Jo Anne, who went by Jo Anne was his second. Then there was Mary, his third with whom he had three daughters. Maxine, yet a fourth, and his last marriage was to Beverly who lived with Nick in Alaska. If there were more, I found no evidence, but it's certainly possible.

Uncle Nick with his dog. 1950's

I wasn't aware of his first two wives until delving into his life. I found Nick's second wife Jo Anne when I was researching grant deeds at the county records. I thumbed through page after page in the humongous books for the name Aleck. In one of them I was very surprised to see the names Nick and Jo Anne Aleck. I went to the corresponding microfiche and found the pair had married on January 17, 1949 in Carson City, Nevada. After buying a house together it was soon discovered that Jo Anne was a polygamist. Mentioning that she was married to another man apparently wasn't important to her at the time. A property agreement and settlement was entered into in Nov. of 1951, leaving Nick with their house, and by January 7, 1952 the marriage was annulled.

My mother once told me Grandma wanted Nick to marry a good Greek woman but he wasn't thrilled with the idea. After Laura and Jo Anne were out of the picture she jumped at the opportunity to keep the bloodline clean. Grandma was determined as she and Grandpa convinced Nick to board a train with her and travel to the east coast. Destination was a visit with Angelica's childhood companion from the old country. This friend and her husband had also immigrated to America, settling in Keene, New Hampshire, and raised a family of their own. Nick "fit the bill" so to speak. The families were friends, he was baptized Greek Orthodox, was young, and personable. And so, in keeping with the tradition of arranged marriages it was decided Mary would be Gus and Angelica's new daughter-in-law. Nick needed a nudge to wed a woman he wasn't hand-picking himself, so the nudge, or bribe as it turns out, was his parents agreeing to buy him a brand new car, throwing in some extra spending cash. In exchange, Nick would place a ring on Mary's one-hundred percent Greek finger. With two past failed marriages it was a pipe dream to be sure, but since Gus and Angelica's arranged union had worked, maybe there was still hope for their second born son.

After their Greek Orthodox marriage in July of '54, Uncle Nick moved 3,000 miles away to start a new life with his bride in Florida. Mary owned twenty-five acres of land at the time, and her own beauty salon. Still naive about the true nature of her husband's work ethic she made exciting plans with him to open a restaurant. In 1957, when Mary was carrying their third child, they applied jointly and received a loan from Alice O'Brian, Mary's very wealthy client with whom she had purchased the twenty-five acres. With that, they opened the Coconut Grove restaurant. Not the famous eatery but still the same name. Mary had also enlisted the assistance of her brother John to help get the establishment afloat, but it wasn't long before both realized her husband was more prone to taking than actually making money. Her brother didn't want to see his sister fail, but also, realizing it was her choice, gave his sis the ultimatum to join allegiance with him or her freeloading mate. Frustrated, Mary was in a pickle, but with her husband's lack of business savvy and constant till dipping, her decision was obvious. Nick was sidelined when it came to business decisions.

Nick and Mary Aleck 1950's

With an unfavorable work life that overflowed into their personal lives, Nick felt the odds were stacked against him. Frustrated with life in Florida, he asked his wife to put five acres of her property in his name, sell the rest, and move their family to Oroville. Moreover, he wanted Mary to take the profit from the sale of the land and purchase the liquor store from his parents. I doubt very much my uncle had asked his parents if the store was even for sale. Well, Mary wasn't having any part of his manipulation, and knew she'd come out the loser. Even though deep down she loved this man, she knew full well her first priority was protecting their children from the poverty she knew was soon follow. Papers were drawn declaring Mary Aleck a free dealer of her own property and businesses, leaving Nick out of the picture. In order for her husband to sign on the dotted line – once again, a payoff occurred, this time to the tune of $10,000. Uncle Nick really had a knack for creating money without lifting a finger.

With three small children at home, one day out of the blue, my uncle drove alone cross-country from Florida to California. Showing up all melancholy, he declared to his parents and mine that his oldest daughter had died and he needed money for funeral expenses. This was around 1959, just four short years after Christiane had passed. He must have been pretty convincing because Grandma gave him $5,000. Feeling horrible for Mary's loss and reliving the anguish of losing Cri-Cri, my mother called to offer sincere condolences, but the response was less than grievous. After the initial shock, Mary told my mom that Nick had been gone for days and she had no idea where he was. As for their daughters, they were healthy and doing just fine.

Now I'm not here to judge anyone, although the word 'scoundrel' has become synonymous with Uncle Nick, but I just can't imagine coming up with such a dreadful tale. His actions bordered on sadistic for the agony all must have felt.

With Grandma's superstition, she was probably conjuring up a chant to break the Aleck curse. Poor Mary had to be fuming with anger while feeling extremely betrayed. I'm not sure if Nick was still in Oroville or if he had hopped back into his car, cash in hand, heading to Florida before being confronted. Either way, I'm sure he was tongue-lashed after deceiving his family in such a cruel way.

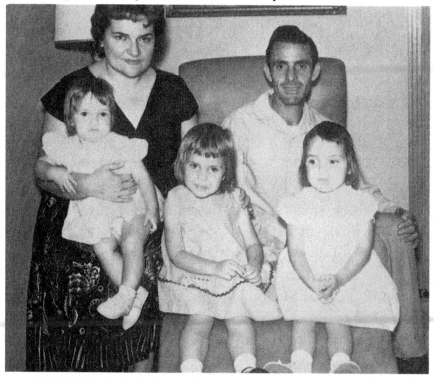

Nick and his family. Far left, Mary Aleck, their youngest daughter MaryAnne on her lap, sisters Alice and Deena, and their Dad Nick. - Picture provided by my cousin MaryAnne - taken about 1958.

Nick did eventually make it back to Florida, but for the next couple of years their marriage teetered. His youngest daughter, my cousin MaryAnne, who now runs her mother's hair salon, Sanibel Beauty Salon in Florida, shared this tale:

"My one memory is the time he came over after being gone for quite some time. Mom was having a little party for some of the

ladies that went to the salon, and when he walked in my sisters ran. I didn't know who he was, but he picked me up, threw me in the air a few times in a playful way then put me down. Mom told me to go to my room. I was maybe three and she asked him 'Where have you been?' His response was 'I don't punch a time clock' and he left."

Uncle Nick with his sisters, Joy left and Bess right. 1940's - after the war.

By 1961 Nick had moved back to Oroville, landing some odd jobs. He filled in at the Oroville Liquor store when the French ladies needed a break. My cousin has a couple of his letters that were written to her mother. It was apparent Mary was all but done with his charades as she had stopped answering the phone. In one of those letters he poses the all-encompassing question, *"Honey, do you love me or not? You don't say you do and I do want to know. Honey, you are cold in your letter to me."* Mary and Nick divorced in January 1963.

I recall during my teen years seeing my uncle standing in the back yard of his parents' house near the grape arbor. He was usually smoking cigarettes, wearing his white t-shirts and ironically khaki work pants. That's when he was married to Maxine, wife number four, who unfortunately had severe drinking issues and drank while he smoked. Seeing Nick standing across the street, and in the Oroville Liquor Store when it was located on the corner are the only recollections I have of my uncle. At the liquor store, I remember him on many occasions opening the floor safe, helping himself to the cash. Seems his hand was never too far from the cookie jar.

Nick and Beverly have plenty of meat for winter.

Uncle Nick spent his later years living in Alaska, where my Aunt Joy and Dad said he had some kind of labor job working around the nuclear testing area on Amchitka Island. In his spare time he continued with his first love, fishing and hunting in the vast Arctic wilderness. I have a picture of him with his wife Beverly, smiling after killing a large elk that is covered in snow. Photos of him in his younger years show my uncle had a definite Greek James Dean edge to him. I can see why the women were drawn to his playful boyish charm.

Nick with his boyish charm.

Tragically, death came at the early age of just fifty after losing his battle to lymphoma cancer. Our family suspects it was a result of the radiation which he came in contact with on Amchitka. Nick passed away in Anchorage, Alaska on Christmas day, 1975; the same year I graduated from high school. My mom said that my father wept and said of his brother, *"Poor guy. He never stood a chance."* To my father and society, Nick had been a failure, with serial marriages and a non-committal life. I think for the most part Nick was a selfish, happy-go-lucky kind of guy who lived life on his own self-serving terms. A scoundrel, yes, he was that, but failure is subjective.

His youngest daughter summed it up, *"So, actually my one memory was a good one of him playing with me. Then it wasn't until I was 18 and engaged that I heard he had died. I wanted to see what he looked like and say good-bye because I knew then that we would never meet, or have a drink, or go fishing, which I love to do and heard that so did he."*

Nick was laid to rest across from his father in the Greek section of the old Oroville Cemetery. He didn't have a headstone but instead an over-sized brick with the initials NGA stamped into it. Early in my research when I was trying to locate the markers for my relatives, I had come across this brick but thought it might be for my great-grandfather Nicolaus. It was only when I inquired at the main cemetery office that I found my uncle was buried there. Since I knew he had been in the Navy I didn't think it was right for him not to have a proper marker. With copies of his military records, I followed the process outlined by the Veterans Administration. Within a couple of months his bronze Veterans grave marker arrived. I made sure it included that he had served in the US Navy during WWII. For some reason, I kept the old brick.

Great Uncle Tom, Gus's brother who had professionally boxed in the early years lived out his retirement in the Oroville area. But the glory days didn't come without a price. Back then boxing gloves were much lighter, making the hard right hook more lethal. After retiring from the ring, Tom, aka George Gilmore, moved back to the Oro Vista. While tending bar at the Liberty Club, my father saw him often and referred to his uncle as being "punch drunk." Barbara from the salon recalls seeing Tom roaming Montgomery Street throwing his hands in the air, yelling and cursing in Greek. He even taught her a couple of off-colored Greek words she remembers to this day. But, his brain had become scrambled eggs. Got so bad he was scaring the women who frequented Aunt Bess's shop so a family effort was put in place to keep the angry little man hidden from public view.

John still recalls his Great Uncle. *"I can remember bits and pieces about Tom. He was short, but had a strong athletic build. Wore dark clothing most of the time I saw him. He was warm around us, but you could tell he was a little off. Punch drunk, I'd say. Didn't speak English well but understood. I remember one time up in the hotel when he and Grandma got into it. No idea why. Both were shouting in Greek and taking aggressive stances. Tom went back to his room afterwards. He came to our house one time to play the boogeyman, but he was playful and had a gunny sack. I think it was around Halloween. We weren't afraid of him, Michele and I. He took us over to Grandpa's small garage where the big wine crusher was kept and pretended to throw us in. He lifted us both up to the top. Dad was with us and laughing. Dad said this is what happens to kids who are bad. I remember him shadow boxing, walking back and forth on Montgomery Street. He was talking to himself in Greek, so I have no clue what he was saying. That's about all I can recall, except Dad saying he had been a pretty good fighter and had suffered from too many head blows."*

Gus may have had him do some odd jobs around the rooming house or bar, but keeping brother Tom under control required a lot of patience with a short leash. At any rate, Tom Aleck lived for another twenty-four years after his last bout. In his later years he moved to nearby Marysville and got a job as a laborer. Then one day he darted out into traffic near the 10th street Bridge, and was hit by a car. At the age of 63 Tom was killed instantly and pronounced dead from head injuries at 3:10pm on April 10, 1958. Three years after Christiane's ill-fated day. Poor mixed up guy must have misjudged the speed of the car. It was ruled an accident and the 24-year-old male driver wasn't cited. It was nice to see the very short newspaper clipping did mention he had been a professional boxer fighting under the name George Gilmore.

Anastasios Alexiou never married, and as far as we know, never had children. Aunt Joy said, when she was younger, she remembered her uncle had black wavy hair and liked to stand in front of the liquor store windows admiring his locks. A much better image to hold than that of a demented little Greek man.

Our family has just two pictures of Tom; one as a young man of twenty-eight wearing a straw hat with Aunt Bess as a baby on his lap. That picture is in the beginning of this book, in Chapter 1. And the other taken in Anaheim Ca. He's wearing a suit with matching flat cap and is quite handsome. Having never known my great uncle, I'm glad my mother was able to identify him. Nick and Tom, nephew and uncle are buried side by side with Tom's inscription reading, "Brother" on top, Tom Aleck, 1900-1958, In Loving Memory. They got his birth year wrong, but close enough.

Tom Aleck, the little Greek from Evia who stood tall in the ring.

Chapter 20

GOODBYE GRANDPA & CHILD OF THE 60's

With John Jr. being the first born, he is fortunate to have memories of our parents and grandparents in their younger years. His recollections have added to the virility shared by the Aleck men, as Jojo told this vivid tale as a youngster.

"One of my favorite memories revolved around the Gillette Friday Night fights. Dad and Grandpa Gus loved boxing and whenever Gus stayed at his Linden Avenue home he made it a point to come over to our home to watch the televised boxing. It was great. Dad and Gus sat on the brown sofa in front of our Magnavox TV Stereo Console and I sat on the floor. I remember Dad and his Dad would drink either Olympia or Pabst Blue Ribbon beer. We watched exciting, hard fought matches with such great fighters as Sweet Sugar Ray Robinson, Gene Fullmer, Carmen Basilio (he cut easily), Archie Moore, Jersey Joe Walcott, Ezzard Charles, Carl "BoBo" Olsen, Floyd Patterson, Sonny Liston, and Ingemar Johansson. Dad and Grandpa were really into these fights. They would sit with their butts barely on the sofa, both of them throwing half punches, bobbing and tightening their fists along with the fighters they watched. In particular, I remember Grandpa jumping up and spitting out his unlit cigar when Johansson knocked out Patterson."

Being a little girl when my grandpa was much older, my memories aren't as exciting as John's, although they are still very dear to me.

One of the few family pictures we have with Grandpa Gus. I'm on my brother John's shoulders. My brother Gregg in front, squinting. Michele is holding brother Marc, and Dad, far right.

I recall next door to the liquor store was a narrow restaurant called the Gateway Cafe. Each morning at the crack of dawn when my dad opened the Liberty Club, someone from the Greek-owned diner would hand-deliver him a nutritious hot breakfast. The small cafe had booths lined on either side against the walls with a skinny walkway between them. When I was maybe four or five years old Grandpa Gus, who always smelled of cigars, took me to the Gateway for a bite to eat. Everyone towered above me as Grandpa held my hand and gently sat me at one of the booths. I watched men walking over to shake his hand with jovial back-slapping and comments in a language I couldn't understand. Then he turned and gestured toward me, probably telling them I was Johnny's daughter. Even though I didn't know what was being said in that moment I instinctively knew Grandpa was an important man who everyone liked.

For the next decade his prized vegetable patch flourished in our side yard, packed with onions, garlic, corn, tomatoes, and much more, consumed by both our families. Even as his hair thinned and grayed, Gus continued to enjoy his relaxing garden. I vaguely recall him actually toiling with a hard-earned sweat, but then I was pretty young. What I remember well is the day of June 5, 1965.

As with any other sunshiny day, my brothers and I were outside doing what kids do best – getting dirty while playing with our Tonka trucks in the sandbox my father had built. All of a sudden I heard Grandpa cry out, and even though I don't recall running up the brick steps to the garden, I vividly remember him lying on his back in the corn stalks. As he lay grimacing, the lens of his wire-framed glasses reflected brightly in my eyes. I walked a little closer then froze, knowing something was terribly wrong. Gregg, who was nine at the time, hearing Gus yell his name in Greek had the good sense to tell our mother, who in turn called for an ambulance. My older brother is sure all three of us were in the sandbox at the time. Marc, born in '58, as young as he was recalled that day to the best of his recollection.

"I was very young but I do remember the day I was playing in the garden while Gus, my grandfather was working in the garden. I had my little red fire engine truck with me that I could get in and use my feet and legs to make it go. What I remember is Grandpa was lying on the ground near some tomato plants. Now the garden was on my dad's property where the apricot tree was. I remember him calling my name and when I walked up to him he told me to get help. Being a child, has to be the only reason for how I reacted to the situation for I proceeded to get in my red fire truck and head to Mame's home where I knew my mother was. So I went on my way, stopped so I could push the truck over the brick wall, then again into the emergency vehicle and off to Mame's home. I parked it next to the entry way to the front door and knocked on the door and the rest is history!"

As young as we were, our stories are going to be a little fuzzy, but the sad truth is Oroville lost a great man that day and we lost our grandpa. Just as John only saw Christiane on that horrible day, I don't remember anyone's face except Gus's, but I do recall seeing the old style ambulance pull away with him in it. It was a Saturday and my father was working at the Liberty Club. I'm sure he got someone to cover, even if it meant grabbing a customer to stand behind the bar. Fortunately, my mother and both my grandmothers were already home. This was to be my first encounter with death as Gus was rushed to Enloe Hospital in Chico and pronounced dead at 11:20am from a massive heart attack.

After having made his way to America and living his dream, Grandpa Gus died doing what he loved the most – tending to his garden. My siblings and I didn't attend the funeral, but I have since visited his grave many times. On the headstone it states, "Native of Greece" along with the spelling of his Greek name. With Grandpa being a proud Greek I'm glad my father included the personal touches of his birthplace and Gus's given name. Once again I found a discrepancy in a birth date. His headstone and last driver's license state he was born March 20, 1894. And yet a copy of his WWI and WWII draft notices show he was born December 23, 1888. So when he died he was 77 and not 71. This coincides with his age of 33 when he was married in 1921.

Gus and Angelica at the Linden house in front of their grape arbor.

Grandpa was driven to prosper, but had a giving side and was generous in helping family instead of hoarding his wealth. One day, for no apparent reason he gave my mother a five dollar gold piece. My mother told me he liked her and just gave it to her. His heart was always in the right place and I would have loved to have been old enough to know him better. I can still envision his old Cadillac parked across the street, Gus standing next to it wearing a wool jacket and gray slacks, fumbling through his keys. From what I've learned, his life was a balanced blend of family, friends, pleasure, and work, with a side dish of mistresses. I'm sure he was greatly missed and respected by fellow Greeks and non-Greeks alike. Rest in peace, Grandpa. I'm glad I got to know you a little better even though it's fifty years later.

Being children, I don't recall us grieving his loss, but I'm sure it was heart-wrenching for my father and grandma. We were busy filling in the rest of our summer vacation before September rolled around. When I started third grade my parents enrolled us into St. Thomas Catholic School where John and Michele had gone. In fact, they attended the school when it first opened in the fall of 1955. John told me he and dad and a lot of other volunteers had helped get the school ready after the contractors had done their jobs. There were windows to wash, paper to remove from beams, desks to set up. John was happy amongst the menfolk, being a part of the male bonding. It was also a good way to refocus their grief from the recent loss of Christiane.

I liked St. Thomas much better than Eastside, the public school we went to previously. When I was in the second grade there were a couple of mean fourth-grade girls who used to bully me. Both of these brats would grab one of my wrists and twist their hands back and forth making my forearms feel like they were on fire. When we were kids we called them "Indian burns," and they hurt like hell!. The fourth-graders were a lot bigger than me so to avoid their torture at lunch time, when the other kids in my class headed out to the cafeteria, I hid in the coat room. Listening intently until my teacher closed the door, I slowly and very happily crept from my hiding place. No one even noticed I was missing, except maybe my nemeses. There was a side door in the classroom that led to the street. I usually sat on the stoop where finally, I was able to eat my lunch in peace. Those kids really ruined that school for me.

This is me at my first Holy Communion in front of St. Thomas School. 1965

Since the teachers were less than helpful keeping them away, my mom decided Catholic school would be a safer environment. With our house a little over a mile away we either rode our bikes, walked, caught a ride with another parent, or took a cab. Most of the time we walked, except in the cold rainy weather. It was an adventure as we would take a shortcut and walk along a dirt ledge running parallel to the railroad tracks that took us down to the rails. Once in a while we'd have to stop for a train, which was exhilarating as a child. We always grouped together, and thinking back now, it was a very sweet time in our lives.

The cab rides were the worst. Since my mother never learned to drive and Dad worked days, it was necessary to call Yellow Cab Taxi as a last resort. There was a very heavy-set driver who usually drew the short straw to pick up the Aleck kids behind the high school. He was the largest man I had ever seen up to that point in my young life and his old Rambler leaned considerably toward the driver's side when he maneuvered himself behind the wheel. The fare was 50 cents and we always had the taxi driver drop us off a block ahead. Armed with umbrellas, it was better to brave the short distance, be it pouring rain or below freezing temperatures than to be thoroughly embarrassed showing up in such a fashion.

After Stephanie was born in '66, affectionately called "the Caboose" by my father, my mother, an avid walker, enjoyed pushing her stroller for daily strolls during sunny weather. Out of the blue, Mom and baby sister would be waiting for us at the stroke of three, and as a family we'd journey home chatting about our day while taking turns pushing the baby stroller. Most of the time though, when it was just Gregg, Marc, and myself, we'd walk the few blocks to the Liberty Club. There we were, me in my plaid uniform with blue, green, and golds, and two little boys wearing white button-down shirts with salt and pepper pants. Good little Catholic school-children walking along Oroville's skid row of the 60's.

The man we called Uncle Tom at my grandparents' side yard at the Linden house. From left to right my cousin Alford Harvey, John Jr., cousin Duane Harvey, and Michele. Notice the double garage doors to the right that led to where the grape crusher was kept. Autumn 1952

Along the way a scattering of men along Montgomery Street leaned against the buildings, usually a little soused, puffing on stogies, or just getting a little air. We were never afraid since they knew who we were and had great respect for our family. There was one aging gentleman we called Uncle Tom, even though there was no blood relation. He was very short, about five foot or less with gray hair and matching mustache. He always wore a dark suit with a vest and had a pocket watch tucked at the end of a chain. He had a subtle smell like the mustiness of the inside of an old drawer. Tom usually wore a round brimmed straw hat which I never saw on anyone else except my grandpa. He was a fellow Greek who was good friends with my grandparents, and lived upstairs in the rooming house helping Angelica with odd jobs. He knew our family well. If he was out on the street we'd always stop before reaching the bar to say hi and he'd talk to us with his thick Greek accent, sounding much like my grandfather.

What was really sweet is that he always gave us some of his loose change. He'd reach into his pocket and reveal nickels, liberty head dimes, and sometimes even quarters laid out in his worn weathered hand. We never asked, but he liked to give us each a coin and sometimes even a half dollar which brightened our eyes, because we knew it equaled tons of candy from the local five and dime. Uncle Tom was just a really nice old guy who I suppose had no family of his own, and we brought a little joy into his everyday life. Now, decades later, he brings a little joy into mine as I think of his kind gentle soul.

Once we made it to the bar my dad would greet us as if we hadn't seen each other in months. He'd shout a big, *"Hey, look who's here,"* while smiling and walking to the other end of the long bar. His customers would turn from their stools and give us all a wave of the hand and shout outs like, *"Hey, look! It's Johnny's kids,"* and from the women, *"Aren't they cute in their little uniforms?"* We felt very proud to be an Aleck, as though we owned the joint ourselves. Dad liked to joke with his patrons, calling us his little Freaks, because we were half French and half Greek. It always got a good laugh, with us saying, *"Oh Dad"* in embarrassment, but in reality each of us loved the corny name and the attention it brought. In fact, I proudly boasted to the kids at school I was a Freak and why, having pride in my European roots. Reaching the end of the counter we'd each get a soda which was usually a small bottle of 7-up or Coke, and a bag of chips or a Slim Jim, which I'd devour.

After our afternoon squeeze from Pops, we'd skedaddle next door to the liquor store. The storefront still had the 1940's architecture back then with large display windows on either side and about a two foot vertical tiled band below the glass. The entryway was laid with tiny one-inch square tiles in shades of light and dark brown. We'd run past the displays filled with stacked liquor bottles and enticing advertisements to quench your thirst, then push through the extra wide glass paneled wooden door, complete with brass handle. Mame was usually sitting behind the counter and greeted us with more smiles and grandmotherly hugs. I can still recall the fragrance of her lovely Estee Lauder scent as she'd hold us tight, giving out smooches on each cheek in true French style. Many times I noticed Mame with rosary in hand or the beads sitting on the lower counter just in reach while she took advantage of the idleness between customers. I wonder if she was praying for herself or the customers who frequented the store.

I loved playing in the old liquor store. In the back room there were boxes upon boxes of liquor stacked four and five feet tall. On the right-hand wall was a row of old wooden refrigerator uprights for sodas, beer, and wine with Mame's *fromage* and lunch meat stashed for an afternoon snack. On the other wall there was a small closet-sized bathroom with an even tinier round sink. Over the bathroom were creaky wooden steps that led to an upstairs narrow area covered in layers of dust. Being small we were able to crouch down through a crawl space that led to the front of the building with poorly painted widows overlooking the street below. Up there we were directly above the tiled entryway and spied on people walking up and down the sidewalk. It was even dirtier in this space and I remember feeling sad after finding a dead bird that had flown in, but couldn't find its way back out.

Johnny, when he worked as manager of the Liquor store.

The back storage room was a child's paradise playing chase round the boxed maze, or camouflaged in nooks for hide and seek, and even army with make believe Tommy guns. When we needed a rest we'd slow it down by hovering around Mame, or do silly things like try to count the dozens of liquor bottles displayed on long narrow shelves climbing the walls like steps. There were hundreds of bottles of vodka, gin, whisky, and the like covering two walls. The counter where Mame spent her days consisted of a wooden display case with a glass front and top. The old dovetail drawers held small bags of pipe and cigarette tobacco, Zig-

Zag papers, round cans of chew, lighter fluid, flints, match books, wooden matchstick boxes, and anything else one would expect to find for lighting up, including a small assortment of pipes. Other drawers had cases of cigarettes including Marlboro, Camel, Pall Mall, and Chesterfield. And yet another had aromatic wooden and hard cardboard boxes of cigars like King Edward Imperials.

Those were fun to look at as a kid but the true treasures lay in the compartments filled with juicy fruit, spearmint, and Bazooka bubble gum. Candy bars including Snickers, Milky Way, Almond Joy, Payday, Big Hunk, Hershey, and many more that packed the old drawers. My favorites were Almond Joy and Butterfingers, and naturally, we were able to pick one along with another soda if we were still thirsty. Many times I would just play nearby or sit with my grandmother. I'd watch, sitting in her office chair with legs dangling as she rang up bottles of booze on the old wooden cash register, counting back change in that wonderful foreign accent. A familiar accent that was never foreign in our household.

My grandmother in 1960.

After a little begging, our grandmother would give us each a nickel and we'd race to the front door again. Outside in the entryway to the right of the door sat a tall yellowish upright scale with a mirrored front. We'd stand at the foot, reaching high to feed it the nickel from Mame. I had to get on my tiptoes to read the sixty or so pounds I weighed back then. Checking our weight was only half the fun. The scale always spit out a generic fortune for the day. For us kids it was like digging for the prize in a Cracker Jacks box.

I was in the third grade at St. Thomas during '64-65, my last school year before Grandpa passed. During that time I remember Gus who I considered generally all-business, occasionally dropping by, but he never really talked to us kids. He and Mame would parley their business talk then he'd sit on her chair in front of the black safe with gold lettering behind the counter. Leaning forward he'd carefully turn the knob this way, click, click, click, then that click, click, until finally cranking the brass handle, swinging the heavy thick door open. Pulling out some rolled coins and bills he'd hand them to Mame and sometimes she'd hand him some money secured with a rubber band. He'd always count her bundle first then stack it with the others. Next he'd grab a small notepad filled with numbers, scribble down some more numbers then put it back in its place, closing the door with a turn of the handle and a spin of the dial. I didn't understand the business end, but always enjoyed watching my grandparents as they worked.

Around Easter, for many years my grandmother would put three silver dollars under a tissue so we couldn't see them. She would sit in her swivel chair while each of us took turns pointing to the coin we wanted. The last person would get whatever coin was left, but we didn't care, knowing it was still a silver dollar. After removing the tissue we'd each pick up our coin, beaming in smiles while comparing the dates, flipping them back and forth in admiration. In hindsight, I see how sweet it was for her to play this little game with us, and to this day I still have ten silver dollars, all given to me by my Mame.

My brothers and I, all dressed up for Easter. Me, Marc, and Gregg.

One of the small adventures my brothers and I used to go on with our dad was the occasional trip to the dump. It's not nearly as fun today as it was when we were kids. These days there's a large metal building where you drop your trash off while a frontloader pushes it around into piles. It's practically a sterile environment compared to when we were kids. Back then it was like landing on another planet where the 'dump people' lived.

After our big yard clean-up where Dad trimmed bushes and cut small tree branches, us kids helped by dragging the cuttings to his truck. Johnny took over from there by tossing them into the bed, then tying the heaping load down, checking it twice. Mom stayed behind, happy, I'm sure, to have the house to herself as Gregg, Marc, and I piled into the cab of Dad's Ford pickup. Once on the outskirts of town we'd gently weave along the narrow Pacific Heights road shaded by hundred-year-old oaks and overgrown scrub trees. At first the smell of the nearing dump mildly wafted throughout the cab, but as the funk grew stronger us little ones would pinch our noses, saying *"pee-yew,"* then gasp dramatically and squeal, *"I can't breathe,"* with anticipated giggling.

Reaching our destination, Dad turned onto a dirt road as our family entered the 'dump people' zone. I swear it was home to displaced kin-folk from the movie Deliverance. Their tiny *houses* tucked under scrawny tree canopies were thrown-together shacks made from discarded plywood and sheet metal. This was where I learned the meaning of, *"One person's trash is another man's treasure."* Piles of rubbish lined both sides as we crept slowly through no-man's land. The opening was just wide enough for two cars to pass one another while Dad scanned the area for the perfect spot. He'd maneuver the truck, backing her up like a pro. At the end of the garbage trail was a wider turn-around area similar to a cul de sac, so you never had to back all the way out. Once he shut off the engine the fun began as we shoved open the door and scampered out like piglets to a mud hole.

Not yet in my teens, I was afraid of the 'dump people'. They looked like they hadn't bathed in months. Their clothes were drab and dirty, covered in dark smudges that matched their faces. I don't think they brushed their hair. I could tell their teeth were rotten or missing when I saw them laughing and talking with each other. I never saw them talk to the *'new arrivals,'* such as we were. Checking out our pile of branches they continued picking through a fresh collection of trash since ours was worthless to them. But sometimes our mother would get it in her head to throw out a bunch of our old toys, or bikes, or whatever she considered junk. Recycling wasn't a *thing* back then. That'd bring a scary smile to the 'dump people's' otherwise blank stares. I'd watch as they'd pick through our fresh gems even as Dad was tossing them out. After a load had been picked clean, what was left was set on fire and tended to by the 'dump people' with wide-tooth metal rakes, shovels, and hoes. There were many smoldering heaps all around us with a powerful punch-of-a-smell I can still recall to this day. The smoke was omnipresent. I swear the stink stuck to our clothes and nose hairs, 'cause I could still smell it even after we got home.

After the back was unloaded, Dad would pull the Ford forward a little. I was the first to scramble to the rear of the truck-bed and grab the broom. I loved sweeping out the dirt and leaves left behind. When I wasn't even as tall as an upright scoop shovel, our Pops used to clean the back patio and I'd hold the handle of the huge spade as he swept the dirt from around the wood pile into it. I remember him saying, *"Whatever you do in life, you gotta do it 100%, even if it's just sweeping the floor."* I think that's why I always tried to grab the broom first. After Dad closed the tailgate, we all jumped back onto the bench seat in the cab as fast as we could, slamming the door shut. The place was swarming with flies and there was always a couple that'd sneak in to hitch a ride with us back home. As my dad drove slowly along the burnt mounds, I'd see those 'dump people', rakes in hand, staring back at our tiny faces pressed against the rolled up window. They really were a creepy bunch, but I always felt safe with Dad by our side.

With a cluster of children to care for any help my mother could get was much appreciated. My dad's shirts and pants had to be ironed and usually starched since this was before wash and wear came into play. My dad hired a kind lady who took care of this for his wife. After the clothes were washed and dried my mother stuffed them into a pillowcase, which to me seemed counter-productive, only adding more wrinkles. Us kids would pile into Dad's old Cadillac or Mercury and take the short drive to the south side of town. In those days you didn't see many black people or other ethnic races in downtown Oroville. Except for some of the janitors at the high school, I do believe this was my first introduction to the black community with much of the neighborhood in the South Side being dark-skinned. As when my dad was a child living on C Street, the community wasn't annexed to the city of Oroville. With sidewalks non-existent, many rundown houses, and yards overgrown with tall weeds, it was clear to me the people living in the area didn't have a lot of money.

Sometimes we'd stay in the car, but most often we would tag along with dad as he carried the over-stuffed pillowcase and a hefty handful of wire and wooden hangers to the quaint little home. Once inside, it was noticeably smaller than our house with an ironing board set up in the living room. I never knew the name of the woman who did the ironing but my dad always referred to her as the "colored lady." The term African American or Black had yet to be born. She and my dad laughed and joked together, and in retrospect, with her being close to the age of my Greek grandparents, they probably knew each other from when Johnny was a boy. There was usually a candy dish somewhere in her living room and she'd offer us some, fussing about how cute we were and how big we were getting. She was portly and jolly and I never saw her without an apron or a big ole gummy smile since she had no teeth. I liked going to see her even though I was very shy, and usually clung to my dad's pant leg. Today I recognize the "colored lady" had good energy, and for a wee one with my upbringing, she was different from anyone I had ever met.

As we got a little older the High School across the street became our extended playground. We rode our bikes all through the campus and I chipped a front tooth while racing one day, hitting a tree then nose-diving into my butterfly handlebars face first. We also enjoyed borrowing our dad's ski rope for a little street surfing adventure. One end would be tied to the sissy bar on the back of my bike and someone would hold the other end while balancing on an old time narrow wooden skateboard. Then the person on the bike would peddle like crazy and pull the skateboarder down Linden Avenue. We didn't wear helmets or pads, but somehow we survived.

We played all the sports, including football, baseball, and basketball. There were several outdoor basketball hoops set up by the PE department where we would play some one-on-one or HORSE. In the grassy area was a softball diamond equipped with an old wooden backstop with chicken and goat wire. Marc was notorious for hitting the "longball," or home run, and must have broken at least a half dozen windows on the old boys' gym a good hundred and fifty feet away. The field was big enough for us little ones to play touch or tackle football, and we'd get the neighborhood gang together, playing games worthy of the Super Bowl. Staying out till dusk we only came a-runnin' when our mother stood at the grassy edge outside our house and yelled as loud as she could in that sweet French accent, "DINNER." Ah, to have those days back again.

We always slept with our windows wide open in the hot summer months. That's when Oroville's temperatures reach triple digits, barely cooling in the evening. Living less than a 1/2 mile from the train depot, in the quiet, stillness of the star-scattered skies, every night a lone whistle could be heard blowing in the distance. As it neared, the roar of the powerful engines grew louder. It wasn't close enough to rattle our windows, yet as we lie contently in our beds after a long hard day at play, the hum of that slow moving train with its whistle blasts was a familiar soothing melody to us kids, providing comfort food for our tired little souls as we drifted off to sleep.

Mom was an avid bridge player when we were kids. So much so, she even taught us little ones how to play so there was always a foursome available at home. Her bridge club took turns hosting their games amongst its players. When it was our mom's turn we'd help her set up two card tables with eight chairs in the living room. In the kitchen a fresh pot of Yuban coffee percolated in the slender shinny coffee maker. A tray of homemade cookies made our young mouths water, but Mom always made plenty so she could set some aside for her family. The real temptation was a more decadent dessert chilling in the refrigerator, like strawberry cream pie, or a layered Jello dish.

When the bridge players arrived it felt like an invasion as they chatted their way to the coffee cups, filled napkins with dainty cookies, and wound their way toward the card tables before finding their seats. Decks were shuffled and as the dealer dealt, a hush fell upon the room while the ladies re-arranged and studied their cards. It bordered on eerie as the women silently counted their points, and then suddenly, as if orchestrated, "One diamond, two spades, three no-trump," --- the bidding had begun.

Gregg, myself, and Marc goofing off on the ivy hedge in our back yard. No computers or iPhones needed when we were kids. Mid 1960's

The gals came prepared for the long evening with packs of Virginia Slims and Salem cigarettes as their survival gear. Even though my parents were non-smokers they kept a stack of ashtrays in the house for those who were. In the '60's, smokers trumped all, smoking wherever and whenever they wished. The rest of the world accommodated their habit, never giving it a second thought. Even if it was 40 degrees outside, on game night, our windows were wide open, beckoning the fresh air to enter.

My brothers and I were supposed to be in bed, but instead we used to sneak down the hallway in our PJ's, hugging the wall, getting as close as we could to hear the gossip being spread. They only talked between hands, and as the evening wore on their laughter was unbridled. They must have forgotten us little ones were *trying* to sleep. It was an exciting night for us youngsters watching the grown-ups hard at play, until one of the ladies would spy us on her way to the powder room.

My brothers and I played all the sports, including tug o' war, with me as the rope. Gregg on left - Marc on right, at the Grand View house- 1960's.

The next morning the house smelled like the Liberty Club. I helped my mother empty the stinky ashtrays, pick up lipstick smeared coffee cups, snack on the cookies, fold card-tables, and drag back the dining room chairs to their usual spots. The windows were still wide open as my mother, like clockwork, whipped out her trusty can of Lysol.

Hanging around my big brother was a little different. We soon learned being an Aleck meant you donned a pair of boxing gloves at least once in your life. As a teenager, brother John took it upon himself to introduce Gregg, then nine or ten, and myself, around seven or eight, to backyard pugilism. Marc was too young. John taught us how to bob and weave, jab, throw straight or overhand rights and cover if we got stung with a hard shot. He did this by beating the heck out us, playfully. Then, he had Gregg and I spar for technique. When he felt we could defend ourselves he had his high school buddies come over with their kid brothers and have little impromptu boxing matches. They even bet six packs on who would win. Egged on by the teenagers, the battles lasted until someone quit or John broke it up. Well Gregg had three fights and won all three. I was the only girl and had three matches total, winning two decisively and the third was a draw. John Jr. called it before I ended up with a bloody nose or black eye so he wouldn't have to explain to our parents. Yep, those were fun days and I can still throw a punch. John won a lot of beer.

Feeling his oats one day my oldest brother threw down the gauntlet to see which Greek was top dog as he challenged the old man to slip on a pair of gloves. *"Hardest I ever got hit was from Papa. Boy, I saw stars, and that was with gloves on. I was peppering him and he stepped on my foot! I had the reach on him and I was just peppering him. He couldn't break through my defense so he just stepped on my foot and knocked me right into a bush. We were boxing out in the back yard and I was in high school. I won golden gloves, okay – I wasn't half bad. I had been in a lot of boxing matches and had been hit hard many times, but none as hard as Dad's. I was never knocked off my feet until Dad threw that punch. I was about 5'10" and weighed 150 pounds back then. Weight-wise, we were about the same, but I was a little taller. He just decked my ass!"*

Big brother, in his late teens, loved taking us younger kids hunting. I had bought a 12-gauge shotgun from Aunt Bess's second husband Ken when I was about eleven or twelve. We only hunted dove and jack rabbits, but Gregg had ventured on to deer as he got a little older, eventually trading his gun for a camera. On one outing I shot and killed a jack that was within fifteen feet from where I stood. It let out a loud cry as it was dying. Up to that point it hadn't really dawned on me that I was killing living breathing creatures. I walked over to the rabbit, now dead, and felt tears roll down my checks. I never shot that gun again and sold it shortly afterward.

On one of those occasions, Gregg accidentally left a dead rabbit in the back of the pickup. He was going to throw it out, but Grandma, who was outside, told him it would make a good dinner. Handing it over, she proceeded to slowly waddle to our back yard, placing the rabbit on our old wooden picnic table. With just her bare hands she started gutting it right there tossing the innards on a newspaper my dad had laid out. I think I gagged a few times, but was so mesmerized I couldn't walk away. Then she took the furless, gutless bunny and snapped off the hind and front quarters so it would fit better in the pot. Even though our family enjoyed a good cottontail and noodle dish prepared by our mother, none us kids were having any part of this meal. The next evening, Angelica, and son Johnny were the only ones brave enough to partake of her jackrabbit stew. The rest of us probably ate meatloaf.

Grandma Aleck brought many of the old ways with her to this new world. When I was very young, one afternoon my dad was lying in bed very sick with a horrible deep cough, fever, and no energy. He asked his wife to tell his mother because she would know what to do. With my mom and brothers and I gathered around in the bedroom, Grandma entered the room with something wrapped in a towel and set it to one side. After a few moments diagnosing my dad's illness, she instructed mom and us little ones to get some cotton balls, glasses, and matches. With that she proceeded to take one cotton ball at a time, spit on them, and then secure the moistened cotton ball to the inside bottom of a short fat high-ball glass. We had given Grandma the long wooden matches my dad used to light fires in our fireplace. While my dad lay on his stomach, she lit the match and caught the cotton ball on fire. As soon as it was burning Grandma quickly turned the glass upside down and placed it on my father's back. With no oxygen the flame was extinguished on contact leaving the glass filled with smoke, and when the smoke cleared my eyes bugged as I saw the suction had created what looked like a big reddish boil on my dad's back. As very young children we were given a glimpse into old world Greece and stood silent in utter amazement. She continued this process all over his back, and when finished, removed all the glasses, leaving perfectly round 1/2 inch raised "boils." I found out later there is a variation of this practice today called cupping therapy.

With his back covered in circles my dad rolled over onto his back while Grandma flipped open the corners of the towel she had brought and revealed something called a mustard pack. It was a folded yellowed towel that contained a concoction of herbs and dry mustard passed down through the ages. She secured the pungent pack against my dad's chest, then leaning down and speaking in their native tongue, gently tucked him in as though he was a small child again.

The next morning it was like a miracle. My dad's fever broke, and he was up with our family having breakfast. Had I not seen it with my own eyes I may not have believed it possible, but I am so glad I was present to witness this strange yet healing phenomenon.

Barbara, the gal who had worked in the salon, shared one more story about Mama Aleck regarding her home remedies. *"I had been in a boating accident. My water ski flew off me and slammed down on my leg. I could hardly walk, so Mama Aleck wanted to put leeches on it to suck the blood. No way was I going to let her. Instead, I settled for chopped onions in a huge bandage around my leg. They sent me home in a taxi. Well, the other customers said I stunk, and for the driver to take me home first. Believe me, the onions took the pain right away. But I smelled like onions forever. She had all kinds of remedies."*

I had to wonder where my grandmother would have found leeches.

For the Alecks, the '60's was a wonderful time~

Chapter 21

LOUISE - RIVER RATS - AND GRANDMA

After graduating from high school in '65 Johnny Jr. enlisted in the U.S. Air Force, on July 4, 1966 starting his own life's journey stationed half way around the world in Germany. It made me think of our father's words as he patrolled the streets of Frankfurt; believing the bombed remains caused by the Allies would never be rebuilt after the destruction the Nazis had wreaked during his younger years. Two decades later, those devastated by the holocaust were still healing while much progress had been made toward reconciliation.

Living in Europe, John had the good fortune to visit our great-grandmother Louise, now in her early eighties and in failing health. John made the journey to the South of France as Grand Mame` MeMille had continued to live in Nice with her daughter's financial help. Being the first born, Jojo's command of the French language was much better than the rest of ours. It came in handy as great-grandmother and great-grandson spent a good three or four days catching up on family tales. Even though she was being cared for in a nursing home, Louise's mind was still clear and she was aware of who John was from her quick visit back in the 1950's. It must have been such a wonderful and unexpected surprise for Madame Wacker to have her oldest great-grandson a visitor after all those years.

About a year after their visit my brother received a phone call through the Red Cross, advising him to call his parents. My mother gave John the sad news that Grand Mame` MeMille had passed away. It was the end of an era as our great-grandmother Louise Wacker Stoll passed in her slumber on January 25, 1968. Having experienced life through two world wars she lived the next two decades without the comfort of her daughter, granddaughters, or great-grandchildren. Even though Louise and Simone, mother and daughter had a strained relationship, I know there was love in their hearts. One can only hope that over time all was forgiven. I think Simone finally realized her mother had the best of intentions for her when she insisted on the arranged marriage with someone who she thought was a strong capable man to take care of her only daughter. What Louise wasn't aware of is that her daughter was ahead of her time, and was perfectly capable of taking care of herself.

I have pictures of Louise with family members from my grandfather Jean's side. Some are taken in the cemetery in Nonancourt where her parents' and husband's remains lie in their crypts. Her extended family, although not blood related, looked after Louise in her senior years and kept in close contact after her daughter had moved to the states. My grandmother, mother, and aunt continued to write letters and catch up with holiday phone calls.

My great-grandmother Louise, center, surrounded by family at the cemetery.

Louise with Jean Andre's cousin Marie Therese and her husband Jean at the Basilica of St. Thérèse, Lisieux in France. 1963

A very sweet picture and maybe one of the last of Grand Mame` MeMille.

My brother was blessed to have attended her funeral on our behalf. Her remains were brought back to Nonancourt where she was laid to rest in the same crypt with her husband Emile. In my research I was able to contact the only cemetery in Nonancourt, giving them information about my ancestors. They were kind enough to take pictures of the two crypts and email them to me. I showed them to my mother and even though she was very young at the time, she remembered going there when Sebastien and Emile had passed. Louise Alexandrine Stoll Wacker was 83 when she joined her beloved husband Emile once again.

For some, life as we know it was ending, while for others a new chapter had begun. With Colette's good looks, naive nature, and beautiful French accent, it's a wonder she still hadn't married. She told me that when she first came to Oroville my dad had set her up on a double blind date with the only Frenchman he knew. Tata, as we affectionately called our aunt, said that although he meant well, it was disastrous. She had zero desire to get to know this stranger whom she considered a "smooth operator," and her actions that evening showed it. I'll bet my parents had a good laugh as Colette's facial expressions would have been priceless. Fate has a way of working things out as the liquor store would have its advantages. There was an older gentleman who would stop by to purchase a bottle here and there of his favorite spirit. It wasn't long before he struck up a conversation with Colette, eventually asking her out. Joe was in the construction trade and worked on the Oroville Dam project. The fact that he was Catholic and attended the same church, St. Thomas, made him acceptable in Simone's eyes.

After a short courtship Colette and Joe Huston married on September 22, 1962. For the first time in her life my aunt, just shy of her 34th birthday, ventured from her mother's nest to build her own. Within the year Joe found a better paying job in Chico where the pair moved and eventually bought a house. Eleven months after their marriage, Colette gave birth to my cousin, Trisha, an only child.

With extended family. Back row left to right, my cousin Trisha being held by Simone, Joe Huston with wife Colette, Monique in very back, and Angelica far right. Front row, Gregg, Marc, Mary-Jo (Joe's niece), and me making a face. Easter of 1964

While Colette was getting to know her husband, Monique found herself a weekend beach warrior as our father found a way for the family to beat the summer heat taking our family practically every weekend to the sandy beaches of the Feather River. Dad had been eyeing an early 1950's 16-foot wooden inboard Mercury that the Burks family owned, but could only afford half the asking price of $1,200. Big brother John, who had been saving from summer jobs, stepped up and lent our dad the other half. With that, we became a boating family as my dad proudly christened his new toy Big Bad John. The Chris Craft looking vessel and our family became regular fixtures on the Feather River while my older siblings and father thoroughly enjoyed slalom skiing on the water's glistening surface.

Brother John and Dad with our boat "Big Bad John"

Mom really was a good sport considering she never learned how to swim, yet being a dedicated mother and wife, automatically prepared salads, baked beans, and fried chicken for all. I can still remember dad dumping ice over the goodies packed in a large silver ice chest. When I think back, planning and preparing all that food, plus rounding up us kids took an extra dose of parenting skills.

Monique sporting cat-eyed sunglasses with our Caddie in the background. June 1963

Admittedly at the age of seven, I wasn't a fan of being pulled behind a powerful boat while trying to balance on two skittish skis. Having to wear glasses since second grade, I'd leave my pair on the shore with my mother so they wouldn't get lost. As a result, I was never able to clearly see the hand signals from the boat tender which added to my lack of confidence. I was always amazed I didn't drown, with each fall bringing me a nose full of water, so finally, three summers later at the ripe age of ten I declared to my father it was time to hang up my skis for good. Fortunately he was just fine with my decision, and had I known, I would have quit much earlier, but I had feared he might be disappointed in me. By my father allowing me to sway from his joy of skiing, I learned at a young age just how blessed I was to have such a fair and loving dad. From then on I enthusiastically took on the responsible roll of boat tender, and felt special as I rode shotgun with my father at the wheel. I guess one could say I was a daddy's girl.

Me, getting ready to ski on doubles before I decided to call it quits. My bathing suit was red and the water-skis were red and white. Mid 1960's

My father, on the other hand, took to the water so well that he and my mother became members of the Oroville Boat Club. For a couple of years Dad was the commodore of the club and we still have his red and white boat club jacket from the sixties. He was heavily involved in organizing the yearly drag boat races the club put on before the construction of the Oroville Dam disrupted the water flow. I still have old snapshots of some of the boats that sat in a parking area while waiting their turn. One boat was a root-beer brown hydroplane named WhoFarted and then later, WhoFarted II, which as a kid, made me giggle. There was always an immense turnout to watch these high-performance flat-bottom boats scream across the sparkling blue waters. The quick burst of power as they sat idling at the starting line echoed along the river's banks. When the flag dropped I covered my ears from the high-pitched SCREAM of the jet engines as they sped past with throttles wide open. Each run was exhilarating and I still remember the overwhelming smell of specially blended fuel that filled the air.

Having been a radio man, my dad borrowed a bunch of old Army issue portable radio/phones from the local armory. They had a black hand-piece that slid inside a small heavy narrow square box that was covered on the outside with an Army green canvas, and wide sturdy matching strap to carry it over your shoulder. The weight was due to the large batteries stored inside so they could be used without wires. Keep in mind, this was before the digital age of Nextel and cell phones. On the top were knobs and buttons only my dad understood. Prior to race day these old Army radios were stored at our house and us kids used to play with them, pretending we were soldiers, just like our dad.

Unfortunately there were two horrible accidents that left their mark on all those who were there that day. One was the complete disintegration of a speed boat named Citation. The driver, Renee Andre miraculously lived with only slight paralysis to one of his arms and later went on to race Citation II. The other was the Cobra in which the driver John Lawson was not so fortunate. After breaking the record of over 200 miles per hour, just at the finish line his boat went airborne flipping high into the air then splashed down hard on the water's surface. My dad and others, positioned in a boat just for such emergencies, took off in haste praying the driver was okay. Sadly, there would be no rescue that day as Johnny grabbed hold of the limp driver by his life jacket and with help, pulled his lifeless body into the boat. It was an eerie day as all of a sudden the sky filled with black clouds followed by crackling thunder, lightning, and an ominous downpour.

Through the sixties and into the seventies, many of the members of the Oroville Boat Club had become more like family than good friends. The building of the Oroville Dam put a stop to boating on the Feather altogether, but the club still met for an annual delicious meal at Table Mountain Tavern. Big Bad John would still take the Aleck clan on excursions around the lake and Loafer Creek, but it wasn't the same. A group of families within the club became known as the Red Mountain Gang, self-named for the cheap Carlos Rossi wine they liked to drink. Our family was a part of this fun-loving bunch of partiers. Gatherings at one another's houses was a common occurrence, I suppose in much the same way the Greeks came together for good times. All would pitch in, helping the others with weddings, baby showers, and even in times of crisis. These families became an extension of our own, and to this day, I feel like the other kids in this group are more like cousins and siblings instead of just friends.

My high school years came as the seventies rolled around. Grandpa Gus had planted about six Mission olive trees near the street back in the 1930's at his house on Linden. I'm sure the fruit from these trees was put to good use in their heyday, but when my grandparents had grown older the olives would turn from green to purple and eventually fall, leaving black stains on the street and sidewalk below. Other high school kids used to pick the olives off the street or from the trees and have olive fights, throwing them at each other. Whenever I saw this I would yell at them to knock it off. It would enrage me to see the disrespect they had for other people's property, especially because these were my grandparents' trees and I felt protective.

If Grandma was outside at the time she'd take it a step further as my brother Gregg recalled. *"Grandma Aleck used to turn the hose directly on the kids. She was a formidable woman! One time when I was a junior or senior I saw her stomping across the quad, dragging about 12 ft. of garden hose during school hours. I have no idea who she was looking for and I didn't stick around to find out."*

There were a few years when Angelica went out in the cool autumn season with a metal bowl in hand and picked the ripe olives within reach. At four foot eleven, her selection was limited. I saw her doing this one day and decided to join. Grandma was wearing one of her dark-colored dresses that day, and as we sat on her short concrete retaining wall, she used her dress as a makeshift basket. Taking the olives from the pan she dumped them into her dress. Grandma's concentration was intense. I could hear her heavy breathing and the occasional licking of lips as she used a paring knife to make four precision slits into each olive, then place them back in the metal pan. It wasn't long before her fingers turned purple from the juice. I tried a few cuts myself and found out it wasn't so easy. The olives were pretty small, and being uncured, were hard to cut through. She always cured several jars, and to this day I have never tasted a better blend. I treasure this memory of us together as I have very few recollections of spending one-on-one time together.

I think one reason we didn't get real close to Grandma was because she still lived as in the old country and didn't bathe all that often. She ate a lot of garlic and onions and had a distinct odor about her. Pungent is the word that comes to mind, although there were times when she wasn't that bad, especially outdoors, and if there was a breeze blowing in the right direction. As children and teenagers it was difficult to see past this. Mom didn't care for her coming over to the house due to her hygiene, or lack thereof, and would whip out a can of Lysol right after she left. Many times Monique even went so far as to lock the front door when she saw her slowly crossing the street toward ours. I stood about a head above the windowsill back then and she'd tell my brothers and I to hide, telling us to shush with her finger to her lips. As young as we were, it was more like a game of hide-and-go seek as we'd sit below the window doing our best not to giggle too loud. We'd hear the knock on the door and our eyes would widen as we covered our mouths. After a few minutes one of us would peer over the top of the sill to see Grandma, now much heavier than in her youth, stroll ever so slowly back home.

Today it pains me to think of what a lonely dejected walk that was. My mother had her reasons, as she and Angelica had a strained relationship ever since I can remember. Mom had always felt that both Gus and Angelica had taken advantage of her husband's loyalty to family and his strong work ethics. I was told my grandparents dangled the proverbial carrot in front of my father, promising year after year to make him part owner of the Liberty Club. But the truth is they never did. It was the money made during it's heyday, when Monique saw her husband put in twelve hour days, even working on Saturdays, that she felt he should have had a part interest in. As a result, Monique resented her in-laws, while doing her best to look out for her own husband and family. She was also aware Nick's umbilical cord was still connected when it came to the thousands of dollars Angelica fed to him through the years. Money she knew was made by her husband's dedication as the consummate bartender. Yes, there was friction. The untidiness of my Greek grandmother's house and her old-country way of living was another reason my mother barely tolerated her husband's mother. Monique even mentioned something about a curse Angelica had placed upon her when she was pregnant with one of us children. At any rate, as I said, my mother had her reasons.

I don't remember Angelica being an affectionate grandmother. In fact, I don't recall ever getting hugs, kisses or cards on our birthdays, but I know she loved us because she loved her son. When I was a teenager I went to her house and visited her a couple of times and asked about our family tree. It was difficult to be in her living room due to the prevailing odor that filled the room. I had a notebook and wrote a bunch of hard to spell names down, but through the years those pages have long since been lost. I know now I was still too young to appreciate the rich history she accumulated throughout her life. I didn't know to ask questions about her life in Greece or that of her parents. I didn't think to ask what it was like when she came to America, or living during the depression. I had the time, but never thought to ask the right questions.

My dad and his mother would chat from time to time, visiting in the street after he'd come home from work or on weekends. On many occasion I would stand with them just to listen since they always spoke in Greek. I found it very intriguing to hear the harsh enunciation of their native tongue, though I didn't have a clue as to what they were saying. My dad would do his best to help me make that guttural Greek sound, but my vocal chords were far too pasteurized to take on a second language as challenging as theirs.

I spoke with my cousin Alford, Aunt Joy's son, about our Greek grandmother and he shared this story from when he was about ten. The year would have been around 1958 and the setting, the Oro Vista.

"I was up there with my brother Duane for some reason, not sure what, and some guy soiled his bed. I mean, it was really a mess. Grandma was yelling at him in Greek so I don't know what she was saying but I know it wasn't good. She grabbed him by the back of the neck and led him to the stairs. He was still drunk and having trouble walking. When they got to the staircase she threw him down, still yelling at him in Greek. I don't know if you remember those stairs but they're pretty steep. Then she looked at me and my brother and waving her finger, said, "You don't see nothing." After that we ran down the stairs past the guy and got the hell out of there. I never saw him around again."

It was my brother Marc who found our grandmother. *"I was a junior in high school. I remember I was home getting ready to leave the house for my U.S. History class when Dad called and said he couldn't get a hold of his mother. Dad asked me to get the key to Angelica's home which was located by the door near the garden. When I opened the door Grandma was laying on her left side on the couch near her phone with the lamp light still on. Her feet were still in the sitting position. I knew something was not right, and when I touched her she was cold with no response. I went back across the street and called Dad to give him the bad news. By now I was late for class and I remember how difficult it was for me to knock on the classroom door so I could tell my teacher what happened. I was teared up pretty bad. I must have reported what happened to the main office because I did not attend school the rest of the day. I do remember when I got home Dad was already across the street. When I went to see him I could tell he had been crying."*

I can't even imagine what it must have been like for my brother and father to have found Angelica in such a state. My dad was a very caring son, making sure her needs were met, be it goods from the grocery store or just one-on-one visiting time. Especially after Gus had passed. Even though I signed the guest book, which I found while emptying my parents closet, I don't recall going to her funeral. It's a total blank except for the mental images of people dressed in black showing up to our house carrying casseroles and side dishes. In a leaflet that was also in my parents' closet, I read that Father John Angelis from the same Greek Orthodox church she and her husband had been married in officiated the graveside service. She was laid to rest beside Gus and across from her brother-in-law Tom and son Nick. One fairly large headstone is shared by both my grandparents.

With Angelica's passing, my dad became the sole proprietor of the Liberty Club. The convenient Oroville Liquor store closed its doors for the last time, and the liquor license was sold along with its inventory. I don't know who got the money, but I know it wasn't my dad; although I did hear a rumor from an older gentleman who knew our family. He said, *"Your grandmother gave the liquor store to your uncle Nick before she died. Boy, your dad was mad! Real mad!"* With the pampering that went on between Grandma and my uncle, it wouldn't surprise me one bit if she had. Apparently Bess had been cut out of the will because Don had threatened to sue Gus over the barber shop/salon business. Gus had paid for all the furnishings and my uncle had the nerve to sue. Not sure if he ever did, but I know Gus would have won. Grandpa's will had never been revised so Bess was out of luck. Although Joy said that "Mama" told her she had some bonds stashed away, and upon Gus's passing in '65, Grandma cashed them in, giving some of the funds to Bessie.

Besides the liquor store, the Oro Vista Rooming house was closed for good. I have just a few memories of the Oro Vista rooming house from when I was very young. My grandmother had a room in the front that for years she had shared with her husband. I can still recall most of the rooms being occupied back in the sixties, but I didn't feel right wandering too far from her view. From its glory days, beginning in 1914, by the seventies, the Oro Vista had become a flop house of sorts. Just a handful of tenants still stumbled up and down the precarious staircase. Grandma had turned over the management duties to a one-handed guy by the name of Jim Bennett, with a pot belly and balding hair, who also managed the liquor store after it was relocated to the corner two doors down in the same Washington Block building it was already in. At one time Gus and Mr. Damon owned the historic building together that still sits on the corner of Myers and Montgomery. My grandparents' law-breaking side gig employing prostitutes had ended years before. It was time for the last stragglers to take their leave of the Oro Vista, since my father had no interest in keeping the doors open.

After Grandma died, the interior of the rooming house remained untouched for several years except for the addition of layers of dust and pigeon droppings. Behind the locked door at the bottom of the staircase, each room still had the original dressers from the 1920's, 30's and 40's. During the 80's, my mother had many of the old chests refinished and gave them to us kids. With money tight, she worked out a deal where she bartered many of them to have others restored.

An old oak roll top desk and swivel chair still sat near the top of the stairs that served as their front office while they had a small room in the back as their official office. I imagine great-grandpa Stefanis spent a great deal of time at that old desk when renting out rooms to fellow Greeks. In the desk I found an old black tin box with thin stripes around it that

I've seen in old movies. There was an envelope from George Gilmore addressed to his brother Gus written in beautiful script. I doubt it was his handwriting. It was post-marked September 15, 1930 with a two-cent stamp affixed in the corner. Too bad there was no letter inside. On top of the desk and propped against the wall was a board with room numbers and at least fifty assorted skeleton keys hanging from hooks. Far more keys than the sixteen rooms. I left the board and decided to keep the keys.

Sadly, my father sold the old desk much to Gregg's dismay. My brother told me there was still a lot of history in the form of letters and ledgers packed in those drawers that were left behind. I wish I had thought to look through them and salvage what I could. They were probably tossed out as rubbish by the new owners. It's really a shame dad sold it before Gregg could save the irreplaceable treasures that would have shed a little more light on our grandparents' lives.

Brass spittoons still sat at various locations with no one wanting to touch them. A sign was tacked to the wall that read, *"Please don't spit on the floor."* Gregg kept that. Soiled mattresses atop old box springs were eventually tossed, and I imagine the heavy metal rails and headboards found new homes in antique stores, or more likely at the city dump. With the Oro Vista Rooming House having been such a huge part of my great-grandfather's and grandparents' lives it's really sad to see what became of the old place. Especially now that I have learned so much more about their lives. Just as people have a life span, I believe the same holds true for businesses. When Grandma drew her final breath, the Oro Vista Rooming House also exhaled its last.

Now that I have become acquainted with Grandma's years in America, I think she had a good life. It was completely different than that of her sister's back in Greece, but I doubt she would have wanted to trade places with Anastasia. My grandmother did fall in love with Gus and the ease they felt around each other is evident in a picture I have of the pair in their elder years. They're sitting at their small kitchen table the way I remember them. I would think after her husband passed, the will to live may have slipped by a little at a time. My cousin Lydia, Alford's sister, lived with our Grandma for about ten months when she was a teenager. There was a warm loving side to Grandma as Lydia shared this moment with me.

Grandma and Grandpa at their kitchen in the Linden house. Early 1960's

"I remember fixing an old record-radio player while living with her. There were some old Greek records and other songs that she asked me to play. She was smiling and also had tears. It was a poignant scene and memory. I think she had a lot of depth to her that was not as visible on the surface. She was probably missing Gus and her homeland at the time. I do know she sent money to her sister in Greece for her family at times. When I see pictures of

where she came from I can see why she would miss it. It is a very beautiful place on the Aegean Sea."

I was happy to learn that during the late 1940's and 50's Angelica had traveled back to Greece to visit her sister Anastasia and husband Spyros. I have a picture of grandma with her three nephews, Anastasia's sons. The nephew's sister, Eleni or Helen in English, was already living in Oroville by then. The photo came in handy when through Helen's daughter we were able to contact our second cousin living in Athens, Greece. She was suspicious about who this American was that was contacting her. I emailed the picture of Grandma with her nephews, proving that indeed we were related since one of the nephews in the photo is her father. I have since stayed in touch with her brother.

My only wish is that I would have had the foresight to have gotten to know my grandmother better. In my rather mundane life, I now know hers was fascinating, but I'm sure to her, as with my father, it was just her life and no big deal. The death certificate stated, as with Gus, his wife had died from a massive heart attack. With her son Nick having passed just two and a half months earlier, I wondered if Grandma didn't die from a broken heart. Nick was always a mama's boy. Being alone, I do hope it was quick and relatively painless.

Angelica Stefani Aleck, born July 17, 1900, deceased March 11, 1976. Although her headstone says she was born in 1900, the fact that she was 23 years old in 1921 tells me she was actually born in 1898 and passed at the age of 78. Some day we will meet again, and be reacquainted forever.

Angelica Stefani Aleck

Chapter 22

THE LIBERTY CLUB

Everyone in Oroville knew where the Liberty Club was on busy Montgomery Street. The huge red sign with the neon white letters L-I-B-E-R-T-Y displayed vertically, and the shorter word CLUB written horizontally below, had been there since the 1950's. My mother said she thought the new sign was gaudy, after it replaced the much smaller, less conspicuous signage from the 30's and 40's.

With each new day either Gus or Johnny, father or son walked their "open arms" friendly demeanor through those club doors. Everyone had a name, a story, and the duo knew them all personally. After Johnny returned from the war he continued to gain the experience of running a full bar, learning all he could from his dad. By the late 1950's Gus had stepped aside, allowing his very capable son to run the place. The younger Aleck could practically do it in his sleep. Johnny continued the tradition of doling out both respect and compassion to his extended downtown family. Some of which were hard drinkers and could easily spend their entire paychecks or monthly social security income within a few short days. Many didn't have bank accounts, so Dad took it upon himself to help out by becoming their private savings and loan.

My father became the money manager for about six of these patrons. After cashing their checks he'd hold back most of their money, handing out allowances throughout the weeks. He set aside what they needed for living expenses and made sure their money was spent accordingly. Dad kept a small notebook with dates and payouts for each guy and did this month after month for years. That way they didn't spend it all on booze before the month was up and continued to keep a roof over their heads which for some, was upstairs at Grandpa's rooming house. Without my Dad's help, many of these men would have been homeless.

Johnny the bartender had a great sense of humor, handing out colorful nicknames, like Okie John, Hardrock, Mikey-Mike, Broom Hilda, Archie, Tokay Tommy, and Squirrel to the regulars. Getting a nickname from Aleck earned respect from the others. Many of these patrons didn't function well beyond the Liberty Club doors. They required a helping hand and Dad's big heart was a constant, like when he helped retirees get their pensions. He would write out detailed instructions as to what these men or women needed in order to sign up for Social Security. Then Pops would call Yellow Cab and have them driven around to gather what was needed, until finally having the taxi take them to the S.S. office then back *home* to the bar.

Your bartender Johnny. Inside the Liberty Club

Likewise, when a member of his second family became ill and didn't have a way to get to the hospital or doctor, again he arranged for their transportation. Even Jojo didn't escape being put to work by Johnny's soft heart. Once John Jr. got his driver's license he'd often get a call from Johnny Sr. to take Hardrock or one of the other colorful revelers to the VA hospital. I even remember staying in the car with my brothers when dad went to the County Hospital to visit the little Greek we called Uncle Tom during his final days.

The holidays were yet another opportunity for Dad to demonstrate the caring man this old paratrooper had become. When Jojo was a young teen and I was just a toddler, Thanksgiving and Christmas morning would find our thoughtful mother roasting the biggest turkeys she could fit into the oven. Cooking for our brood became second nature and a passion, as our mother whipped up mashed potatoes, string beans, stuffing, gravy, cranberry sauce, and pumpkin pies. But she didn't cook just for us. For several years early in the afternoon my parents gathered one of the fully prepared feasts and hauled it down to the Liberty Club. When the pair entered through the swinging red doors the men and women cheered with heartfelt thank-yous and appreciation over the piping hot glistening bird with all the fixin's. For many, these two holiday meals would be the only home-cooked supper they'd have the entire year. It was for this reason and many more the men and women who called the Liberty Club home were truly grateful.

Continuing his love for friends and family, during my teen years, my Dad sponsored a fast pitch softball team for me and my friends through the Liberty Club. It became a family affair with Marc as our coach and my family cheering at every game. On rare occasions even Mame piled into my dad's mafia-style dark charcoal gray '65 Lincoln we affectionately referred to as The Tank, to cheer on her granddaughter. Naturally our team was called "The Liberty Club" as we donned green jerseys, with white striping, and black letters. Many practices were held at Mitchell Field less than a mile or so from the club. Even though we still weren't 21 yet, after practice a couple of us would make a pit-stop at Dad's bar, guzzling down an ice cold orange pop whilst devouring a hot dog. It was just one more perk of living in a small town.

My parents in the 50's when they'd take home-cooked meals to club patrons.

When I was in my early twenties, from time to time I'd help dad around the bar. Often I would run to the bank for him, carrying a bank bag full of checks to nearby Central Valley Bank. Back then there was a big barrel-chested Irish beat cop by the name of Officer Russ Bergman who everyone called Officer Bergie, or just Bergie for short. If I was within his eyesight Bergie would jog over and patrol beside me the block and a half to the bank as a precaution. Apparently, gingerly swinging a white money bag clearly marked CENTRAL VALLEY BANK could have proved disastrous. Since I knew so many people downtown, robbery was the last thing on my mind, but it was nice to get the personal escort just the same.

I recall one occasion when I stopped in at the club to make a deposit for Pops. He was real busy with a bar full of yakking customers, and was still listing the checks on deposit slips when I walked in. I quietly waited in the loud over-stimulating atmosphere Dad had grown accustomed to. As I waited, a guy who I would later learn went by the name of Chuck, struck up a conversation with me. While he talked his eyes drifted, unable to focus and the foul smell of his breath encouraged me to take a step back. I continued to be cordial since he was one of Dad's paying regulars, but as he started to make verbal advances I became very uncomfortable. My father still had his back to us, listing the stack of checks and wasn't aware of the nuisance Chuck had become. By the time my father finished and turned around he saw his customer pawing at my arm trying to get me to sit on his lap. Johnny yelled at him to knock it off, but in his stupor Chuck either didn't hear or ignored the warning. By now I was pulling my arm away while maintaining a polite attitude, knowing Dad was about to intervene. I certainly wasn't prepared for what was to happen next.

The guys had been playing a dice game called horse when I walked in. All of a sudden Dad grabbed the leather dice cup, then raising his arm up high, smashed it down on Chuck's thick paw that lay across the bar. I mean, it was a loud BAM and I could feel my jaw drop, shocked at what he'd just done. Drunk Chuck hardly flinched as he turned his glassy gaze toward my dad and said, *"Hey Johnny, what'd you go and do that for?"* To which my dad pointing his dagger finger, and growling beneath his breath shot back, *"That's my daughter. You take your hand off her and treat her with respect."* Chuck apologized profusely to both of us, and afterward, even in his intoxicated state, Chucky never bothered me again. I could not have been more proud to be this bartender's daughter.

I owned a dark electric-blue 1974 Ford Ranchero back then, with light blue tuck and roll upholstery, matching shag carpet, new rubber-n-wheels, and air shocks, so I could raise the back end and look cool. This came in handy as my dad, always cutting corners, enlisted my help to take a load every couple of weeks of emptied beer and liquor bottles to the dump since recycling hadn't taken hold yet. I'd pull up to the old bluing metal back door to the Liberty Club in narrow Miners Alley on a Saturday morning. The same entrance that had been used to enter McClungs speak-easy back in the 20's and still has McClungs written on a very old wooden sign above. At least six to eight dirty metal trash cans were lined against the red brick wall filled with amber bottles and reeking of stale beer. Knowing I was waiting out back, Dad would come out with sleeves rolled to his elbows, brandishing stout hairy forearms. Together we'd heave those cans full of bottles into the back of my Ford. I was pretty strong back then, but my dad even into his mid-fifties had super-human strength. With a full load, I headed to the dump where I was able to drag the cans to the edge of the tailgate, then tipping them over, cover my ears from the thunderous crash of glass busting below.

Back door to the Liberty Club in Miners Alley. Notice JM McClung is still visible under the numbers 1966. Photo courtesy of local Oroville photographer Wayne Wilson.

It was during this period I had the big idea that maybe I would take over the family business. It was obvious all three of my brothers had no interest in running the Liberty Club and with my sentimental nature I couldn't bear the thought of the club in someone else's hands. I was like a little gnat buzzing around my father's head, repeating, teach me, teach me. Mixed drinks weren't my strong suit since I never really cared for hard liquor, so the learning curve would be rather steep. Still, I was up for the challenge. One day my pestering paid off when Dad told me to come down to the club at such and such time. This was my chance to make my Daddy proud!

The next day I punctually showed up to a packed house. It was the first of the month and with it came social security and disability checks to be cashed. There wasn't a bare barstool to be found. Archie, who ran the back-room card games, had all the tables filled with gamblers vying to win the big pot. The smoke was sickly thick and once again, the room a-buzz with booming voices and howling laughter. Suddenly, my excitement dissipated to anxiety. What the heck was I thinking?

Dad motioned for me to come around one end so I could meet him behind the bar. I had never stood back there before and now I was downright unnerved! Johnny scooped up the bank bag and said, *"Okay, I'll be right back."* The blood rushed from my face, *"What? You can't leave, I just got here."* He laughed as he walked around the bar and heading toward the swinging doors, shouted, *"You'll be fine, the guys will tell you how to mix their drinks, don't worry I'll be right back."* And with that, my father, along with my confidence, left the building.

Without moving my head, my eyes scanned the faces all staring back. I surveyed the endless bar down one end and back up the other. I was petrified! Blood continued to rush from my cheeks. Suddenly a voice stood out from amongst the chatter, *"Hey little lady, how about you pour me a red beer."* Red beer, I thought, what the heck is that? *"Here, let me help you."* Since he was sitting right in front of me he leaned over the bar and pointed to some glasses, *"Grab one of those, and down there in the ice box you'll find a can of tomato juice."* I grabbed both and set them on the bar. Directing me to one of the beer taps, he continued. *"Now take the glass and tip it a little then s-l-o-w-l-y fill the glass almost to the top."* He gestured with his hands, *"Slow now so it don't foam too much."* So I did as he instructed and it wasn't too bad. *"Good, now just pour some of that red juice on top and slide it over."* Hey, this is pretty easy, I thought. He told me how much it was and how to ring it up on my dad's shiny metal cash register.

I can do this, this isn't so hard, or so I thought. Next thing I knew others were ordering drinks, all kinds of concoctions I had never heard of. My head swirled. I over-poured and they probably under paid. A century went by and finally my dad strolled in chuckling and being pretty darn proud of himself. Back behind the bar he asked how it went. *"You did that on purpose didn't you?"* I half smiled, admiring his tactics. Grabbing a rag, he wiped down the bar and just kept on smiling and chuckling a little cackle I'd grown to love. His customers were all laughing and said I did a good job, but since I had been so slow some of the guys were still thirsty. Relieved my father had returned, I stood back and watched the master at work with never a movement wasted. It was obvious he was King and this was his domain. Johnny had been a fixture in this working man's bar for over three decades. He held the utmost respect from his regulars and deserved every bit of it.

In hindsight, I do believe his little stunt was a conspiracy. He had planned this all along because he had no desire for his daughter to become a bartender. Pretty sure I excused myself shortly afterward saying I had something to do. Lesson learned, I gave my dad a big hug and went on my way. I don't recall ever getting mad at him. How could I? He always had my best interest in mind, and had his own humorous way of showing it. I never had to do anything for him to be proud of me. Just being his daughter gave him pride enough.

Dad knew as the owner of a small town bar, one had to wear many hats. I'm sure this was a huge factor in making my first experience pouring drinks my last. It wasn't as simple as I'd thought, and I certainly didn't possess an arsenal full of jokes and stories to keep them coming back for more like Pops did. But my father also knew one of the most important and sometimes dangerous jobs was as a peace keeping bouncer. My brother John recalls one of many situations where dad's army toughness came in handy.

Back in the '50's when Johnny Jr. and Michele were still in grade school they were sitting in the family car parked on Montgomery Street, waiting for our dad to get off shift and take them home. Walking home from St. Thomas school they didn't feel like drudging the rest of the distance which was mostly up hill. As they sat patiently waiting, my brother happened to notice Sheriff Gillick walking on the sidewalk toward them.

"The next thing I know the doors fly open and Dad is throwing these two guys out and one of them bumped into Gillick and both of them fell into the street and into the gutter. Gillick was not happy but he got over it. And the other guy went flying on his ass and Dad came out there and gave them verbal hell. Then he saw Sheriff

Gillick and he went over and helped him up. That's when he was young and strong as an ox."

Another time, the inevitable happened as a trip to the hospital made the local newspaper. In the newspaper photo my dad lay stretched out on a gurney outside the bar. The caption, *"Aleck defends clientele; hospitalized after attack."* The article starts by stating, *"The same day an interview appeared in the Mercury-Register with Liberty Club owner-bartender Johnny Aleck defending the bar's clientele, he was assaulted by a patron and taken to Oroville Hospital by ambulance."* It continues by stating the attacker's name with a picture of him being handcuffed along with his age, 35, and address. The clipping resumed, *"When officers and medical personnel arrived, Aleck was lying on the club's floor semiconscious in front of the bar. According to police, Brown was sitting on the floor next to him."*

"Brown was charged with felony assault with intent to do great bodily harm. He was booked into Butte County Jail about 12:30 p.m. and remains held on $5,000 bail. As of press-time today Aleck was still under observation at Oroville Hospital and is listed in satisfactory condition. A nursing supervisor said Aleck was expected to be released soon. Approximately a dozen patrons were inside the bar when the assault occurred. Witnesses at the bar said Brown reportedly entered the club in an obvious state of intoxication and was asked to leave by Aleck. Refusing to do so, witnesses said Aleck walked around the bar to tell Brown in a more direct manner to leave. According to police, Brown responded by allegedly striking Aleck several times in the face, knocking him unconscious."

The thought of my dad who at that time was in his mid-fifties, being accosted in such a brutal way made my blood boil. Fortunately, he came out okay but it could have been far worse. I recall my father later saying, *"He cold-cocked me. I didn't even see it coming."*

The article continued: *"In an interview appearing in the Mercury-Register Friday Aleck was quoted as saying he felt harassed by his fellow business people who believe his club and others on Montgomery Street don't belong in Oroville's downtown prime shopping area"* They inserted his quote, *"Every time business gets slow in Oroville, they want to blame Montgomery Street for it,"* Aleck said. *"I have people come in from all walks of life. I don't have to apologize for any of them."* In the interview Aleck said his club provides services for customers such as cashing checks that other businesses won't. Aleck accused his fellow business people of *"insulting the backbone of Oroville."*

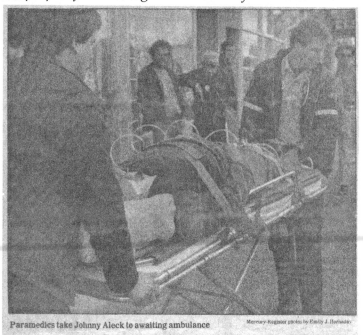

Paramedics take Johnny Aleck to awaiting ambulance

Mercury-Register photos by Emily J. Hornaday

Aleck defends clientele; hospitalized after attack

My dad on the gurney after being knocked out. No date is listed.

I remember those days well, hearing my dad grumble about a certain detective on the police force who he said was targeting his business. Just from reading the newspaper article, it was as though the writer wanted my dad to eat his own words. It was obvious the coward that struck my father wasn't one of Johnny's regulars. There were many reasons the downtown businesses started to dwindle, the least of which were the bars in the area. They had been around since Oroville first sprung from the earth, providing services decade upon decade. The local reporter may as well have kicked my father while he was already down.

The tide had turned in his home town. With the completion of the Oroville Dam in 1968, although many of the families remained in the area the revenue a community enjoys with such a massive project had all but dried up. And now what had once been the outskirts of Oroville was developed with small shopping centers, super markets, and gas stations along the new Oro Dam Boulevard. With companies now having an alternative location to set up shop, the downtown area was no longer the hub of Oroville. It's not an unfamiliar sight in many cities across America where a once thriving Main street became a ghost town when the outlying areas grew.

My parents began to feel the pinch. To make matters worse, in 1975 Oroville shook from a 5.8 magnitude earthquake. Many homes and businesses sustained minor to moderate damage. All the old brick buildings downtown, including the Liberty Club were inspected. In the end, thousands of dollars of retrofitting was expected for my dad to stay in business. Again, according to Jim Lenhoff, Oroville's historian, a specialist from Sacramento was brought in to carry out his own inspection, and found the buildings were still in great shape, which saved my parents thousands. But the months of waiting for the final report caused undue stress to my father's already taxed body. To help make ends meet, my mother continued to work at Woolworths, where she had been since '79. These were very difficult times for Johnny and Monique as the pressure was slowly testing their own relationship.

You can see the huge Liberty Club sign to the left of the picture. The martini glass is visible between the sign and the building. When the Liberty sign was put up in the 1950's the liquor store sign from the 40's was taken down. Notice the streets are practically empty. Used with permission by James Lenhoff. Taken 1980.

Before the liquor store was relocated a couple doors down to the corner of Myers and Montgomery in the Washington Block, Simone, now getting up in age, decided it was time to call it quits. Instead of days behind the counter, she took on the challenging task of being my father's full-time bookkeeper. Back in November of '56, just months after my parents had moved into their new home on Grand View, Simone and Colette bought the house where Dad and Mom had been living, making them all neighbors.

With Simone living right next door, I vividly recall her walking the worn path between our houses with a frown and a fist-full of ten-key calculator tape wanting to know where our father was. Routine money squabbles that took place between Mame and her son-in-law overflowed to our parents along with the contagious tension that mounted. The saddest part is my mom started to drink a little and then a little bit more. Wine had always been her choice and now she was drinking almost daily. I couldn't help but draw a parallel between her and her father. I know it was difficult for my dad as he tried to make ends meet while keeping his wife happy. As teenagers and young adults, life's complications were unfolding right before our eyes. Looking back now, I regret not being able to fix it, but the inevitable is just that... unfixable.

As if their situation couldn't get any worse, the Liberty Club was robbed by what to this day we believe was an inside job. Our family is sure it was the boyfriend of one of the night bartenders, but my dad was never able to prove the accusation. In the club against one wall sat a huge heavy safe just a few feet from the front doors. It was at least three or four feet tall, wide and deep, and had been there since the bar's beginnings, and possibly the former owner as well. As quoted in the newspaper, Johnny would cash many of the payroll checks from cannery workers and others who in turn spent a portion of their earnings at the bar. One night when the safe was full due to the 1st of the month, someone torched and then blew open the massive steel doors, cleaning it out. In all, over $8,000 was stolen and I'm not entirely sure it was covered by insurance.

In hard times it was just one more jolt to send a man to drink. During the fruitful years Johnny's patrons used to buy him shots, which in the past he turned down or pretended to drink. But with his financial woes, and a wife who was becoming emotionally absent, a little burn in the throat didn't sound half bad. I'd get a call to see if I could give him a ride home. I knew he'd been drinking, which was out of character for my Dad. With the police station sitting on the levee just up the hill from his bar, I'm glad he had the good sense not to drive himself home.

Johnny behind the bar looking tired, but still has a smile. Late 70's early 80's

The eighties rolled around, and with it, the economic dust devil continued its swirl around downtown Oroville. One by one, iconic businesses such as Hills Furniture, Warmacks, and City of Paris closed their doors forever. I mourned for my childhood as it crumbled. Even though by then I had moved to Sacramento, I came home to visit often and was saddened every time, wondering which shop was next to fall victim. I could see a difference in my parents as well. They seemed tired and the home was showing its age. In order to keep up with the bills, my parents borrowed against the house more than once. Even though they should have been close to making their final mortgage payment, life continued to kick them in the teeth.

The Liberty Club with the sign above the swinging red doors. To the right is Don's Barber Shop, and further right, is the entrance to the Oro Vista Rooming House above with the three large windows. The liquor store was just to the left of the Liberty Club - not pictured. Photo provided by Butte County Historical Society. Early 1970's.

With age now a factor and the weight of the world upon both their shoulders, a decision had to be made. The once thriving Liberty Club had become a dying old friend. I'm sure both my parents knew this day would come, but was my Dad able to pull the plug? Johnny was already on high blood pressure medication, and his wife continued to deny reality through a bottle. My siblings and I felt helpless on the sidelines with none of us in a position to help. In 1985 I moved from Sacramento to Reno, Nevada and although I was aware of their struggles, I didn't know just how dire the situation had become.

Finally, after exhausting all other options, my parents had but one viable solution. It was time to put their friend, the Liberty Club out of its misery. Emotionally, it must have tormented my father, having spent the majority of his life behind that bar. There were many memories of his younger days working side by side with his father, and he now felt that he had failed him. Joking around with brother Nick during the bustling heyday was a thing of the past and no matter how hard one searches, there's just no road that leads us back to the good old days. The building, liquor license, and inventory were sold so my parents could breathe again. The City of Oroville bought the Liberty Club building for $150,000. After the back taxes and debt were paid just a small chunk of change was left.

With the bar now sold the contents had to go. Through the decades, customers had enjoyed giving Johnny the bartender antiques or oddities, knowing they'd earn a place of honor somewhere in the Club. Some of the treasures came from clientele who, when short on cash, would have their tabs settled by my Dad accepting a quick barter. I imagine this could have been one of the subjects he and Mame disagreed about during those heated bookkeeping arguments. Hanging from the rafters was an array of one-of-a-kinds such as an old bicycle, an ox yolk, and ancient pair of Levi's. Even a woman's brassiere that my dad found one day while restocking the ladies' bathroom hung from the rafters. The bar reflected my dad's unique personality and all the patrons loved it! Over time the souvenirs had yellowed from the rising smoke of customers sitting comfy on their bar stools with a sip and a puff to pass the time.

The inside of the Liberty Club – a working man's bar. July 1987

The better pieces always found their way to our house to be displayed in the yard or inside our home. Some of the items really were just junk, but many were interesting and held value. Despite years of neglect, the salvageable pieces were set aside with a handful divided amongst us kids. Dad had a small brown truck and I talked him into having someone help load the last of the old relics, and haul them to my house in Reno. With the contents emptied and escrow now closed, our family's Liberty Club doors were closed and locked for the last time.

With the bed of their truck filled, my parents drove to Reno where I had arranged to have an Old West Sale. The sale was a success and all of us had a great time. To be honest, they both were more relaxed than I had seen them in years. Relieved, is the word that comes to mind as my dad enjoyed his ice cold Oly's, and shared a story about every trinket to would-be customers. My mother chimed in with her sweet French accent as everyone hushed to listen. To this day we still have a picture of the two of them with great big smiles holding the riches from the day.

Loving life - Dad and Mom after the old west sale. Mid 1980's

It wasn't long before the last remnant of a bygone era would be removed forever. The huge neon Liberty Club sign would no longer stand as a reminder of the immigrants who settled in Oroville at the turn of the 20th century. It would no longer light the evening sky along Montgomery Street. The glow of its bright lettering and neon torch perched atop, like that held by Lady Liberty, would be extinguished forever. I liken it to the changing of the guards, except there was no other guard to take over.

The local newspaper dated November 2, 1988 had as its caption: *Historic facade renovation*. The picture shows the mammoth Liberty Club sign as it lay on rain-soaked Montgomery Street with several onlookers in the background. The caption below read: *Liberty Club sign lays in street after being taken down*. Part of the sign had a a neon martini glass, complete with stir stick and olive that was affixed alongside the words, L-I-B-E-R-T-Y, reminiscent of 1950's art deco. The glowing landmark really was massive, being at least fifteen to twenty feet long, and hanging a good ten feet off the sidewalk. It could be seen from blocks away up and down Montgomery Street. Above the red swinging doors were an array of neon stars that blinked one set red, another blue, and then the last of all, red, white, and blue. As a youngster I'd sit in my dad's car as he ducked in to grab something from the bar, mesmerized by the shooting star effect. If the window was down even just a smidgen, I could hear the crackle of the quick electrical buzzing with each changing of the lights.

Removing the sign was supposed to be the kick-off to a million dollar restoration project on Montgomery Street. The drizzling rain didn't hamper a turnout of about a hundred people. As the sign was removed, for some reason it felt more like a public hanging as our families' marquee gently swayed as it hung from the crane.

To us it was more than just a sign; it represented a chunk of our heritage. The big event was also attended by political dignitaries, including Congressman Wally Herger, Assemblyman Chris Chandler, and State Senator Jim Nielsen. Nielsen commented, *"We're not tearing down, we're building up."* A total of thirteen historic buildings in the downtown district were slated to get new facades, starting with my dad's bar and three others on Montgomery St.

The newspaper caption read: "A crane lowers the cocktail sign at the old Liberty Club Wednesday beginning a $900,000 rejuvenation on Montgomery St." November 3, 1988.

This was the front page article as it appeared in the Mercury Register from 1988:

Removing the old Liberty Club sign Wednesday afternoon was a little more emotional for one Oroville family, the Alecks, who first opened the downtown bar in 1937. Michele Aleck, daughter of

Johnny Aleck, attended the ceremony Wednesday afternoon when the Oroville Redevelopment Agency broke ground for a Historic Facade Rehabilitation project by removing the Liberty Club sign.

Michele's grandfather, Gus Aleck first opened the club in 1937. His son Johnny worked there while he was still in high school in 1937. After World War II in the fall of 1945 Johnny Aleck returned to operate the club until he became a half-partner in 1965.

The Liberty Club was open along Montgomery Street for 50 years.

Johnny Aleck said his father opened the club after he was hurt in a mining accident. His father named it the Liberty Club, Aleck said because he was a patriotic person. "He just believed in liberty," Aleck said

Aleck remembers the downtown area years ago. "In that era we were cashing $30,000 to $40,000 worth of checks a day," he said. "Downtown Oroville was really thriving." There was a two story J.C. Penney store, two shoe stores, a jewelry store. Chinatown was booming and Oroville was considered Little Reno."

Oroville has changed so drastically he wonders if the proposed movie theater in the old Liberty Club will work. "Thinking of today, I don't know if it is going to work," he said. "Oroville had an attitude back then. The downtown area was the place to be."

As for the end of the Aleck's Liberty Club era with the sign they "designed ourselves and paid $5,000 for," Aleck said although the sign is gone, he is pleased the developers are keeping the "liberty" in the name of the new Liberty Cinema Four.

"I still miss my customers and friends," he said, "but times change." I raised seven kids out of it. We didn't do too bad."

Historic facade renovation

The Liberty Club sign on rain-soaked Montgomery Street. November 2, 1988

The sign was junked and although, according to the paper, the developers of the proposed Liberty Cinema Four said they were, *"going ahead 100 percent,"* adding that the 1000-seat movie theatre would open in May of 1989, it never came to be. After all the hoopla, the only change I noticed in downtown Oroville was the absence of my family's Liberty Club sign, and a new look to its entrance. I cried when I read the article.

Liberty Club pictured above with drawing
Liberty Cinema Four that never happened.

Sean and Lori Pierce of Oroville, who appreciate local history, acquired the long wooden Liberty Club bar that a contractor was going to take to the dump. The larger portion of the bar has a new home around the corner from my dad's club at the old Grey Nurse Hardware store. The smaller section is being used as a counter at Red Fly Clothing. And if you're ever in Oroville, the blue neon martini glass with its red olive that was once a part of the Liberty Club sign now hangs in the Red Fly window, just a few doors down from where it once glowed in the night sky.

With the shooting stars and swinging red doors long gone, replaced with large windows and a single glass door outlined in red, Gus and Angelica wouldn't recognize the place, nor would my father. But a wonderful woman by the name of Joyce Townsend opened a candy store where the old bar once flourished. She named her new venture Liberty Candy in honor of my family, and the Liberty Club that once bustled between those same red brick walls.

Chapter 23

MAME

For as long as I can remember, my grandmother had snow-white hair, not gray, but white, and thick with soft waves. She wore it short yet full and it was always perfect. Her teeth, though slightly crooked, never diminished from the warmth of Mame's smile. Like many members in our family, she wore glasses the entire time she was in my life. Her accent was even thicker than my mother's, which made it nearly impossible for my friends to join in our conversation on the days when she stopped by for a visit. Just like my other grandmother, she wore only dresses, and in the winter I loved her camel hair three-quarter-length coat. Just as in her youth, Mame's ensembles were tailored for a perfect fit, yet never over-stated, wearing shades of beige and tan with an occasional grey accented with colorful scarfs. It was obvious both in demeanor and dress, Simone was still a woman of class and sophistication.

From the time Jojo was about two until he began kindergarten, Mame and Colette babysat him and my older sister while our parents worked. They conversed exclusively in French, so my oldest brother became very fluent *en Français*. As a result, on his first day of school he had to learn English as a second language.

John was an avid small game hunter. With BB gun in hand he terrorized *les moineaux*, or sparrows, from the surrounding trees. Like our dad, my oldest brother was a deadly shot and always targeted the head. After he killed enough to fill a dish, he proudly toted his trophies to his grandmother. Together they'd prep the small birds as

Simone cooked up another masterpiece. With gobs of butter, garlic, onion, and of course, white wine, the pair enjoyed this delicious delicacy, tiny bones and all. Today it seems a bit garish, but in the 1950's, and with a French grandmother, it was perfectly normal. As John grew older he traded his BB gun for a shotgun, bringing home dove, pheasant, and even pigeons that Mame enjoyed cooking as a treat the entire family enjoyed.

When we were younger our family took one vacation a year to San Francisco and stayed at the Handlery Hotel, which was called the Handlery Inn back then. The three of us kids shared a room with Mame, while my parents had their own adjoining room. April 1965

Back yard safaris hunting snails was another favorite boyhood memory. The pair searched the garden vegetation in the evenings when the snails were plentiful, snatching and placing the slimy mollusks in a metal bucket. It was the perfect way to keep her garden from being devoured while providing the opportunity for another traditional gourmet meal, and time with her grandson. Just as in France, Mame purged then smothered the escargot in the same flavorful blend as *les petit moineaux*. On one of the family trips to San Francisco, Simone purchased a few dozen decorative Escargot shells. From then on she'd fill the shells with simmered morsels and serve them with simple yet exquisite side dishes for just the two of them to enjoy.

When my brother was in high school, he and some jock buddies managed to swipe a few bottles of whiskey from our grandparents' liquor store. Teenagers will do that. They figured a safe hiding place was in Mame's garden, but they figured wrong. Stuffing the bottles in a small duffel bag, the boys dug a hole in the soft soil, burying the loot. Knowing her garden intimately, it didn't take long for Mame to notice the loosened dirt. She poked her hand shovel around and felt something hard beneath. Simone was a little puzzled until she uncovered the bag and heard the familiar clanking of bottles. Instinctively, our wise grandmother suspected her mischievous grandson. Mame took the evidence to our dad, and after confirming the serial numbers on the bottles came from the Oroville Liquor store, John was brought in for questioning. He gave it up quickly, and faced a good old-fashioned grounding that lasted an eternal two weeks. I know for a fact this didn't detour young John Jr. from his adolescent ways, but he did learn where not to hide his stash.

Mame's manicured yard was always in order with rose bushes and petunias providing vibrant colors. A small flower bed of her favorite red geraniums were seemingly always in bloom. She had a yellow push mower with no motor. My grandmother provided the power. I can still hear the sound of the blades twirling and the smell of freshly cut grass as she mowed her lawn while getting a tremendous workout. It was no easy task, as I tried it many times and after just a few minutes, gave up exhausted. When I was strong enough to pull the cord on our gas-powered mower at the age of ten or eleven I took over the lawn mowing duties for her. I used to walk down to the nearby gas station with a one gallon metal gas can and 25 cents in my pocket to purchase fuel for the old Toro. I mowed, edged with hand clippers, raked, and swept the front and back yards once a week. She always paid me $5.00 each time for the two-hour ordeal, which was a lot of money for a kid, and I greatly appreciated it. Plus, I knew mowing at her age had become a struggle.

My mother told me that throughout her life, our grandmother still made her own cottage cheese that she had learned to make as child. I wish she would have shared her cheese making process with me, but wise Mame probably thought I would have found it boring. As a youngster and even into my teens, she was probably right. But I'd jump at the chance to learn her old-school ways today.

Simone's cozy three-bedroom, one-bath house was immaculate with tasteful streamlined furnishings. Living alone, it only required tidying up from time to time after us grandkids had touched everything in sight.

Still a devout Catholic, Mame spent a portion of each afternoon in devotion as she whispered Hail Mary's and the Lord's Prayer, keeping track on her beaded rosary. She filled her days with various activities from watching favorite TV programs like the Price is Right, to playing game after game of solitaire with a worn deck of cards. She always had a crochet project in progress. Before finding the letter revealing the abundance of baby clothes she made and crossed the Atlantic with, I had no idea just how crafty she was, but I was aware of her crocheting talent. Having me pick my favorite colors, Mame crocheted a beautiful afghan I still have to this day, in blues, purple, and red. Full of patience, she even crocheted an entire dress for herself in a soft gray, that my mother pointed out in an old black and white photo from the early 50's of Simone wearing it.

Simone wearing the soft grey dress she crocheted, with grandson Jojo. She also sewed the outfit he has on. Taken on Manzanita Street with part of Table Mountain visible to the left of the picture. Approximately 1951 or 52.

Her bookkeeping duties for the Liberty Club consumed a small portion of the day allowing her the opportunity to babysit my little sister while our parents worked. I still have the short story Stephanie wrote years later about a typical day spent with our grandmother when she was a child. She mentions games of dominos, and go-fish, along with building trains from blocks where Mame excelled. My little sis was fortunate to have learned to crochet upon the lap of a master and continues to this day.

Christmas chaos. Grand View house 1960's

The holidays were very special in our family, and naturally, Mame spent the majority with us while we all enjoyed many Thanksgivings at Colette's. We still joke about our aunt's lumpy mashed potatoes. On Christmas Eve, before going to midnight mass, us kids would find our biggest pair of shoes and eagerly place them near the fireplace. It's a tradition in France to put out shoes instead of hanging stockings. Then on Christmas morning it was magical to see our shoes filled with goodies, and discover the abundance of toys left by St. Nick. After we played with them for a while, and still in our pajamas, we couldn't wait to run next door to Mame's. We knew, warming in the oven was a small stack of home-made delicate crepes. Before opening our presents, my brothers and I would run to her kitchen and gently peel the crepes from each other. After sprinkling a generous amount of sugar across the middle we'd roll the crepe into a fun finger food. The buttery sweet flavor melted in our mouths as we sipped on a soothing cup of *cafe au lait*.

With our taste buds delighted by these sweet rolls of deliciousness, we stood every year, mesmerized by our grandmother's nativity scene. Knowing she had packed the one-of-a-kind manger on her very first trip to America was more wonderful than words can express. Mame never had a Christmas tree, but more than made up for it with her enchanted village. My mother told me even Lala and Daucy, Jeans' partners in crime from the Vichy days, were spellbound by her *crèche*, as it is called in French. She would set different sized boxes on a flat cabinet surface, and lay a sheet of gray crumpled paper over the top of the squares, making the terrain appear mountainous with a valley below. Using snippets from the base of our Christmas tree, she placed them in strategic areas, then sprayed the branches with fake snow. Within the unique nativity scene was an over-sized baby Jesus, and smaller Mary and Joseph with the three wise men. A flock of sheep with shepherds and townspeople roamed the lower levels. She even had a fisherman standing on a bridge over a tin foil river with a fish at the end of his line. Twinkly lights outlined the landscape with one poking through the back of the manger to light up the inside for a better view of the baby Jesus. As a child, it was whimsical! Many years later and after our grandmother had passed, the box of treasures holding all the pieces to Mame's Christmas world were stolen from my younger sister's storage locker. It sickens me to this day.

About the late 1960's, Simone had a friend who came to visit by the name of Margarette. We always referred to her as the French lady, which is ironic because we were surrounded by French ladies. Margarette was slender and a little taller than my grandmother. She wore glasses and kept her grayish hair short. Like the others of her generation she wore only dresses. Margarette worked her entire life as a professional nanny and apparently was quite good. I was to learn they met on the Liberty Ship that brought Simone and Colette to the states. Colette said it was a smaller vessel and everyone, including the sailors, got seasick on board. During their two week voyage the three French women became constant companions. Upon their arrival to the U.S., Margarette gave her contact information to Simone as she was going to be living with her niece in New York. So now, years later, and both retired, Margarette decided to come to California for a short visit which was extended to a two-year stay.

They had their French culture in common, only speaking their native tongue when conversing, and got along as if they had known one another forever. And in a way, they had, since over the past two decades they corresponded through letters and phone calls. Then just as quickly as she had arrived, Margarette moved back east to live with her niece again, eventually passing away in her early 90's. I do believe this was the only real friend Mame had made in the states. I don't remember anyone else visiting her and I know she never left her home to visit anyone else. If she did have friends, I'm certainly not aware of who they were outside our family.

It was during the early 1980's Simone's health began to decline. As did her father, she developed lung issues. Her respiratory doctor had his practice in Chico, which also had, in her opinion, a better hospital. With doctor appointments more frequent and the desire to live closer to Enloe Hospital, Mame came to the conclusion it was time to sell the house she had called home for some thirty years. I wonder if it was a hard decision to make. My mother would take over the bookkeeping duties, and except for their daily visits there really was no reason to stay. Moving to Chico would also provide my grandmother the opportunity to spend more time with Colette, who had recently become a widow with Joe's passing in 1981.

My grand-mere had learned how to live frugally after her husband had lost their fortune. Her house was paid in full, so to provide an additional income to her Social Security, she sold it to a young couple and carried the note at eight percent interest. A balloon payment was written into the contract as an additional nest egg. She had come to America with hardly more than the clothes on her back, and a small scattering of keepsakes from the affluent high life of the 20's and 30's. Even with her meager earnings behind the liquor store counter, she had done very well for herself.

I was still living in Reno when Mame sold her house and didn't learn about it until after the fact. Maybe she thought I'd be too upset and would have tried to stop her. I probably would have. After my grandmother moved, my dad had a fence built between the two properties where we once roamed free. I recall the empty feeling I felt coming home for visits and not having my Mame next door anymore.

She rented a clean two-bedroom downstairs apartment on The Esplanade just a few blocks from the hospital and her doctors. Simone was able to keep the majority of her furniture so it was nice to see her in familiar surroundings. We had always been very close and corresponded through monthly letters to stay in touch. Back then a person had to pay extra to make long distance phone calls so the art of letter writing was a wonderful alternative. Cell phones didn't exist yet. To this day I still have three precious letters written in her own pen.

Mame in her green robe spoiling me with another delicious meal, at her apartment in the early 1980's.

In one letter she tells me it's okay to call her collect so we could talk. I doubt I ever did. I wouldn't have felt right having her pay for our call. In others, she talked about her breathing treatments she was getting three and four times a day, leaving her weak and depressed. Mame was full of thank-yous when she received a letter or card from me. I usually enclosed pictures of where I lived and a picture of myself. There was an open invitation in every letter from her to visit when I could and *"your room is waiting for you."* When I was able to stay over, she insisted on cooking a very tasteful yet simple meal. My favorite was chicken smothered in tomatoes, onion, garlic, and white wine with a side of rice pilaf, and cool cucumber salad. I still have some of her delicious recipes. I'd always stay the night in the spare bedroom she had dubbed my own.

I thoroughly enjoyed these visits and sometimes would ask questions about her younger days. Mame loved to talk about the French countryside with its abundance of flowers, perfumeries, and the blue green Mediterranean Sea. I could tell she missed her homeland. With several opportunities to do so, she never exposed the truth regarding her husband and his prison term. The shame still lay just beneath the surface, too painful to share with her granddaughter. In fact, she never spoke about him at all. Mame was very good at deflecting questions and turning them to a query about myself. Always wanting the best for me, I would receive counsel on certain situations in my life, be it relationship or work. To this day, the one-liner I remember most from her well-intentioned heart was, *"I pray you find your way."* I wasn't one to stay in one place, relationship, or job for too long and she recognized the butterfly in me.

On one visit, for fun I brought my camera and took some pictures of her. One in particular was of her wearing her green robe with black-roped trim, eating a bowl of ice cream. We always ended the evening before retiring with a favorite sweet treat, and now having read my mother's journal, I know ice cream had been her favorite for a very long time. I dabbled in different art mediums back then and from that picture drew a pencil and charcoal that turned out to be a very good likeness of her. Framed, she was thrilled to receive it as a Christmas present. There were a couple of other water colors I painted and hung for her in her home. She loved the paintings not because they were all that great, but because I had done them just for my Mame.

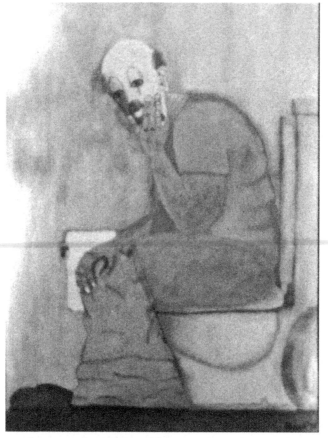

A painting only a grandmother could love. I hung it in her bathroom. The clown's shirt and hair were orange, with blue pants, brown shoes, and a dirty yellow background. She loved me~

In her younger day Simone could walk for miles without breaking a sweat. In France as well as in America she loved to walk as it was good exercise. Now though, her breathing had its challenges. Still wanting to enjoy the sunshine, we would walk arm in arm around a couple of blocks in her neighborhood. As time went on it was just one block, and then just to the corner and back.

By the spring of 1989 the relationship I was in ended and I temporarily moved back home with my parents. I slept on a single bed in the same room I had shared with my two brothers when we were little. It wasn't long before I found a place to live in Chico and rented a room from a former high school friend. My grandmother's health had taken a turn at this point, so other living arrangements had been made for her. After almost ten years it was time to give up the comfortable apartment where Simone had been able to maintain her independence. Both daughters took turns having Mame live with them for six weeks at a time. The furnishings were divided between Monique and Colette, with each taking a bedroom set for Mame's new rooms. I recall my dad getting her all settled in the car when it was time to take Simone to Colette's. I have to wonder how my grandmother felt about being uprooted every six weeks. But in all reality, she was fortunate to have two loving daughters to care for her in such an ailing situation.

Her cough could be heard down the hall and into the kitchen. Sometimes on my weekend visits I'd see my frail grandmother dressed in a nightgown sitting on the edge of her bed. A diminished version of the woman I'd grown to know, but her inner fortitude unbelievably strong, struggling to stay alive. She had an oxygen tank in her room and the respiratory therapist made visits often to give Mame her breathing treatments. It was torture to hear her cough so deeply and fatiguingly. I recall watching her emerge from the bedroom thin and slightly hunched over, exhausted from coughing. I'd help her to the bathroom where she rarely closed the door for fear if she fell no one would know.

My grandmother was as sweet as pie, and is very appreciative getting her own strawberry pie on her birthday. Grand View house

And yet when my sister Stephanie had her first child my grandmother mustered up the strength to see her beautiful great-granddaughter who was given the middle name Simone. We all decided to pay a visit to the proud parents and newborn that lived just a couple of blocks from my parents. When my dad got out of the car he was carrying my grandmother's portable oxygen bottle while she walked behind him on the narrow pathway with her walker. I had driven from Chico and arrived at the same time. My dad, always happy to see one of his children, waved and started talking to me as I approached. Well, Pops got a little excited and started walking a bit too fast for my grandmother. All of a sudden I heard in her weakened voice, *"Johnny, Johnny you're going too fast."* My poor grandmother had the thin oxygen tube wrapped around her ears and my dad was unknowingly pulling her forward. He heard her in time and stopped full of apologies. No harm was done, and from my perspective it looked quite comical like something out of Laurel and Hardy.

Hospital visits became routine as her condition worsened. It was on one of these stays when I had gone to visit with her that she told me the story about her youth and eating too many plums. It was nice to see her smile as we laughed together. Mame always kept a pair of small slightly curved scissors in her purse. On several occasions she asked me to find them and if I wouldn't mind cutting her fingernails for her. How could I mind? It was an honor to do something so small for one I loved so deeply. As Mame's eyelids grew heavy and sleep fell upon her tired body, I knew it was time for me to leave.

It was the winter of 1992 when the phone rang. My mother spoke in a hurried voice, *"You need to get here now if you want to say goodbye."* I was about a ten minute drive away, including parking and running through the hospital doors. I wasted no time. Upon entering her room I found my parents and Colette by her side. We exchanged quick hugs and I noticed everyone's eyes were welled with tears, which prompted my own. Mame was not conscious, her breathing shallow, with an oxygen mask placed over her nose and mouth. Mom and dad were on one side with Mom closest to her mother. I took my spot across from my mother with my aunt next to me. Even though she was breathing, it was as if my grandmother was already gone. I placed my left hand on her thin shoulder and with my other, took her hand in mine. We all talked gently, telling her it was okay to go HOME. We told her that it was time now to be with her parents and her grandparents, and my mother and Colette named them one by one. Christiane is waiting, and how wonderful it will be to see her again. I could feel myself choking back a rush of tears, especially since my mother and aunt were no longer able to contain theirs. Even my dad was weeping as his wife cried upon his shoulder. Simone truly was a second mother to him. I continued to gaze upon Mame saying, *"You can go HOME now, we're okay, you can go HOME."*

It wasn't long before she took her last breath. As she did, she squeezed my hand hard. Mame always had a strong grip and there it was again. At the same time I felt her body give a quick shiver, for lack of a better word. And just as quickly, her grip was gone and so was she. I turned to my aunt as we embraced and wept with my parents doing the same. When I was somewhat composed I turned back to Mame and removed the oxygen mask from her face. I didn't know what to do next. I had never witnessed another's passing. Was I supposed to lift the sheet over her face? Instead, I just looked at her one more time, and touching her shoulder, whispered, *"I love you, Mame."*

My brothers asked if I wanted to be a pallbearer. As unconventional as that was for a woman to help carry a casket, again, I was honored. John and Marc were in the Air Force at the time and were very handsome in their dress blues. Mame would have been proud. Michele's two sons and Colette's son-in-law at the time took their places on either side. The Catholic Mass was held at St. John the Baptist Catholic Church in Chico. There are many steps leading to the front doors and as strong as I was, holding my end was difficult, but I didn't let on. The attendance was mostly family and a few close friends of my mother and Colette's that also knew Simone. In reality, Mame's life was her family, no others were needed. I sat with the other pallbearers and wept during most of the service. Afterward, we carried her coffin down the aisle as tears continued to stream down my face. My parents, my aunt, everyone cried.

After the graveside service we gathered back at Colette's house. I still have a picture of my two six-foot brothers in their uniforms holding Jillian Simone, Mame's great-granddaughter who had just turned one year's old the month before. It was a somber day, surreal in many ways.

John and Marc in their dress blues holding their niece Jillian Simone at Colette's house. February 14, 1992

While writing this chapter I recalled in my youth hearing stories that my grandmother had been mugged while walking home from work one day. I never knew any of the details, and as the years went by, had forgotten about it altogether. Now that it had resurrected in my mind, I had to know more. Even though her memory was beginning to fade, thankfully, Colette vividly remembered that disturbing afternoon.

It was the mid 1950's and just like any other day, Mame, who was pushing fifty, was walking home from another shift at the liquor store. As she approached their duplex, while still living on Montgomery Street, a man came from out of nowhere, grabbing her purse and striking her in the face with his bare fists. The force knocked her to the ground, then shocked and in terrific pain, she let out a terrified scream. Colette heard her mother's cry and flew out of the house, finding a tall skinny man standing over Simone with her purse in hand as she lay bleeding. When the assailant saw my aunt he took off running down the street. Instinctively, Colette quickly called the police who were ever-present in the downtown area in those days. She said they came immediately and after Colette gave a brief description of the attacker and stating he had her mother's blood on him, the police were in hot pursuit. It wasn't long before they caught their man who was sprinting down Montgomery Street, still carrying my grandmother's purse.

Meanwhile, Colette helped Simone to the house and tended to her wounds. My poor Mame was in horrible pain with a black eye, split lip, bloodied nose and abrasions. She had hit the concrete when she fell, which resulted in a large bump on the side of her head. She was taken to the doctor and patched up, but it would take time to heal both physically and emotionally. When she was healthy enough to go back to work, Simone, still immensely traumatized, kept a watchful eye of her surroundings. Had the tall skinny man attacked my grandmother out of ear shot of her daughter, I wonder what the outcome would have been. I'm just so happy she survived as Mame played an irreplaceable role in all our lives.

You had to have a strong constitution to get though such an ordeal, and I remember my grandmother as being an uncommonly strong, independent woman. It is apparent from what I learned she had been this way her entire life. John Jr. reiterated her resilience when he mentioned, *"She was an amazing woman who was a pillar of strength when we suffered the loss of Christiane."* The events of Mame's journey surely played a part in who she would become.

Her life encompassed a plethora of emotions. The simple carefree life of a child with great love for her father who would become a disabled veteran after the Great War. The torment of a loveless arranged marriage, coupled with the joy of having two beautiful daughters. Then the betrayal of her husband, both in marriage and character. She went from riches to rags, survived both wars, lost an unborn child, and began a new life in a foreign country. Mame felt an even greater loss with the death of her grandchild Christiane and toward the end, settled into her senior years with dignity in spite of her chronic condition. It wasn't an ordinary life by any means.

Simone Sebastienne Clementine Wacker-Poulain joined her heavenly family February 10, 1992 at the age of 85. Not a day goes by that you are not on my mind, and always, you rest in my heart.

Simone Poulain

Chapter 24

JOHNNY

After they sold the bar my father and mother took a much needed vacation. Traveling north, they made stops in Montana and Idaho, visiting with Marc's and Gregg's families. The clean mountain air was invigorating, and after having been strapped to the Liberty Club during its downward spiral, finally being able to take in deep breaths and relax was way overdue. A change in scenery was the perfect remedy to re-open their hearts as Johnny and Monique were like young lovers once again without a care in the world.

The pair also spent some time visiting their eldest, John Jr., and his lovely wife Shirley. At the time, John was a Chief Master Sergeant in the Air Force and Senior Enlisted Advisor to the Wing Commander. Because of his rank and position it was John's duty to attend upper echelon military functions. At one of these intimate barbecues, my parents, who were in town, were invited as guests. Mom, who by now had heard her husbands "broken record" war stories one too many times, made it a point to tell Jojo to keep an eye on his father so as not to bore the others. John wasn't concerned, but as the evening wore on wondered where dear old Pops had wandered off to. As he stepped outside to a large patio he heard his dad's animated voice. A crowd of high ranking officers, including the General himself, had huddled around and were hanging on Johnny's every word. Dad was in story mode. You could see WWII come to life for these officers who had never seen combat. Their admiration apparent as this paratrooper, this NCO, (non-commissioned officer) vividly described bloody encounters, and German ingenuity with their use of radio-controlled miniature tanks designed to explode behind enemy lines. He described escaping sniper fire while riding a motorcycle through Anzio's mud, and the bitter cold resulting in high casualties suffered by both sides. Dad's graphic details and emotion put you there. They were in awe and held complete respect for this seasoned veteran as he shared first-hand accounts fighting on the front lines during WWII. Young Johnny Jr. could not have been more proud.

With the traveling bug out of their system they returned once more to the real world. What was left from the money from the sale of the business along with my mother's income needed supplementing. Seven months before the Liberty Club sign was removed, my mother retired from Woolworths, after nine years of service. She went back to banking which she had done in the '60's, taking a position as a teller at First Interstate Bank which later became Washington Mutual. One day she was the unlucky teller to have a bank robbery note slid into her hands. She gave the bandit the money and he left without incident, but she was visibly shaken. To make matters worse, the local paper blundered by printing her full name and home address in the robbery write-up. She was more afraid of possible repercussions than she was at the time of the hold up.

Central Lanes, the old bowling alley, was still open for business back then and my father was able to get a job doing what he knew best, bartending. Even though he had the evening shift, Johnny enjoyed seeing familiar faces again. It wasn't long though before the bowling alley fell victim to the changing economy. It was sold, torn down, and replaced with a Rite Aid. Still needing money to pay the bills, my dad came full circle. As he had done as a youngster running the streets of Oroville, Johnny found himself once more delivering newspapers.

And so this is how Johnny and Monique, the young couple with movie star good looks and a torrid romance were to live out their golden years. My brothers and I helped out when we could, paying for new tires, an air-conditioner, or forty bucks here and there. Dad became accustomed to taking the good with the bad. He knew how to enjoy life in spite of hardships, playing with the family dog, chit-chatting with friends, and getting his hands dirty in the yard. He expressed to me more than once he'd be just fine living in a tent like he did as a kid. The material realm was never important to my dad. Johnny's life's purpose was sharing his huge heart with family, friends, and even strangers. That's what brought true joy into my father's world.

My younger sister Stephanie with our dad on her birthday. Dad was a total family man. Grand View house kitchen 1960's.

My parents were still doing their best to recover from the financial trials that plagued them. I know it was a difficult time with many unproductive arguments ending unresolved. But the same can be said for other couples with money issues. One thing I am absolutely certain of is that in spite of their money woes Johnny and Monique's love was genuine. They held on to a deeper level of devotion; one that truly withstands "for richer or poorer, till death do us part." Beneath life's layers of disappointment and heartache I would still see them sneak a hug and a kiss. My father would give a little swat on his *chérie's derrière,* saying, "*Ooh, la la!*" And just as when I was a child, mom and dad would cuddle on the couch, half watching some silly TV show. With dad's arm draped around his beautiful wife she would eventually drift off into blissful slumber upon a shoulder that had become so familiar to her cheek.

Still in love after all these years~ 1986

Mom and Dad's 50th wedding anniversary photo. June 30, 1995

Their fiftieth wedding anniversary came to light on June 30, 1995. A huge back yard party was planned, with members of the Red Mountain gang, and many of our extended family members excited to revel in the event. Even my Texas nieces made the long journey to celebrate this milestone. My parents still remained stunning, as us siblings strutted around like peacocks filled with pride to have such loving parents. Michele and Stephanie, the consummate decorators, strung twinkly white lights through the crepe myrtles and along the fence line for a Mediterranean ambiance. Vases of gardenias and small candles accented each round table throughout the patio, extending to the cozy grassy yard. Greek, French, and big band music filled the air as all anticipated the renewal of vows for *Monsieur et Madame Aleck*. John did the honors of introducing them with an R-rated commentary bringing ooh's and ah's to all with great pleasure. As husband and wife stood before the pastor, my parents insisted on having all six children stand with them.

Displayed for all to admire were many old photos of my parents in their youth, including their wedding photo and a new black and white we had not seen before. It was of the wedding party from 1945, all arm in arm, including Colette and Mame. Colette had it framed and presented the priceless photo as an anniversary present. Brother John gathered my dad's army dress jacket along with his medals, the red beret of the 509th, and a folded American flag that once flew over the Capital in Washington D.C. and had them displayed in a shadow box.

Another table was filled with beautifully wrapped presents in silver and gold print. And as a special gift, a gorgeous Grecian garden fountain was presented from all of us children and nephews. As dusk fell, my father, aunt Bess and fellow Greeks joined hands and danced in true Greek fashion. Smiles were infectious as all involved in this wonderful occasion clapped and cheered, shouting *"opa"* from the depths of our hearts.

Johnny with fellow Greeks Spiro Theveos, and Aunt Bess showing how it's done! Watching are Jim Banos on left, and Jack Watts clapping, who was married to my Aunt Joy. June 30, 1995

Two years later in '97, it was time to make a dream come true. For a number of years the old 509th PIB Geronimo unit had met at various locations for an annual reunion. On April 1, 1963, two decades after my dad's battalion was dismantled, the old unit was brought back to life as the 509th Infantry Regiment (Airborne/Mechanized), bringing in a new crop of Army-tough soldiers. At the reunions the original WWII veterans like my father mingled amongst the newer veterans. The old soldiers, now a little heavier, some with canes, and others with health issues were highly sought after to share their incredible stories. In the past, the timing had never been right for my parents to make the trip back east to catch up with Johnny's fellow war heroes. Somehow, they managed to scrape up the money and in 1997 flew to St. Paul, Minneapolis to be with the old gang again. They had a fantastic time, with my father in all his glory. Many of the Gingerbread Men who had either been taken prisoner, were wounded, or like my father, had walked off the hill that momentous day, had since passed, but there were still enough to relive what the rest of us still read about in war books. While there, Johnny was able to get the phone number of an old buddy, Ray Chapin, but upon speaking with his widow Rita, was to find that Ray too had passed.

Johnny G. Aleck's dress uniform jacket and medals from his days with the 509.

Shortly afterward dad received a card from Rita with a handwritten note including five black and white photos Ray had kept. Taken in the fall of '44 they were of the young paratroopers while combing the Maritime Alps. (These pictures appear in chapter twelve.) While reading "Stand in the Door" I came across a photo of Chapin, McCann, and Pope, as well as Lt. Sol Weber, who if you recall, almost got his throat slit when he jumped in a foxhole with my dad at Anzio. Now I had a few faces to go with their stories. The Geronimo reunion was a great getaway for them both, and as it turns out, the last cross country trip they would enjoy as a couple.

On May 21, 1999 the phone rang, *"Your father came through okay. His stomach hurts a little but probably just gas,"* my mother casually expressed over the phone. *"What are you talking about?"* was my reply. She proceeded to inform me that dad was in the hospital after having had knee surgery. I knew he had been struggling with pain for a few months, generously rubbing asper-cream and taking Tylenol like it was candy. For some reason, just as when Mame sold her house, I wasn't told my father was having surgery until after the fact. *"Dad wants to talk to you."* *"Okay, put him on."* *"Hi Bunny. I'm okay, my stomach is hurting but that will go away."* Bunny was my childhood nickname that ONLY my parents were still allowed to use as I got older. I could hear the pain in his voice. I told him I didn't even know he was going in so soon. Once again, he said it was no big deal and didn't want to bother anyone. He sounded tired so we said our goodbyes, and handing the phone to my mother we did the same.

The next morning my partner and I loaded the Jeep with plans to spend the weekend in Redding with her parents. With no news from Oroville, I figured dad was just fine and we were literally walking out the door when again, the phone rang. Keep in mind, this was well before cell phones were in every hand. My girlfriend told me not to answer, but fortunately, I didn't listen to her. *"You have to come quick, something's wrong with Dad."* Stephanie's voice was frantic. The conversation was short as we wasted no time driving the twenty miles to Oroville. When we arrived at the hospital I found my mother sitting in the nearby waiting room, stunned and being comforted by my sis. I went straight to his bedside in ICU, unaware of anyone else in the room. My Dad was sitting up in the hospital bed when the first thing I noticed was his eyes. They wandered in two different directions which was very unnerving. Then I saw his arms were strapped down to the bedside rails. Someone, maybe a nurse, said it was because he had been pulling his monitors off.

"Dad I'm here, I'm right here." I whispered, placing my hand on his strong shoulder. *"Bunny, untie my hands, I'm trying to drive but my arms are too short. Please, can you just untie my arms."* His gaze was straight ahead while his eyes were clearly unfocused. He continued in a calm voice, *"Come on, Bunny, you can untie them, I can't reach the steering wheel."*

My heart sank. I can't even describe the helplessness I felt in that moment. I heard another voice from the room telling us he was on morphine. Even with the heavy dose at least he knew it was me, but at the same time, I couldn't figure out what was going on. Surgery had been just a routine knee replacement. What had happened to my father? WHAT THE HELL WAS WRONG?

They only allowed two family members by his side at a time. Again, I don't know who else was in the room with me, possibly a nephew or one of my brothers. I left my dad's side to check on mom. She was in a state of shock from this completely unbelievable situation. To be honest, we all were. Our dad was invincible. Surely a knee replacement wasn't going to end the life of this brave soldier. I asked why he was so sick, but they had no answers. Tests were being run and we'd have to wait. I don't think the doctors even knew. The one thing they were certain of is that he had a high fever and severe abdominal pain.

More family members were called, especially those out of state who needed to make travel arrangements. In small groups they showed up at the airport as John drove to Sacramento to bring them to Oroville and some rented cars. Even baby Kendyl at just 3 months old, my parents newest great-granddaughter, flew out from Texas with her parents and older sisters. With empty bedrooms at my parents' house, some stayed there while others got hotel rooms. The ICU waiting room overflowed to the hospital halls with just our family. We all took turns keeping vigil at his side, two at a time. It became too much for mom to see him like this, so she spent most of her time in the waiting room, praying and being consoled by all.

Three days passed and his condition grew worse. The doctors asked permission to do exploratory surgery on his digestive system with his white blood count soaring. Monique gave the nod. It wasn't good. They did a bowel resection but found the majority of his intestines had become gangrened. We were told there was a slim chance that if they removed all of it and gave him a colostomy bag, he might live. A very slim chance at that. We sat as a family, still in the waiting room and decided dad would never want to live that way if he lived at all. Johnny had decided to have his knee replaced to avoid spending the rest of his life in a wheel chair. With his zest for life, living under such confinements would have killed his spirit. Besides, the probability of him waking after surgery was dubious. Speaking for us all, mom said no because there were too many other unknowns. In hindsight, I believe the doctors were just throwing darts at his dire situation.

On the fourth day he lay unconscious as I stood by his side. A male nurse was seated next to him doing something with my dad's IV. I've always been squeamish around needles and blood and this day would be no different. I was already completely stressed and exhausted, knowing how gravely ill my father was, and made the big mistake of looking down at what he was doing. It was lights out for me as I felt my body crumple and fall into the nurse's lap. The next thing I remember was waking up on the ICU floor with ears buzzing. When I became conscious, a couple of the nurses helped me to a chair, checking my vitals to make sure I was okay. Embarrassed, I sat in the waiting room for a little while then went back to the Grand View house to rest. I don't believe I made it back to the hospital that day for fear I would pass out again.

This wasn't the ideal situation in which to have a family reunion as the patriarch of our family lay fighting for his life. All family members who were going to be there had arrived except for my brother Marc and his wife Johanna. The days were long and anguished. Somehow we were all able to take time off from our jobs, but who could work anyway. We surmised that the gangrene must have developed from a blood clot which is why his gut had been hurting the day we spoke on the phone. As a last resort he was given kidney dialysis, but really there was nothing they could do.

The next morning on May 26, 1999 I was in the shower getting ready to leave for the hospital when the phone rang. To this day I don't remember who called. I just know I broke down in tears. The death certificate read: immediate cause of death cardio-respiratory arrest, due to bowel infraction, due to acute renal failure, due to disseminated intravascular coagulopathy. Basically it was an undetected blood clot as we had suspected from his surgery that ended my father's life. There was talk of suing the doctor and hospital, but we were all too grief-stricken and nothing would have changed the outcome. My mother told me later that just as with Christiane she had a very bad feeling about her husband having surgery. It didn't come in the form of a dream as before, but still an intuitive sense of doom. She shared this with her Johnny, but he thought it a foolish notion. Always the eternal optimist, my father insisted everything would be just fine.

Gregg had just left our father's side and was on his way to the house when Dad passed. John was already at our parents' home doing his best to prepare mom for the worst. Stephanie was at home getting ready for another day at the ICU, and Marc and his wife's plane had just landed in Sacramento. After receiving the news that my father had died, I got myself together and we drove once more to my home town. John was at the hospital waiting for us. I walked through the swinging doors to say goodbye to our father one last time. Except for his grayish face, he appeared to be sleeping. Dad's thick Greek hair and mustache still had more pepper than salt. I borrowed some scissors from a nurse and cut off a small lock. My mother had kept a clipping of Christiane's hair and for some reason I felt I should do the same. To this day I still have the cutting in a little blue bag. Knowing he wasn't there anymore still hadn't hit. It would take a very, very long time to come to terms with what I considered a premature death, even at age 75.

After leaving the hospital we entered my parents' house where many of my nieces, nephews, and siblings had already gathered. I was told mom was in her bedroom and as I walked down the hallway I wasn't sure what to expect. I peered through the doorway and saw my mother sitting on her bedroom floor with a box of old family photos. Some were scattered about as she took the black and whites into her hand, gave them a blank stare, then set them back down. Either Michele or Stephanie was in the room with her, but as with my father, my focus was now on my mother. Whomever it was decided to leave the room for a much needed break. After a few moments, mom glanced my way and mumbled, *"I was supposed to go first."* I walked in and sat on the edge of her bed. My only response, *"I know mom. I know."* She repeated, *"I was supposed to go first, I was supposed to go first,"* throwing her fists to the carpet. *"What am I supposed to do now?"*

She was so lost, so bewildered. The only man she had ever loved, had ever kissed, had ever *known*, was suddenly taken forever. Words failed me as I thought the same, what was she going to do now? Mom reached down and picked up a passport size picture of my dad from when he was in his early twenties. In fact, it had been taken for his passport, one he never had the occasion to use. She knelt at her bedside holding the tiny picture in both hands and kissed it, then kissed it again, and then again. She must have kissed his face a dozen times, sobbing as I slid off the bed and knelt beside her. I bawled while holding her close. *"I was supposed to go first, I was supposed to go first,"* she whimpered through her tears. *"I know mom, I know,"* I whimpered through mine.

My sister walked in and took over the impossible task of consoling our mother. I wiped my tears as best I could and wandered outside. John, his wife Shirley, and Michele were outside waiting for our brother. Marc and Johanna had called earlier from the airport to let us know they were in route, and as I was gathering my composure they pulled into the driveway. Marc walked down the narrow pathway doing his best to be strong. I was in front of the others and as he reached down to give me a hug my buffed six-foot younger brother broke down in tears, weeping like a baby in my arms. We held one another and cried for I don't know how long. Our indestructible father had passed at 11:00am just a couple of hours earlier. It must have been especially difficult for Marc living 3,000 miles away, not to be able to see his dad one last time.

My dad's picture that my mother kissed over and over and over again.

The night before the funeral was the viewing. Being a complete mess, there was no possible way I was going to see my dad lying in a coffin. John asked if there was anything I wanted him put in his casket for me. I gave him an 8x10 photo I had of myself pitching when I played softball. It seemed only right to have it keep my dad company for all eternity.

Since it was Memorial Day weekend, the funeral was rushed, but you'd never know it. John Jr., our new patriarch, somehow had the strength to bring it all together. I sat with our mother, sisters, and niece in the front row. When my brothers and nephews carried Dad's casket to the front of St. Thomas Church we all broke down yet again. It's amazing how much one can cry and never run dry. I don't recall the Mass. We were more concerned with our mother who was still in a daze. After the service, when they carried him back down the aisle, all of us women were the first to follow. I was sobbing so hard I could hardly walk. It was the first time I had seen how full the church was with all the members of the Red Mountain Gang filling many of the wooden pews. I heard my mother's best friend Ann Kumle say out loud, *"Oh, poor dears,"* as we walked past. Louis Armstrong's "What a Wonderful World" filled the air. A song I couldn't listen to for several years without breaking down.

As the men carried our father to the hearse we noticed an older man who stood at attention somberly saluting his casket as it passed in front of him. He held his hand to forehead until the coffin was slid into the hearse and the door closed. This elderly man, a veteran himself, had been one of dad's customers from the Liberty Club who took the time to pay his last respects. There was another man, equally upset about our father's passing. Marc approached to ask how he knew our father. He commented he knew dad from the bar, and that when he was down on his luck, Johnny had been a real friend and helped him out until he got back on his feet. He said he never forgot his kindness and didn't know what he would have done without our father's generosity. That's the kind of man Johnny was. I'm sure there were many others he gave a leg up to.

The funeral is still somewhat of a blur. I sat in the front row of metal chairs with my mom and sisters. There was a flag covering my father's brown casket that the military personnel folded and presented to his widow. The flag remained folded in its triangle shape in my mom's closet for years until the day I found it. Stephanie has it now and whenever there is a family event such as when she got married, the flag, or as we now call it, "Dad" is brought and set in a place of honor. We know he's there in spirit.

Michele and Stephanie put together a huge collage of timeless pictures of our father through the years that was displayed graveside. Later, mom made sure all of us siblings had a copy. What I remember the most from that day was the finality of it all and Taps being played on the bugle. To this day, it is in my opinion, the loneliest set of notes ever played.

A couple of days later we all gathered on the front lawn of the old Grand View house for a picture. Siblings in the back with partners and spouses; Mom in front of us seated on a chair. Then the grandkids and their significant others in front of her, and finally the front row was strewn with grandchildren and great-grandchildren. Our neighbor took some pictures and when I came across the photos while writing this chapter I noticed we were all smiling. Even my mother had managed a half smile, but the heartache and grief would last a lifetime. I never liked the fact that our mother was sitting in a row by herself without her Johnny by her side. So, I looked through some old photos and found one of my dad that was perfect. I had a friend who was good with computers back in 1999 who was able to Photoshop him into the picture next to our mother. Now when I look at this family picture I can smile at the reunion that should have been; one including our dear old dad.

The family reunion that should have been. One including our dear old dad.

Our lives changed forever after our father passed. Looking back, it is clear he was the glue that held our family together. Gregg immersed himself into learning everything he could about our father's military service. His research, propelled through grieving, became invaluable information for this book. He had sent a letter telling of our dad's passing, including some pictures of Johnny, to Charles Doyle, author of "Stand in the Door." Mr. Doyle took the envelope and its contents with him to one of their 509th reunions. Upon reading the letter and looking at the picture of his old friend Johnny, James Batton, the young soldier who served by his side, and was there the day Johnny met his future bride, was overcome with grief and corresponded with Gregg. That's how we were able to get Mr. Batton's tales of their historic moment in history. My brother was to find out not only did he know our dad, but he was with him every day from Anzio to the jump at Le Muy, through the Battle of the Bulge, and was among the handful of fortunate men to walk off that hill with our father at St. Vith. James was at our father's side when they got word that their beloved 509th PIB would be no more. Mr. Batton said of Dad, *"Johnny was real quiet, kept to himself a lot during the war and was a good soldier and friend."*

Brother John shared a few stories about our Rock that we had never heard before. Here is just one of many tales John Jr. was fortunate to have witnessed showing the talented and funny guy we were blessed to have in our lives. When Jojo was about twelve Pops took him to the outdoor shooting range near the airport. Next to them, a guy with a couple of buddies was trying out his new rifle, a Savage 300 lever action, for the first time. Shooting with open sights (not using a scope) and from a bench position, his results at 100 yards were lousy since he was barely hitting the target. He started complaining and cussing that there was something wrong with his new toy. Dad took this all in and politely asked if he could take a look at the "defective" gun. At first the man was a little taken aback, but thought what the heck and handed it to him. John Sr. raised the rifle to his shoulder as junior looked on. Standing as still as a statue he took in a breath, let it out slowly, and squeezed the trigger. BANG, the bullet struck the center of the target. BANG, BANG, two more direct hits. BANG, BANG, BANG, all six shots struck the center. Johnny glanced at his son with a wink, then handing the gun back, said, *"There ain't a damn thing wrong with this rifle. It's the one who's pulling the trigger."* His buddies burst out in laughter.

Michele and I shared more stories from our perspective of our patriarch, as Gregg kept us in the loop on his discoveries. My nephew Eric, Michele's oldest son to whom Johnny was more like a dad, took it upon himself to gather a crew and re-roof my parents' moss-covered wood shakes. And of course we all stayed in constant contact with our devastated mother, with each having our own way of processing this terrible loss.

Unbeknownst to our family, the Red Mountain Gang had its own way of mourning. They had done something very special for the first family member they'd lost. Just a little more than three months after Dad passed, my mother, with my sister's help sent out this email to our family dated September 3, 1999.

Hi,

Today has been very heavy for me. Ann and Kenny came by around 5:00 to pick me up to have pizza. I did not want to go but they insisted and I finally gave in. Well, Kenny started driving all the way down Montgomery St. down to the river. It has been cleaned up and looks very nice and right around the bend under the most beautiful tree was the Red Mountain Gang plus some more friends. I was very surprised and right under the tree was a beautiful bench in the memory of Dad. I cried a lot as you can imagine, but it was so peaceful I knew it was what Dad would have wanted. The river was calm, perfect for water skiing. I could see him smile.

We did have pizza. There is a picnic table that sits ten feet next to it and near a cement path for joggers and bicycles. A perfect spot, so restful just the way Dad would have liked it. It was so peaceful I felt him close to me. One of these days we will have to picnic there. Love you, MOM.

Dad grew a beard for a beard growing contest in town. He took advantage of the new look sporting a top hat. Mom was right it was the perfect spot for her Johnny's bench.

The bench dedication ceremony took place with a local newspaper photographer on hand. My mother had cut out the article and picture from that day and mailed it to us kids, of the freshly-stained bench with the gang and Monique now all in their senior years standing behind it. I still have it to this day.

The caption reads: *"Stan Lane, right, anoints a memorial bench for longtime Oroville resident and business owner Johnny Aleck. Lane used vinegar and oil for the anointment because Aleck was well known for the tasty salads he made. On hand for the dedication were several of Aleck's friends, including his widow Monique. Friends of Johnny Aleck in cooperation with the Feather*

River Recreation and Park District sponsored the memorial bench and plaque in the River Bend Park, located at the west end of Montgomery Street."

DAVID C. NEILSEN II/MERCURY-REGISTER

Part of the Red Mountain Gang dedicating the bench to their good friend Johnny, as my mother stands in the middle clutching her handbag. Newspaper date, September 7, 1999.

My father's bench sits below a towering old Oak tree a little ways back from the shore of the Feather River. His was the first of many to be installed during the infancy of the park. Soccer fields, pavilions, paved parking, and picnic tables are enjoyed today. But on that perfect autumn evening there were just scattered trees, a lone bike path, and my dad's new memorial bench. Through the years other RMG members have passed and now have their own memorial in the form of a relaxing bench for others to enjoy. I have four pictures taken at Riverbend Park shortly after our dad's passing. One is from a distance of just the billowing Oak with Johnny's bench below, and another of my mom sitting on it with her arm around their big black dog Sammy. It is a lonely picture to be sure.

Mom on Dad's bench at Riverbend Park. Autumn of 1999

Johnny Gus Aleck May 3, 1924 to May 26, 1999, you are forever in our hearts and the tears we shed. Dad, you were truly the best father a girl could have ever imagined. I love you~

Johnny

Chapter 25

MONIQUE

Mom took to her wine pretty heavy after her husband died. I can't say that I blame her. She did what she could to stay busy, but never went back to work at the bank, and didn't feel a part of the old gang anymore without Johnny by her side. My younger sister and her family moved in since it wasn't a good situation.

Our mothers grief was more than any of us knew how to address, especially while processing our own indigestible feelings. But we did the best we could. Some loss is inconsolable. Monique went to her church hoping she could find a way to escape the inescapable. She received grief counseling and was asked to put her emotions on paper. Writing them out may help to unburden her desolate heart. In a folder with our dad's paperwork from his funeral, I found grief pamphlets and a sheet of paper with both sides filled with a letter she wrote to her Johnny. It is dated July 24, 1999, just two months after her husband passed, and titled, "Why?"

Why did you leave me all alone and crying in the silent night? Chéri, I know it was not your choice because you loved me too much. I remember that last morning - putting your wallet - your loose change, your watch on the nightstand. Brushing my hair for a last time and saying as always, "I love your hair, it's so beautiful." I was worried, but you were not. You comforted me, "It's routine, Monique. You worry too much, it's fine." I saw you before surgery, it was to be the last big kiss I gave you on your lips.

You were fine after surgery, a little drowsy, but in good spirits. Saturday was fine also and you were walking, had lunch, and anxious to get home. Little did I know it was the last time I talked to you, because when they put in the tubes, I could only be by you and kiss your hand and arm. But I would see you the next day. Then Sunday morning that dreaded telephone call. "Please come, John is having a setback." You were already unconscious. You did not know anyone anymore. You were leaving us. Everything was done, but nothing succeeded and you died, and so did I.

I loved you so much, and I know so did you. You were my whole life, and I cannot stand to be without you, I'm so empty. I feel I am going crazy - you were my life - I am just waiting for the day we will be together again. Our love will never die.

Yours forever - Chéri

Monique

Tears rolled down my cheeks the entire time I typed my mother's final letter to her one and only true love, her Johnny.

The following spring Monique, at the urging of her children, flew to South Carolina to spend a couple of weeks with Marc and his wife. She was treated like royalty, enjoying the history and beauty of the land, but the loss of mom's constant companion was ever-present.

Back in Oroville she realized long days spent at home were unhealthy and found a new calling as a volunteer at St. Thomas School. Monique was a whiz with numbers as well as having mastered the English language. With these skills she assisted the 5th grade teacher in correcting homework and tutoring youngsters. Had she been born in a different era I'm sure mom would have been a CEO of some big corporation. She had that kind of smarts. During high school she always proofread my English papers with what seemed like just a glance and knew which words were spelled wrong while correcting my punctuation. Mom loved to read and could breeze through a romantic novel in just one night. In math as well, she did long division quicker on paper than I could on a calculator. We used to race for fun and she always won, which brought a huge smile and *"ahha!"*

My mother during the 1970's

Being around children again and keeping her mind sharp was the best therapy. As an added bonus, Monique was able to fuss over two of her grandkids, Jillian and Jordan, who were now at home every evening. She continued with her passion of potting and re-potting plants that were abundant in both the front and back yards. With grandchildren by her side she'd share with them wonderful stories about France and the variety of flowers, including her favorite bougainvilleas which my parents had planted in their front yard years ago. Monique loved the feel of the soil between her fingers and the sense of accomplishment from taking an empty planter and turning it into a beautiful reminder of her homeland. In just a short time, her drinking dwindled to a mere small glass of wine with dinner. Even though she missed her beloved husband dearly, it seemed as though life was still worth living, but within a few short years my mother ran into financial difficulty. After dad passed, we found out he had stopped paying on one of his life insurance policies due to money concerns. Had we known, one of us would have paid it for him, but without the additional settlement payout, our mother only had Social Security to live on. Then, for personal reasons, Stephanie and her family moved out.

With my mother living alone in 2004, she gifted the house to me with my promise that I'd give it a much needed make-over. The old Grand View homestead needed more than just a new roof. There were plumbing and dry rot issues and a host of others that cropped up during a partial remodel. I was living in Sacramento then, and drove to Oroville every Friday night, staying with my mom throughout the weekend while acting as owner-contractor.

This was about the time we learned the devastating news that my dear sister Michele had breast cancer, and as a result was spending a lot of time at our mother's house. Naturally, our family was *very* concerned. Since I lived out of town it put my mind at ease knowing my sis was with our mom during the week, as the two were of great comfort to one another, enjoying the same TV shows and movies. While Michele had her own battles, it became apparent that something just wasn't right with our dear mother. After having worked for years as a bank teller, she was now having issues balancing her own check book and would mail the wrong payments to the wrong companies. As time went on, mom couldn't remember how to run the washing machine and seemed unusually more forgetful than usual. Worst of all, our Monique started complaining that she had too many papers to correct at school and that the teacher was taking advantage of her. I reminded her, *"Mom, you're volunteering, you don't have to keep going if you don't want to."* But deep down she knew something wasn't right. The workload hadn't changed, but she had. It became more and more difficult for Monique to grade those adorable school children's papers and it was eating her up inside. When she could no longer play solitaire, it finally hit me. I had a new job by now and had moved back in with her. I was on the road four days a week so it wasn't as evident at first. Looking back, it could have been my own denial. The thought of such an intelligent beautiful woman as my mother having dementia was inconceivable. That happened to other people's parents, not mine.

Then in 2007 I moved to Orange County in Southern California for personal reasons. Michele had gone through her chemo and radiation, continuing to spend most days with mom at the house. I still wasn't fully aware of what to expect from our mother's progressive disease. I began getting phone calls on a regular basis from my older sis informing me of her condition. Then within a few months I was having my own financial concerns as the financial market took a nose dive. When the great recession hit, Stephanie and her children moved back in with our mother. But within a year I was no longer able to afford the Grand View house and my mother's condition had grown worse. I think the reality alarm finally sounded when a neighbor called, saying Monique, wearing her bathrobe, had walked up the street with phone in hand, asking him how to use it.

Monique when Stephanie and her family lived with her at the Grand View house.

Michele was instrumental in finding a clean, well-run assisted living facility. We had to ease mom into the process taking her there for dinner and meeting the residence and staff over a two week period. She had lived for five decades at the home she and her Johnny had built, always believing she would die in their home with its array of memories. Life is never a planned event; it unfolds along the way. On January 1, 2009 it was time to move our mother into her one-bedroom assisted living apartment, be it kicking and screaming. It would take two long years before she finally stopped asking when she could go back home. It broke my heart every time. Even though I lived in Orange County, I was heavily involved with her day to day care as my mother became very needy at first, which is to be expected. Phone calls and emails were daily, and I made the day's long drive to see her when I could. Occasionally she would have some health issue that landed her in the hospital, but mom always pulled through.

Then in the spring of 2010 Michele lost her courageous battle with cancer. I was fortunate to have lived with her for about five weeks, caring for her needs. It's not easy watching your sister slowly fade away, but I cherish the moments we'll never get back. I drove her to her last doctor appointment when it was agreed that the chemo was no longer working and it was time for hospice. Afterwards, she asked me to drive around so she could see the different neighborhoods, the trees, and the houses one last time before going home. So I did, and slowly pointing her finger, she'd say turn here or turn there. Her face seemed to glow as she absorbed the beauty of Mother Nature. There was a blissfulness in her smile indicating that she had made peace with God, and was ready to go *home*. Back at the house her pain was intense. I held her in the evenings as we both cried telling her it was okay to curse God, she had every right to be angry, and who wouldn't be scared. For her last Thanksgiving dinner I brought home KFC when she still had somewhat of an appetite. It is to this day the most memorable Thanksgiving I can recall.

Michele Colette

Michele passed away March 9, 2010 with her son Eric and his wife Corina by her side. Her youngest son Devin was in route, and thankfully her only daughter Chantel and flown out with her family from the east coast a few days earlier. Michele was able to meet her grandson Ben, for the first and last time.

After she died, her two sons and their families, along with some of my siblings and I, came together as a family, and crowded into mom's small apartment. Eric sat by Mom's side and gently told her that Michele had passed. He was amazingly tender and loving with his grandmother as she cried in his arms. As difficult as it was, just as with Christiane, Mom insisted on going to now, her second funeral to bury a daughter. The service was both beautiful and just so sad.

In time, Monique's condition grew worse and we had to move her to a studio apartment within Prestige, the assisted living facility, to another wing where she would get more one-on-one care and attention for her special needs. It's called Expressions and is a more intimate setting which truly feels like one big family. Watching our dear mother mentally slipping away was an emotional adjustment for all. Daily phone calls were difficult due to her continued hearing loss as well as losing cognitive ability. Many times when we spoke she thought she was talking to my younger sister. I went along with it because it was just easier. After we rented the house down south and moved back to Oroville I was able to see her at least four days a week. I spent many hours just sitting and talking or walking beside her as she strolled down the carpeted floors with her four-wheeled walker.

Cinco de Mayo, one of many holidays we spent together at Expressions. Our mother always spent Christmas at either Eric or Stephanie's house.

We laughed plenty as my mother still had her great sense of humor, while we attempted puzzles, bingo, and her favorite game of Yahtzee. More times than I can count, I had lunch or dinner with the small group. I got to know many of the others who lived at Expressions, and even helped serve meals on many occasion, staying until bedtime. After one of the gals helped get her ready for bed, I'd tuck her in and wait until my mother fell asleep, which never took long, and thought how precious our time together was.

No longer able to attend mass, my mother was very happy to receive Holy Communion every week by volunteer Lianna from St. Thomas church. With the loss of her precious Cri-Cri, Mom's faith had been tested, but her solid Catholic upbringing was too ingrained for her faith to be completely extinguished. She expressed to me more than once how much she looked forward to and appreciated still being able to receive the body of Christ. Besides bringing communion, the young woman was there to listen to and pray with Monique, which was comforting during her daily struggles with dementia.

The Prestige bus took us on outings, and before the doors were open to the public they let us into the Butte County fair held in Gridley. Mom was a fall risk so I wheeled her around in a wheelchair to view the beautiful quilts and flower exhibits. Expressions had their own exhibit at the fair of faux stained glass pictures made by the residents. My heart warmed as they pointed out my mother's hanging amongst them. Mom and I rang in the New Year together on several occasions. I had just bought a video recorder and have some wonderful footage of my mother hamming it up for all. She enjoyed a good party even into her eighties. It was during this time I was able to learn more about her past and recorded much of what she said. I even recorded a short video of Monique singing French children's songs her mother sang to her as a child, and in turn she sang to us. I'm so very fortunate to have had this time to spend with her. I know not everybody does.

Monique having a great time at the Butte County Fair in Gridley, CA. August 23, 2012

Then my own health took a turn as I developed a nasty digestive issue. I was no longer able to visit and instead, phone calls had to do. In July of 2013 my niece, Chantel, Michele's daughter, and her husband flew in from New York for a quick visit with Mom's great-grandson in tow. Her brothers and their families all met at Expressions with myself and my girlfriend joining. It was a quick visit for us, and as I left, I instinctively knew it would be the last time I would be seeing my mom, because I had to take care of my own health.

It got to where phone calls weren't even possible since we were unable to understand one another. It upset me to not be able to see my mother, but I had to put energy into my own healing. Even though I was sick, we bought a house about two hours away in a 55+ community where my brother John and his wife lived. I was kept informed as to my mother's health while Stephanie and Gregg visited her when they could. Since mom hadn't seen me for months she no longer continued to ask about me. Her focus was in the present, in the now, which in hindsight was a blessing.

On the morning of June 14, 2014 Monique was her usual cheerful self, enjoying the attention from the gals who cared for her and the morning activities, but by afternoon she was complaining that she was pregnant. With her cognitive decline this was at times a way for her to convey her stomach was hurting which the caregivers had learned to understand. After checking her vitals, other than her complaint, she seemed fine. As the afternoon waned her discomfort grew worse. I received a call that they wanted to send mom to ER. I made phone calls to ensure a family member could meet them there. It was always best to have a relative present as a translator given Monique's thick accent and dementia. It seemed to be routine at the time, although in reality, at the age of 87 nothing is routine.

It was determined her gallbladder was inflamed and mom was admitted. A couple of days later a drainage catheter was inserted to drain it. At first she responded well to the antibiotics, so well in fact that after a week or so she was transferred to extended care. While there her condition took a turn for the worse. Mom became dehydrated and started to go into renal failure. We had them transport her back to the hospital where she remained for several days. With fluids, her kidneys were no longer in danger, but now her body wasn't responding to treatment. Mom was sleeping day and night, not eating and only drinking when someone held a cup to her lips. Now that we were in the age of texting, Stephanie set up a group text for us all, and sent us daily updates.

Even though we all come into this world with an expiration date, one is never prepared for such heart-wrenching news. Two weeks after our mom was admitted on July 2, we received this text from Stephanie:

"I have just spent the last couple of hours with mom. I spoke with her RN. It is time to let mom go. She is not responding to the treatment. The doctor will be calling to confirm. After papers are signed they will stop treatment and make her comfortable. Those who want to say good bye should make arrangements. I'm sorry to send this text."

My heart felt hollow as I felt tears roll down my cheeks. So many times mom was near death and then miraculously she'd pull through. The last time her gallbladder had been inflamed they wanted to remove it and I gave the doctor an emphatic NO. With her age and health I wasn't sure she would have survived the anesthesia. My niece, Jillian, (who was living with us at the time in Orange County) and I drove all night, arriving in Oroville at 6 a.m. When I called the hospital to get a second opinion, I was told her white blood count had gone down and surgery wouldn't be needed.

Now we were talking hospice, but if they took the catheter out there was a chance she would become septic, plus it would be too painful. She wasn't able to return to Expression with the catheter, so as a family we decided she should go back to extended care. The short transport went well as texts continued.

July 3, 2014 text from Stephanie: *"She knows me when awake but only once. It feels like subconsciously she knows I'm there. She calms when I speak or sing to her but she's mostly asleep. She does not yell or scream but will get fidgety."*

Later that same day: *"The last time she knew me she smiled said my name and asked if she was going to get better. Then she said she needed God. I told her she was better today."*

July 4, 2014 text from Stephanie: *"Mom is very alert today. Said she was in pain. We gave her something for that. She said she did not feel good and that she was sleepy. Most she had talked in a week."* Eric was even able to feed his grandmother a little ice cream and pudding, her two favorites.

Later that evening I asked how Mom was doing. Stephanie's reply, *"Still pretty good. Last night I was singing a French child's song and she started moving towards me until she was almost to my head. Then she started mouthing the words. Then she started making the sounds. It about broke me. Milan [Stephanie's husband] was crying. Then she told me she loved me. These little moments are gifts."* Mom slept after that and completely stopped eating and drinking.

July 7, 2014 text from Stephanie: *"Mom was just given the anointing of the sick. The priest just left. Eric, Corina, and myself were with her. She is still the same."*

July 8, 2014 sent 10:03 a.m. from Gregg: *"Mom passed in total peace at 9:50am. She quietly drew her last breath as the chaplain and I watched and she was gone. She's with Dad again."*

Stephanie walked in just minutes later. The manager of Expressions, who we consider family, was also there at the moment Stephanie walked out of mom's room in tears. They wept together. I'm so glad my sister was able to be there for mom through those wearisome weeks, and Gregg was by her side at the end.

We had a beautiful graveside service officiated by Father Roy from Saint Thomas the Apostle Catholic Church, and a family friend through Jillian, Marisa, soulfully sang Amazing Grace acapella. A spray of white, yellow, and a splash of deep bluish-purple flowers lay across her light blue casket. Another family friend Andrea, who spent a lot of time at the house with Stephanie, shared humorous anecdotes about our mother. And the 5th grade teacher from St. Thomas school spoke highly of Mom, praising that our mother had received the presidential award for 500 hours of volunteer service. My girlfriend took many pictures so we wouldn't forget. After the funeral we all gathered at the Eagles Club where some of the members had prepared a delicious buffet. Stephanie had enlarged photos of our beautiful mother that were displayed on a table for all to marvel over, including of course, our parents' wedding picture.

Jillian put together a collection of photos on a DVD of her grandmother that played on the big screen for all to view. A lovely French song along with *Somewhere over the Rainbow* by the young Hawaiian, Israel Kamakawiwo'ole played softly in the background. There wasn't a dry eye in the room, as we all watched images of Monique when she was in the prime of her life. My mother was absolutely gorgeous with a smile to last a lifetime. How I do miss those years of our youth.

A thoughtfully written obituary collaborated by John and myself included a picture of Mom as she looked in France when she met our dad, and another taken in 2005. Now in the age of Facebook, my sister posted her own write-up with two timeless pictures of the sassy, French lady we called Mom. Many kind words followed, as well as little stories people shared.

"I remember your father as a war hero returning from Europe with a beautiful French Bride. At the time I worked at Johnson's Pharmacy. I can still vision your mother dressed to the nines, walking into the Liberty Club. The buzz was, that Johnny was one lucky guy." R.H.

Our mother was definitely easy on the eyes. During the sixties we teasingly called her Jackie-O since she wore similar outfits as the former first lady, but in my biased opinion, Monique was much prettier. My dad kept a small worn picture of his bride when she was in her thirties for several decades. It looked like our mother was working at a raffle of sorts and was wearing a very sexy outfit with black stockings and a gorgeous smile. I thought it was sweet that her picture never left his wallet and was still there the day he died.

Dad had unwittingly set the tone of jealousy early in their marriage as Madame Aleck's green streak continued to run through her veins. When they were younger my parents used to go to dances with Dad's dance card always full. Unless it was a slow romantic song mom never did gain the confidence to dance in public. As she put it, she had two left feet. There was one attractive woman who always flirted with our father, and to be fair, he may well have flirted back. But he was always faithful after the infamous affair when mom was still in France. At one of those dances my mother wasn't happy that this one particular woman had been dancing with her Johnny. Sitting on the sideline, Monique deliberately stuck her foot out and tripped this hussy as she walked by. The victim went down with a THUD as my mom said not a word, but instead proudly turned her head, basking in triumph. With the room somewhat dark, it appeared as though the woman had accidentally tripped. Not able to prove otherwise, nor wanting to cause a scene in a tight-knit community, the gal played it off.

After that incident you'd think she would have taken a hint that Monique was like a rattler when it came to keeping her man. Still, the woman wasn't yet ready to raise the white flag. This same widow, who for social reasons, my mother had to pretend was her friend, used to call and ask if Johnny could come over to fix this or that. Mind you, Dad did masonry and woodwork in the backyard, but was never much of a handyman indoors. So as not to appear jealous, Mom always made sure all of us kids piled into the car, acting as unwitting chaperones, just in case. Thankfully, as their love grew, the jealousy dwindled and Monique was able to relax, knowing her husband would always remain hers and hers alone.

I've never taken it for granted that we had such loving parents. My mother always tucked us into bed each night with a kiss and a smile. Even as teenagers she'd make her rounds to our bedrooms, wishing us sweet dreams, or *fais de beaux rêves, en Francais.* She loved us all equally, extending that warmth to her grandchildren. With the dysfunctional childhood she endured as a youngster, Monique was determined her own family would enjoy just the opposite.

Knowing how tough it is to be a teenager, my mother was concerned when she suspected her fourteen year old daughter might be gay. After weeks of repeatedly grilling me on if I liked girls and saying it was okay if I did, finally one day in frustration I blurted, "Yes, *I think maybe I do.*" Well, as it turns out, it wasn't "okay," as my Mom started to cry and declared herself a failure. The truth is, in the summer of 1971, before my freshman year, I wasn't even sure what the word "gay" meant. But, my mother, with her sixth sense was always right, and knew even before I did. She could tell some of the gals I played softball with were lesbians, and noticed I never talked about boys.

Unable to adjust to a daughter who wasn't interested in having a boyfriend, two years later, Mom insisted I see a psychologist. Back then, doctors focused on a term they coined, "The Generation Gap." Once there, my parents never thought to question why the psychologist had us fill out one of his tests to see if *we* had one of these gaps. While my Dad sat silent, Mom questioned as to why I was *different*, and if anything could be done to make me *normal*. Looking back, I'm not sure how a test disclosing how well my parents and I got along, correlated to my being gay. But, the man behind the desk was the one with the PhD, so my parents and I obliged. After he analyzed the results, the good doctor was thrilled to share that the three of us were the closest matched family he had ever seen. In fact, there was virtually no generation gap between my parents and myself. In addition, at the age of sixteen, and admitting I was gay, he said I was one of the most well-adjusted teenagers he had ever come across, but offered no solution to *fix* my perceived abnormality. As our family walked back to the car my mother grumbled, *"What a waste of ninety dollars."*

True, thinking there was a cure for her daughter's *condition*, she didn't get the answer she wanted, but I believe the point missed, was that Mom and Dad had done a pretty good job of raising me, regardless of my sexuality. Over time, the fact that I was a lesbian became as normal as white bread, and my mother welcomed my girlfriends just as she did the romantic interests of all my siblings.

The Aleck clan. Left to right: Stephanie, Marc, Marianne (me), Gregg, Michele, and John Jr. 1990's

Those who knew my mom knew she was a very strong-minded woman. She held her ground, and as I learned through her journal and letters, fought for what was hers. The determination and self-confidence she possessed became the core of who her daughters and granddaughters would become. As a result, we are all strong-willed independent thinkers, sometimes confused with being stubborn. Maybe the bond I had with my mother was the reason no generation gap had been detected.

Her countless hours preparing meals for our family also didn't go unnoticed or unappreciated. I still know the recipe for my Mom's world famous clam dip by heart. Our family enjoyed cultural dishes such as moussaka, paella, spanakopita, and baklava. Our parents had annual *cioppino* feeds at our house filling a huge pot full of white fish, clams, mussels, shrimp and crab basking in a seasoned tomato based stew. She always made her own sauces, and mom's pot roasts melted in your mouth. The enticing aroma of these wonderful meals drifted throughout our home daily. Our friends never hesitated to come over to raid the fridge. And of course on our birthdays, she pampered us by preparing our favorite meals while baking a yummy moist birthday cake. Food equals love, and it was obvious our mother was very devoted in sharing her selfless love day in and day out. Thanks to her delicious doses of culinary delights, all of us children know our way around a kitchen, and then some.

Our stylish French lady juggled homemaking and work outside of the home in an era when most women were still waiting for women's lib to open that door for them. And somehow, even with a litter of us kids running through the house, she did it with ease and complete dedication to her family and to the man she adored. We were her life, and she shared that motherly instinct among her grandchildren and great-grandchildren as well. I see clearly just how blessed our family was to have had, not just one, but two dedicated and very loving parents.

Upon learning of our mother's passing, my sister Michele's best friend from high school shared her memories with me. *"She was such a classy lady. I remember breakfast at your house, your mama serving "café au lait" coffee with milk to all of you. I would never try it, but she always offered it to me. Your mama loved to shop. I remember her showing us all these items she had hid under her bed away from papa John's eyes. She would bring them out gradually so he wouldn't get mad. Monique always looked so perfect, a lovely lady."* - Shannon.

One of the caretakers at Expressions shared her love for our mother. *"She would always sing to me in French and then ask me to sing her an American song and all I could think to sing to her was Amazing Grace and she loved it. When Sandy [not her real name] and I sent her out that night, she wasn't talking, but as some of the EMT's came she was instantly happy and flirtatious. I miss her so much."*

Another attendant chimed in, *"When I started at Prestige your mom was in 218, and I didn't know anything about dementia. Your mom was crying in her room. She told me that she just found out that all her daughters were on a plane and it crashed and she lost them all. Well I went and told the front desk and they told me she was wrong and that you were all fine. The next day she was crying again and I asked what was wrong. Monique told me that one of the girls that worked there stole her rings and she told the front desk and they weren't doing anything about it. So I helped her call the police and made a report, because if they weren't going to do anything to help her then by God I was. The police showed up and needless to say Management called me to their office to explain what dementia was."*

Monique in her one-bedroom apartment.

For several months I would get daily phone calls so my mother could talk to me and know I was still alive. It was a very emotional time for all of us.

And yet one more, *"She always thought she was pregnant and when we would tell her that she wasn't she would say bull shit and for us to get her a doctor. She was full of life and would attempt to teach us French but some just didn't catch on to it. And the dancing – she loved to dance."* Even with dementia my mother kept her sense of humor, and it was nice to know she had finally dropped her inhibition to shake a leg.

I asked Annie, one of my mother's closest friends and member of the RMG about a phrase, *"Chéri, I bite you,"* that I heard often growing up and wondered as to its origin. *"We were at Bev and Spiro's, partying of course, when Johnny decided it was time to go home. After asking Monique several times to go he went out and started the car, then came back in for her and reached for her arm and she said, "I bite you, John."* Well it struck us all *funny so we kept saying it. They stayed a while longer."* That phrase morphed later into *"Chéri, I bite you,"* which drew a good laugh every time it was heard.

When our father passed, we were so shocked and devastated that the grieving was intense. With our mother it became a matter of when, as she had come close several times. Our family had more time to prepare while the dementia was slowly taking her from us. Still, when that moment came I broke down in tears, but was so grateful for the years we had together. I'll never forget her cute little ways and that wonderful French accent. I've shared her advice many times to, "consider the source," when someone uses hurtful words against another, or "misery loves company." I can still hear enunciations that were unique only to Monique like when she'd say son-of-bitch under her breath, I'd laugh as it'd come out, *"so-mama-beach."* She'd come a long way from her strict Catholic upbringing. If you'd ever met my mother, you'd never forget her, and you'd be smiling just like I am now.

On our mother's grave marker is my parents' black and white wedding photo in a 5x7 oval. The inscription reads in part, *"With her Chéri Johnny again"*. Monique Marie Louise Poulain-Aleck born February 24, 1927 joined her family in the enlightened afterlife July 8, 2014. I am comforted knowing our ancestors who once traveled this earth are now our heavenly family, with my parents reunited with each other, Christiane, Michele, their parents, and all those who have moved on before us.

Like my father said in one of his many letters, "There's only one Monique."

With so many loved ones now gone from my own life, I've come to a place that when I think of those I've lost, there is joy in knowing the day will come when we will all be together again. That's not to say I don't miss them every day and cried plenty while I wrote their stories.

When my mother was living at Expressions, even though she suffered from dementia, her condition at that time did not affect her long term memory. She clearly understood what I was saying, and was so very excited when I told her I was writing the story of her life, and that of our family. When I visited we ate brie and crackers, while I read the earlier chapters about the adventures of our French and Greek families. She loved the tales of when everyone was so young. (I didn't tell her the truth I had discovered about her father.) Monique would sit on the edge of her small red sofa, leaning forward, clinging to every word, every inflection. I'm sure a flood of memories came to life as I read. After all, this was her life, the story she had wanted to write, and my mother was excited to hear more every time I walked in.

Each of us has our own beliefs of what to expect at the end of this ever-surprising junket we call life. After shedding these bodies do we continue for all eternity in spirit, or do we reincarnate to start yet another trek on earth, or possibly even another planet? Obviously, I don't have the answers, but I do have my thoughts. I am confident there is an afterlife where all is revealed. One where our families are waiting for us, and exuberantly greet all who arrive at the crossroads. I believe the beauty and energy that will consume us in that moment is impossible to describe by mere mortal words. Upon drawing our last earthly breath I'm convinced there will be one huge family reunion in heaven. And that, my friends, brings me great comfort when I'm missing them most, and is a very happy beginning indeed.~

About the Author

Marianne Monique Aleck was born in Oroville, a small northern California town. She grew up with a special bond between herself and her parents, since she was born on their twelfth wedding anniversary, and shares her mother's first name. She enjoyed life as a child of the '60's much like any other kid, but was always keenly aware of her family's rich European heritage, having been raised by a full-blooded French mother and Greek father. Words like *tais-toi, cochon,* and *kapeesh* were routinely used by both parents, and the Aleck kids knew full well their meaning. When schoolmates came to visit, due to her mother's thick accent, her friends would ask Marianne to translate. With six children, the Aleck's large boisterous household was not unlike the one portrayed in the movie, "My Big Fat Greek Wedding," that shares family dynamics Marianne can laugh at and relate to.

Ms. Aleck attended Catholic school from 3rd to 8th grade, and early on possessed a passion to be a writer. In high school she opted to take not one, but two English courses each semester including journalism, and even wrote a sports column in the school's local Tiger-Tales rag. One of her favorite English teachers, Ms. Denise Jones encouraged her enthusiasm to put thought on paper, providing stimulating classes with this teenager earning mostly A's. Marianne recalls handing in a poem once, and having it retuned by Ms. Jones with, *"Write only about what you know,"* jotted across the top. Marianne knew she was right, and never forgot those words of wisdom.

After graduating, Ms. Aleck enrolled at local Butte Junior College where she took a creative writing course. This time however, Marianne's wordsmith confidence was shattered as she was never able to raise her grade above a C. Believing her abilities were merely average, the beautiful cherry wood pen her parents had once bought for her as a gift, would now be used for an occasional poem, letter, or short story, minus the lofty goals of someday becoming a real writer.

With no hopes of authorship and leaving college after her softball eligibility was up, her work career became an assortment of survival fillers, never finding satisfaction or passion, just a paycheck. After turning twenty-one she even tried her hand at learning the family business, but it wasn't meant to be, so her meandering trail of menial jobs continued. Finally at age thirty she convinced a contractor to hire her in the male-dominated world of construction. Working with her hands was satisfying work, and she loved learning the trade. After four years in the field, Marianne took and passed the exams for her California Concrete license. The gratification of taking a barren piece of land and turning it into a house foundation, concrete steps, or walkway fulfilled her creative side. But just two years later in 1995, she injured her back, had surgery, then went into construction material sales for the next eight years.

Through it all, family remained a constant, and she never ventured too far either geographically or emotionally from her roots. Even though Marianne never married or had children, she holds family in the highest regard. In her retirement years, and with the added bonus of free time, Marianne at last was able to focus on her true passion; to write. This time it was propelled by an obsession, not a letter grade, writing from the heart and writing about what she knew – her family. For several years she was consumed with finding and completing the story of her ancestors.

During the discovery stages in writing her book, she realized she had all the necessary documents to apply for citizenship with France since her mother Monique was a French native. And so in 2012, with the assistance of the French Consulate in San Francisco, Marianne became a card carrying French citizen, and is very proud to say she has both American and French citizenship.

She plans to travel to both France and Greece with her partner of eight years and visit the landmarks of her ancestors. While in Greece she hopes to meet distant relatives still living in Athens, whom she found while researching and writing the adventures of, The Liberty Club.

Individual Acknowledgments

Monique Aleck - I thank my wonderful French mother for so many reasons. For writing and saving her journal, love letters from her husband, letters from her family, and Christiane's treasures. I could never get enough of the stories of France you shared through the years. But just as importantly for being a wonderful loving, spunky, strong-minded woman who lead a remarkable life and made it look so easy.

Johnny Aleck Sr. – My father, the rock of our family. I thank you for leading by example. For having a rare zest for life that propelled you, even through great hardships. I acknowledge your years in the Army, fighting on the front lines under such extreme conditions I cannot even imagine. Your life was a pleasure to learn about and to write about. Even though you weren't perfect, in my eyes you are and always will be a living example of what a man should strive to be. How fortunate I am to have had you for 42 years of my life.

My French and Greek Grandparents all of you were amazing! Thank you for living lives that were so much more exciting than my own.

John Gus Aleck Jr. - My wonderful brother who willingly shared many stories from his youth, war stories told to him by our father, and had the foresight to record our parents life stories which were invaluable in writing this book. Also, your continued input through-out the books evolution. You were my go-to guy!

Gregg Gus Aleck - My other wonderful brother who also provided personal stories and had done extensive research into our dad's military service. Also, thank you for your continuous availability to verify small nuances known only to our family. Again, invaluable to the writing of this book. My other go-to guy~

Aunt Colette Poulain Huston - My mother's sister who took the time to translate and read my mother's journal, as well as add stories and feeling into the lives of our French family. What would I have done without you?

Anne-Marie Wheatley - My French translator who translated the documents and letters I had that were all written *en Francais*. *Merci* for revealing the truth about a family secret that had lay dormant for so many years.

Matt Anderson - WWII historian and authority on the 509 PIB. Thank you for offering and taking the time to read my father's war chapters to ensure accuracy while doing small edits. I would have been embarrassed to have published a book with the errors you found.

http://www.509thgeronimo.org Thank you~

Loïc 'Jack' Jankowiak - My friend from France who keeps the lives of the US paratroopers alive through your website http://www.1stabtf.com and WWII reenactments. Your encouragement, knowledge of the Champagne Campaign, and assistance with the French language has been a joy. I look forward to reading your book when it is finished.

Gregory Kontos - My Greek friend, thank you for finding documents from my Great-grandfather, Grandfather, and Great Uncle used in this book. Plus helping to unite me through emails and pictures with relatives we found still living in Greece. Someday I hope to visit them. If anyone is searching for your Greek ancestors contact him on his Facebook page GKfamilytrees:

https://www.facebook.com/Gkfamilytrees?pnref=about.overview
Thank you Gregory~

And to those who contributed individual stories, or pictures, you added a whole new dimension that I could never have imagined. I've listed you in no particular order, because all are invaluable to me.... merci beaucoup~

Marc P. Aleck - brother

Stephanie Aleck Cole - sister

Lydia Harvey Plaster - cousin

Alford Harvey - cousin

Joy Aleck Harvey - aunt

MaryAnne Banta - cousin

Andrew Ithurburn – cousin

Paul Ithurburn - cousin

Ann Kumle - friend

Barbara Evans - friend

TJ Whetstone – friend

Wayne Wilson – friend

Shannon - friend

Roy Hayes - from Facebook

The wonderful caretakers at Prestige and Expressions

I'D ALSO LIKE TO THANK

Steve Baker who put me in touch with author Joy Redmond, who put me in touch with my fantastic editor.

Edward M Wolfe - my fantastic editor.

Bev Slover - my volunteer beta-reader, for your spot-on suggestions, good-eye in catching errors missed, and for your overwhelming enthusiasm and support for The Liberty Club.

Facebook - for providing a platform from which to launch and share The Liberty Club.

Joyce Townsend - For naming her store Liberty Candy in honor of my family's bar and for making sinfully delicious candy.

Sean and Lori Pierce - For doing their darndest to preserve Oroville's historic buildings and for saving mementos from the Liberty Club.

James (Jim) Lenhoff - Oroville's historian, for his vast knowledge and willingness to share *all* he knows about Oroville and the tid-bits he shared with me for this book.

The Oroville branch of the Butte County Historical Society

AND FINALLY

Lori Fishburn - For being the best partner on the planet and giving me the space I needed to think, type, re-hash, discuss, dream, obsess, cry, delve, and "let the house go" for several years. Your unwavering love and commitment to our relationship (and hiring a housekeeper) is a testament to your strength that drew me in. You don't have to be a book-widow anymore :) I'm back~

References

Various Wikipedia pages were used to reference certain details about such events as The Franco Prussian War and:

Greek Immigration to the United States -
http://immigrationtounitedstates.org/529-greek-immigrants.html
WWI - Battle of the Frontiers - etc.

Battle of Verdun 1916 - http://www.wereldoorlog1418.nl/battleverdun/

USS Block Island CVE21 - http://www.ussblockisland.org

Anzio - http://www.history.army.mil/brochures/anzio/72-19.htm

Operation Dragoon-Southern France-
http://www.history.army.mil/brochures/sfrance/sfrance.htm

509 PIB - http://www.509thgeronimo.org

Ancestry - ancestry.com

BoxRec Boxing Records - boxrec.com

BOOK REFERENCES

Battle of the Bulge - "Stand in the Door" by Charles H. Doyle and James M Phillips

Battle at Sadzot - "Bloody Clash at Sadzot: Hitler's Final Strike for Antwerp" by William B. Breuer

Images of America - Oroville, California by James (Jim) Lenhoff.

OTHER

Oroville branch of the Butte County Library - Mercury Register newspaper archives

Butte County Records

Sutter County Records

Marysville branch of the Yuba County Library - Appeal Democrat newspaper archives

Father James - Annunciation Greek Orthodox Church, Sacramento, CA

Plumas County: History of the Feather River Region. Info by Jim Cook. Photo from the Plumas County GenWeb Project